MYSTERIOUS ANCIENT AMERICA

An Investigation into the Enigmas of America's Pre-history

Paul Devereux

ISBN 1 84333 594 8

A catalogue record for this book is available
from the British Library

First published in 2002 by
Vega
64 Brewery Road
London, N7 9NT

A member of Chrysalis Books plc

Visit our website at www.chrysalisbooks.co.uk

Printed in Great Britain
by CPD Wales

Illustrations:
Photographs not sourced by the author are credited in their captions.
Credits for figures are also given in their captions as appropriate.

Design: Profiles
Jacket design: Design Revolution, Brighton
Copy editors: Anna Kiernan and Richard Emerson
Indexing: Indexing Specialists

CONTENTS

INTRODUCTION

THE OLD NEW WORLD

The Americas have an ancient and mysterious past. This is sometimes overlooked because Europeans effectively discovered them a mere 500 years ago, and because the United States, a powerful and vibrant young nation, developed in a part of them. This book sets out to explore this shadowy dimension of the New World by providing an informed digest of what is known about its mysteries. The information has been gleaned from the findings of many scholars, scientists and explorers, as well as from my own research. In the following chapters, I sketch a portrait of the enigmatic face of ancient America – and 'America' is taken here to include both American continents, north and south, for in the course of the book we will range from the frozen northlands of Canada, across the deserts, plains and mountains of the United States and through the lush tropical forests and arid regions of Central and South America.

Even the nature of the European discovery of the 'New World' is veiled in mystery. The contacts made by Columbus and other explorers and exploiters in the 15th and 16th centuries were accepted as the beginnings of what became the permanent European extension to the Americas, effectively signalling the end of American prehistory (its 'dreamtime'). However, it is likely that a European presence in the form of the Vikings was felt much earlier. The possibility that they had made contact with North America arose out of the *Sagas*, medieval Icelandic narratives that probably represented the written versions of earlier oral lore. According to the *Sagas*, some Norse folk had originally migrated west from Scandinavia to settle in Iceland, some moved on to Greenland, while a few intrepid sailors such as Bjarni Herjolfsson and Leif Eriksson explored a land even farther west – temperate places they called 'Markland' and 'Vinland'.

Was this simply myth, or the memory of actual encounters with the Americas? There followed many decades of scholarly bickering, until Norwegian explorer and author Helge Ingstad decided to settle the matter. Ingstad attempted to establish where Eriksson and the other long-ago Vikings who sailed out of Greenland might have made their various American landfalls, and undertook field expeditions along much of North America's eastern coastline. In 1960, his investigations paid off when he found a remote archaeological site consisting of grassy humps and hollows at L'Anse aux Meadows on the northern Newfoundland coast. Ingstad and his archaeologist wife, Anne, spent several years excavating the site and revealed it to be the remains of eight sod buildings, including houses and a smithy. These structures consisted of walls of piled turf and turf roofs originally supported by wooden frames. Three of the buildings had multiple rooms, and were typical of ancient Norse dwellings found in Greenland and Iceland. Scientific dating methods showed the L'Anse aux Meadows site to have been an early 11th-century Viking settlement. But at first it was thought not to have been Vinland, for that name is assumed to relate to vines, and surely no vines could have grown there owing to the harsh climate. However, it has subsequently been found that grapes could be cultivated in the New Brunswick region on the Canadian mainland south across the Gulf of St Lawrence from Newfoundland. Some archaeologists now believe that 'Vinland' was the term for the whole region.

If it has taken all this time to begin to untangle this pre-Columbian European contact with America, it is hardly surprising that some wonder what even earlier transatlantic contacts there might have been. And this conjecture has extended beyond the discovery of America into speculation about the origin of the American Indians themselves. Did they arrive from the Atlantic or the Pacific sides of America – or both? How long ago? The speculations have become wild and bold: could the ancestors of the Indians have been refugees from ancient Egypt or a stricken Atlantis? Such theories have been strengthened by more specific questions, such as who built the pyramids and the gigantic ceremonial earthen structures of the Americas? Were the curious, engraved lines on the southern deserts really landing strips for ancient astronauts? Why are there massive, 3000-year-old carved stone heads apparently depicting negroid people in Mexico? Who designed the great cities and astronomically aligned temples of the ancient New World? What was the purpose of the giant effigies and patterns to be found laid out on landscapes throughout the Americas? What was the supernatural life of the ancient American Indians like—the secret rituals, magic and sorcery? And do American Indian mythic themes reveal hints of a strange history?

These are some of the historical issues that I will discuss in full. In doing so, I will present alternatives to some of the more popular notions and misconceptions that have grown up around them revealing alternative theories that are, perhaps, even stranger. But during the course of this book we will also find that there are many questions that remain unanswered about the people and artefacts of America's remote past, or for which answers are only just beginning to materialize.

PART 1

MYSTERIOUS ORIGINS

WHO ARE
THE AMERICAN INDIANS?

CHAPTER ONE

FANTASTIC HISTORIES

The first Europeans to follow Columbus to the New World were amazed at what they found, and with good reason. At the time of that European contact it is thought that the total American Indian population was about 44 million. This broke down into two million in North America, 25 million in Central America, seven million in the Caribbean and ten million in South America.[1] Within these regions, people spoke some 2000 languages. There were many different cultures, ranging from nomadic hunter-gatherers to great states with cities containing sophisticated architecture and highly organized societies. In North America, Europeans came across giant earthworks covering many acres, laid out to precise geometrical ground plans, and mighty earthen mounds. In South and Central America they discovered pyramids and citadels, mysterious writing carved on stelae (inscribed upright pillars) and temple walls, great road systems and monumental stone buildings displaying extraordinary masonry skills. There were jewels and glittering gold and silver ornaments; there were statues and carved stone friezes. Such awe-inspiring products of advanced cultures encountered by the European explorers and adventurers inspired intense speculation about the origins of the American Indians.

In 1535, a Spanish historian called Oviedo claimed that Plato's Atlantis had been a landmass extending from Spain to the Americas, and that after it had been destroyed, its refugees had become the ancestors of the American Indians. In 1567, Lumnius, a Dutch theologian, argued that the American Indians had descended from the Ten Tribes of Israel, who had been exiled in 721BC. By 1607, a whole range of other hypotheses had been proposed.[2] These included the notions that seafaring people from the Old World had accidentally arrived on American shores having been blown there by storms, or that America had been populated since ancient times by migrations from, variously, Carthage, Rome, Greece, Wales (and most other western European lands including Scandinavia), Phoenicia (modern-day Syria and Lebanon), Egypt, Ethiopia, China, Japan – and even the Canary Islands. Another early theory was that the southern extent of South America had been peopled by immigrants from Melanesia – an idea that was to resurface subsequently in the 20th and 21st centuries in interesting ways. Indeed, versions of several of these early notions and beliefs were reprised.

Welsh Indians

In the 18th and 19th centuries, a rumour was abroad that a group of ancient Welsh explorers had founded an American Indian tribe – or had at least mixed their gene pool with an existing tribe. The rumour was predicated on two elements – legend and the finding of an unusual tribe of Indians. The legend was apparently instigated by a Dr Powell in the 16th century. It stated that the Welsh prince, Madoc ap Owain Gwynedd, and over 100 followers, had sailed across the Atlantic in 1170 and visited America, landing at what is now Mobile on the Gulf shore of Alabama. Powell further claimed that the much later Spanish conquistadors encountered 'Brytish words and names' throughout Mexico. Early in the 17th century, Sir Walter Raleigh noted that American Indians had been heard to utter words seemingly derived from Welsh. In 1666 (by which time there actually were Welsh migrants among the settlers of the New World), Morgan Jones, chaplain to the governor of Virginia, was abducted by the Tuscarora Indians. When he was later released, he claimed the Indians had communicated with him in 'the British tongue'. In the same decade, a story arose concerning a shipwrecked Welshman who claimed that he had been washed ashore and captured by 'white men in Indian dress' and that he found he could communicate with them in the Welsh language. Folklore had it that there was a tribe of white-skinned Indians in the remote vastnesses of the North American continent, a belief that even the American folk hero, Daniel Boone, supported with his claim to have met a tribe of blue-eyed natives.

In 1735, French explorer Sieur de la Verendrye discovered an unusual Plains Indian tribe – the Mandans – living along the Missouri River. These were a light-skinned people who lived in communities laid out with streets and squares. He felt that they showed traces of European ancestry, and in one of their ceremonies they danced around a wooden object, which they said represented the 'Big Canoe' in which a legendary white man survived a great flood. In the 1830s, the artist George Catlin became enamoured of them, featuring them in his paintings. He considered Mandan women to be 'pleasing and beautiful'. So who were these people? In 1792, Welshman John Evans was commissioned to trace the supposed route of Madoc in America seeking evidence of 'Welsh Indians'. He finally reported, 'I have only to inform you that I could not meet with such a people'. Today, we cannot directly enquire of the Mandan, because most of them died from smallpox brought by the Europeans, and once-thriving villages were abandoned – the sites of some of these are still visible and can be visited. What can be deduced about these people suggests that they were simply one element in the medley of tribes who became known collectively as 'Plains Indians'.

There was further speculation that great fort-like structures containing

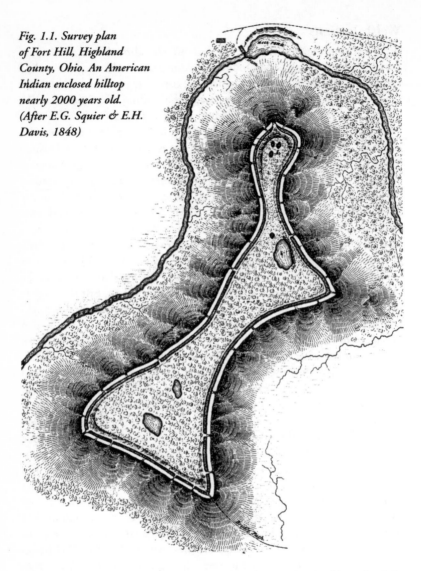

Fig. 1.1. Survey plan of Fort Hill, Highland County, Ohio. An American Indian enclosed hilltop nearly 2000 years old. (After E.G. Squier & E.H. Davis, 1848)

thousands of feet of walling were not Indian features but had been built by the Welsh, as they resembled ancient hill fort remains that are to be found in the British Isles (Figure 1.1). But in 1966, one such site, Old Stone Fort, in Tennessee, was excavated by archaeologists who found that the wall there had been built piecemeal over the first four centuries AD, long before Prince Madoc. Despite the reluctance of the whites to credit the indigenous people with such achievements, it was a structure built by the American Indians themselves, probably owing something to the widespread religious influence known to archaeologists as the Hopewell Culture (see Part Two).

There are, nevertheless, some small but anomalous groups of people still to be found in America. For instance, there is a smattering of farming families living in the border area between Virginia and Tennessee who seem unique. Known as 'Melungeons', these reclusive people display coppery skin colour, straight hair, thin lips and narrow-shaped faces. They appear not to be purely American Indian, Caucasoid, or Afro-American. These somewhat reclusive people are themselves unsure as to their origins, although some of them claim they occupied the area even before any of the local Indians – let alone before the arrival of Europeans. A number of alternative explanations for their existence, other than ancient Welsh adventurers or Lost Tribes of Israel (see below) are espoused by some. For example, it is known that a Portuguese fleet was wrecked off the North Carolina coast in the 17th century, and survivors could readily have inter-bred with the Cherokee Indians inland, forming a distinctive racial blend. A group of Spanish soldiers deserted the armed forces of the cruel Hernando de Soto who proceeded through the region in the same century seeking gold. These disaffected Spaniards could similarly have merged with the local Indians. There are yet further possibilities, including the intermarriage of Indians with local African Americans.

From Egypt, Atlantis, or Mu?

In the 19th century, French antiquarian Augustus Le Plongeon argued that there had been an ancient Egyptian connection with America. His theory was particularly intriguing because he claimed that the Mayan civilization of Mexico had colonized the Nile region 11,500 years ago, thus turning the standard 'diffusionist' idea – that is, Old World to New World migration – on its head. He came to this bizarre conclusion because of his somewhat flawed attempts to decipher Mayan script in the Yucatan. Around the middle of this century the priest Charles Brasseur de Bourbourg proposed a supporting hypothesis, that an Egyptian influence was in evidence in the Mexican pyramids. However he felt that this influence actually originated in the lost Atlantis, some of whose people travelled first to the Americas, then later to Egypt. We now know that during Le Plongeon's and Brasseur de Bourbourg's time, the great antiquity of the Egyptian culture and the relatively more recent chronology of the Mayan civilization was not fully understood.

The Atlantis connection was given a huge boost in the 19th century by the works of Ignatius Donnelly. He was a US politician for part of his career, and a farmer for another part, but it was his writing that brought him fame and fortune. He published his mighty *Atlantis: The Antediluvian World* in 1882, and *Ragnarok: the Age of Fire and Gravel* in the following year. Donnelly's books caused Atlantis to rise again in the modern mind, and he sold vast numbers of copies. They are still in print. Donnelly presented the image of Atlantis as being the mother civilization, spawning later

11

Fig. 1.2. American Indian mound at Miamisburg, Ohio. (J.D. Baldwin, 1872)

developments on both sides of the Atlantic. He compared axes and pottery items from selected Indian tribes with similar-shaped prehistoric artefacts in Europe, seemingly oblivious to the fact that certain basic objects like axes can look much the same from any era or culture. He also saw Atlantean connections with the great Indian mounds of the American upper Midwest (Figure 1.2).

Donnelly used objects known as the Davenport Tablets to support his thesis. These tablets had been unearthed in a burial mound near Davenport, Iowa, by an antiquarian in 1877. They were slates that had rather fresh-looking inscriptions on them depicting, variously, large concentric circles, crude images of trees, animals and human figures, and glyphs, small circles and stars. Did these formations represent a calendar or an astrological chart? Speculation was rife, and the provenance of the objects became a widespread debate. Arguably, the new-looking quality of the tablets, the freshness of the markings, the evidence of compass usage discernible on the tablet surfaces, and the presence of corner holes on one 'tablet' (showing it to have been a roof tile) combine to reveal them as crude hoaxes. What remains unclear is who the hoaxer was: the excavator himself or others? Archaeologist Stephen Williams has pointed out that the artefacts 'verge on the absurd'. The scenic imagery is 'pathetic', the work of the standard of an unskilled schoolchild. Williams correctly observes that it is denigrating to think of the tablets as the work of Indian craftsmen.[3] The tablets were officially recognized as hoaxes only in 1894, after Donnelly's books had first been published. But those who wanted to believe that the antiquities of the Americas had Atlantean connections persisted with their belief in 'evidence' that supported this position.

Russian-born Helena Petrovna Blavatsky, a self-proclaimed psychic and mystic, who was exposed as a fraud on more than one occasion in her lifetime, co-founded the Theosophical Society with American Henry Olcott in New York in 1875. Offering itself as a channel of ancient Eastern spiritual wisdom – some of it authentic, some of it fanciful – the Theosophical Society was amazingly influential, attracting leading intellectuals of the day on both sides of the Atlantic. (It still survives, even if in a now more modest fashion, and its works continue to be published. Its background influence is clearly discernible in modern 'New Age' philosophy.) In 1877, Blavatsky published *Isis Unveiled,* in which she wrote: 'The ruins which cover both Americas, and are found on many West Indian islands, are all attributed to the submerged Atlanteans.' This appears to have been based on a tale she picked up while travelling in Peru with friends. And Atlantis was not the only lost continent she invoked. In 1888, she published her master work, *The Secret Doctrine: The Synthesis of Science, Religion, and Philosophy,* which in part expounds on the idea of 'Root Races' – the seed lines of ancestry of the human race, stretching back millions of years. According to Blavatsky, the Third Root Race derived from the lost continent of Lemuria. She claimed to have gained this knowledge from ancient Tibetan scripts that only she could translate. It was a 19th-century zoologist, P.L. Sclater, who first suggested that this lost land originally existed in the Indian Ocean. Before today's understanding of continental drift, Sclater's proposed continent provided a handy conceptual land bridge to explain such awkward facts as the existence of the lemur in lands all around the Indian Ocean. Blavatsky extended the supposed former continent into the Pacific. After the cataclysmic demise of Lemuria, there rose in the Atlantic the continent we know as Atlantis about three-quarters of a million years ago, according to Blavatsky's chronology. This was the home of the 'Fourth Race'. The denizens of this continent were technically very advanced, and for a time gigantic in stature, thus explaining the massive nature of the great megalithic monuments of the ancient world. Atlantis was itself destroyed about 11,000 years ago, Blavatsky claimed, following Plato's deduced chronology.

Blavatsky's approach was echoed by Colonel James Churchward, whose concerns over 50 years from the late 19th century through to the 1930s centred on the 'Land of Mu' – his term for Lemuria. He claimed he had been taught how to decipher inscriptions in an ancient language he called 'Naacal' found engraved on old stone tablets guarded by a Hindu holy man in India. He stated that these tablets were the source of his information on the great continent of the Pacific. He argued that this land was the original Garden of Eden and had been home to a civilization of incredible antiquity. The continent was finally lost in a concatenation of earthquakes, tidal waves and volcanic eruptions. The Lemurians had been seafarers, and they had established various colonies around the world, including the Americas.

Fig. 1.3. One of the Niven tablets.

One of Churchward's pieces of evidence for this was the supposed discovery by a Scottish amateur archaeologist, William Niven, of 2000 inscribed tablets in the Valley of Mexico. It appears that through the Freemasonry network, Niven was able to get in touch with Churchward, who felt that the markings on the tablets were related to those on his mysterious Naacal tablets, and so was able to translate the pictographic writing on them (Figure 1.3). Both men thought that the tablets were over 35,000 years old. Stephen Williams examined the Niven tablets, some of which are now held in the Peabody Museum at Harvard, and found that they 'definitely do not have the patina of great age' and are totally distinct from all other artefacts found in Mexico.[4] They are anomalies, and seem to be hoaxes like so many of the other 'ancient tablets' that archaeological fantasists of that era were wont to conjure up to justify their claims. There is some doubt, though, as to whether Niven was himself the hoaxer or had been duped by others, for much else that he unearthed has been proven to be authentic.

Egyptian-Mayans, refugee Atlanteans, or colonists from Mu were not the only ones peopling the America of the imagination.

The Lost Ten Tribes

According to the Bible, ten Hebrew tribes – Reuben, Gad, Ephraim, Zebulun, Simeon, Dan, Asher, Manasseh, Naphtali and Issachar – were taken away by the Assyrians in the 8th century BC. Their ultimate fate is not known or recorded, and the whereabouts of their descendants have long haunted the minds of the curious. It was inevitable that the discovery of the New World should provide fresh possibilities for 'finding' the lost tribes, a theory already being mooted by 1567, as I have noted.

In 1650, a Dutch rabbi, Manasseh ben Israel, published an account in which he claimed an Indian guide during his visit to South America greeted him with the words: 'Shema Israel (Hear, O Israel).' The same Indian fellow, Manasseh maintained, told him that many people 'of the same origin' lived in highland areas around Quito, Ecuador. The rabbi used this account to curry belief in the coming of the Messiah, which he felt could only happen when the Jews were scattered all around the world, and that of course included the New World. The rabbi's claims were echoed by other travellers through the Americas, who swore that they could detect vestiges of Old Testament customs in some of the rituals and ceremonial activities of various Indian societies. Such passing similarities were grasped onto as proof of the long-ago passage of the Ten Tribes to the Americas. Such identifications were cultural ink-blot tests, much as were the claims of travellers picking out what they thought to be Hebrew words or phrases in American Indian speech and songs. In the 18th century, for example, an Indian trader, James Adair, insisted that he had picked out the name 'Jehovah', among other Hebrew words and terms, in various Choctaw and Chickasaw chants.

In Britain in the early 19th century, Lord Kingsborough (Edward King) pored over a Mayan Codex – a lime-plastered bark-leaved 'book' of the ancient Mayans – housed in Oxford's Bodleian Library. He became convinced that the tome showed scenes based on Judaic themes such as Adam and Eve and the Great Flood, which indicated that the Lost Tribes of Israel were the ancestors of the Mexican Indians. He spent a fortune publishing several magnificent volumes that reproduced Mayan codices. The venture led him into debt and he died of an illness at 42 years of age while in a debtors' prison.

A related idea to the Ten Tribes lies at the heart of the modern American religion, Mormonism. According to the tenets of this belief system, various tribes left Israel in three migrations during the first two millennia BC and found their way to America. One migratory group eventually split into two tribal factions, the Nephites and the Lamanites. Mormonism states that it was the Nephites who were responsible for building some of the great monuments of pre-Columbian North America, notably the great earthen mounds and fort-like earthworks. The Lamanites, on the other hand, were sinful and acquired red colouring to their skins – these fallen people becoming the ancestors of the Indians, according to this creed. Eventually, the two factions engaged in war with each other and the Nephites lost. A vastly more complex version of this fantastic history was given in the 19th century by Joseph Smith. He had, in turn, learned it from inscribed golden plates – the 'ancient tablet' motif again – given to him on a hillside in New York State by the angel, Moroni, who had been the last leader of the Nephites when in corporeal form.

Sky Gods

American colonists and European explorers were united in one questionable assumption: they simply could not accept that the Indians' ancestors had built the great ancient cities and mighty works without the help of peoples from the Old World. This theme of negating the inherent genius of the American Indians took a new twist in the 20th century: not mere Atlanteans, not Welshmen or Israelites, but *spacemen* were now to be seen as the ancient saviours of the New World and, indeed, the whole world.

Among various early champions of the 'ancient astronaut' theme was British writer Desmond Leslie, who co-authored *Flying Saucers Have Landed* with American 'UFO contactee' George Adamski in 1953. *Flying Saucers Have Landed* became a world-wide bestseller, so Leslie's ideas, which were in part influenced by theosophy, were widely read. In researching the book, Leslie sought evidence for ancient astronauts just about everywhere. He studied the ancient Vedic literature of India, and discussed the references to *vimanas* or 'air-boats', apparently used by the military elite in that ancient society. He was also impressed with seeming references to awesome weapons that, in the context of the 1950s, could be interpreted as being 'nuclear' in nature. Whether these Vedic accounts are literal descriptions of flying craft and atomic bombs or poetic imagery relating to apocalyptic visions is not clear, but Leslie opted for the notion that they were the product of Atlantean technology. The flying saucer is 'only an interplanetary, more advanced, model of the ancient *vimana*', he asserted. Leslie also probed ancient Celtic and European myths, translating into modern terms what he perceived to be the super-weaponry of culture heroes such as Chuchulain of Ireland and Siegfried of Germany. To Leslie, it was clear that Chuchulain, for instance, had the use of tanks and missiles. Leslie's theories are not always easy to decipher but the gist seems to be that in the days before the Great Flood space people came to Earth and founded a hybrid race of terrestrials and extraterrestrials. This race formed the civilization of Atlantis and raised Earth people to new intellectual and spiritual heights.

Other proponents of this theory included George Hunt Williamson (who claimed to have been with Adamski during a supposed encounter with an alien spaceship in the American desert), and a number of other authors such as W.R. Drake, T.C. Lethbridge and Brinsley Le Poer Trench (Lord Clancarty). The best known of them all, though, is Erich von Daniken, whose 1968 *Chariots of the Gods?* was an international bestseller.

The basic technique employed by this Swiss ex-hotelier is to gather up a host of unconnected archaeological mysteries and use them as collective evidence to support his space-gods hypothesis. In the Americas, von Daniken saw rock paintings left by the Chumash Indians of California, and similar prehistoric rock art, as being depictions of spacemen rather than gods, because they looked to his eye 'more technical than divine'. He

Fig. 1.4. The tomb lid at Palenque showing King Pakal falling into the Otherworld.

interpreted ceramic Aztec incense burners as being votive copies of jet engines and consistently opted for mechanistic explanations familiar to 20th-century thinking rather than beliefs relating to the ritual and intellectual life of prehistoric humanity. Von Daniken asserted the view that the ancestors of the Mayans 'were paid a visit by the "gods" (in whom I suspect space travellers)'.[5] Perhaps best known are his claims relating to a burial slab in a Mayan temple and the mysterious ground markings in Peru. The burial slab is situated beneath the Temple of Inscriptions in the ancient Mayan city of Palenque in Guatemala. Carved on it is a depiction of a human figure surrounded by designs in characteristic Mayan style (Figure 1.4). To von Daniken, this assemblage of imagery looked like a helmeted astronaut in a reclining seat piloting a spacecraft. To archaeologists it is the image of the Mayan priest-king Pakal, shown between the worlds of the living and dead, falling into the Otherworld atop the deified plate of sacrifice. His 'helmet' is a smoking axe, a recognized Mayan symbol of spiritual authority.

The ground markings are the famed 'Nazca lines': these consist of geoglyphs (ground drawings) of animals and abstract forms, plus a plethora of long straight lines engraved into the surface of an arid tableland near Nazca. Many of these lines run for kilometres. According to von Daniken, when viewed from the air they look like aircraft landing strips. That there is a similarity is not in doubt, but that does not mean they *are* aircraft landing strips. To von Daniken, they represent a kind of prehistoric spaceport; a landing area for the craft of the ancient astronauts, the extra-terrestrial sky gods. The Nazca lines are certainly mysterious, but in ways far deeper and stranger than von Daniken was able to discern (see Chapter Nine).

CHAPTER TWO

MYTHIC MEMORY

American Indian myths often return to deep-rooted themes, such as the plumed serpent, the 'suns' or 'earths' of mythological earlier worlds, tales of emergence from the ground that describe a range of 'First People', creator beings and culture heroes. Some people feel that certain myths could be distorted memories of early contacts between American Indians and mysterious other peoples or beings, or tell of the Old World roots of the American Indians.

The Bird-snake

The mythic motif of a feathered serpent is found throughout a vast region encompassing Central America, Mexico and the south-western United States. Its origins lie in the mists of remotest antiquity. It first appears to our gaze as a crested and beaked rattlesnake on a relief carving dating to around 800BC at La Venta, the ceremonial centre of the Olmec civilization, currently the earliest known culture of prehistoric Mexico. Then, around AD300, feathered serpents appeared as carved bosses on the exterior walls of a temple (see Plate 1), as well as in temple murals in the great prehistoric Mexican city of Teotihuacan, founded 2000 years ago by an unknown people. The plumed serpent was known as Kukulcan to the Maya, and as Quetzalcoatl to the Toltecs and the later Aztecs – *quetzalli* being the Aztec (Nahuatl) name for the rainforest bird that was sacred to numerous cultures in ancient Mexico (its ample and gorgeously coloured plumage prized for use with ceremonial wear). In the various cultures the plumed serpent seems to have been a mythic depiction of a deity associated with abundance, fertility and, in particular, water. But we know most about the image in its Aztec form of Quetzalcoatl, where it is associated with a creation myth and culture heroes. The Aztec cult of Quetzalcoatl was particularly bloody, employing extensive human sacrifice.

The plumed serpent was usually depicted in non-human form, but an early break with this tradition occurred in Late Classic (*c.* AD600–1000) Veracruz, a state on the Gulf Coast of Mexico. Here was discovered a carved stone device – known as a *palma* – designed to fit on the front of the stone belts or 'yokes' worn by the ceremonial ball players of ancient Mexico. This depicted Quetzalcoatl with human hands rendered as quetzal bird heads. The figure has a conch whorl on its chest, and as this shell produces a distinctive sound when it is blown like a horn, this would seem to relate to the 'wind jewel' associated with the Postclassic (*c.* AD1000–1540) Quetzalcoatl. In the latter part of this period, the god was often shown in human form, wearing the wind jewel like a conical hat, in the role of a wind god. He was also the Morning Star.

The Aztec legend of Quetzalcoatl seems to be conflated with an actual personage or event that occurred centuries before Aztec times, similar in kind to the legend of King Arthur in British myth. According to this version of the legend, Quetzalcoatl was the king of 'Tollan', now identified as the ceremonial city of Tula, capital of the Toltec, who preceded the Aztec culture in central Mexico. In the legend, the Toltec hero-king or god was led astray by drink, and a sorcerer tricked him into committing incest with his sister. Humiliated, he left Toltec country and sailed off eastwards across the Gulf of Mexico, towards the Yucatan peninsula, wearing his quetzal-plume insignia. This was said to have happened in the 10th century AD. Legends of the Yucatan Maya mention the coming of an individual named Kukulcan, the Yucatec term for 'quetzal serpent'. It is said that he arrived at the Mayan ceremonial city of Chichen Itza, and it is true that during the tenth century AD the old city was refurbished and extended with Toltec-influenced architecture. There are also depictions at the site of a masked person behind whom is seen a green-plumed feathered serpent.

This was already a myth that had been confused with actual events and the confusion was to be compounded in the 16th century through the accounts of the Spanish priests who accompanied the conquistadors. Based on what they gleaned from their subjugated Aztec informants, the priests made some unfounded assumptions. According to these Spanish Colonial versions of the legend, Quetzalcoatl was white-skinned and he promised to return. Certain depictions of him in these sources show him bearded as well. Did he promise to return, as in the Old World's Christian belief of the second coming? This has led to the popular belief that the Aztec king, Motecuhzoma ('Montezuma'), who first encountered Cortes and his contingent in 1519, was influenced by this prophecy in the legend. As a consequence, he dithered and prevaricated, unsure whether he was actually dealing with Quetzalcoatl, for here was a strange white-skinned being who came from the east. Had the god returned as promised? This delay gave the Spaniards the crucial initiative that enabled them to conquer the Aztecs. Others have also seen reference to some early, unrecorded contact between the pre-Columbian Mexican Indians and Europeans in the Colonial version of the legend. Was Quetzalcoatl in fact a leader of a European party of explorers or adventurers? Had he – by accident or intent – arrived in Mexico and impressed the Indians with his knowledge, skills and technology, supercharging the natives' innate abilities and so leading to the creation of their sophisticated civilizations? Did he return to Europe but promise to return? Even wilder speculations were that the otherworldly contact with the Mexican Indians was literally that: Quetzalcoatl had been a passing ancient astronaut, in effect a space god. Another adventurous idea states that

Quetzalcoatl may actually have been Christ, for one of the attributes of the Aztec hero-god was that he was the Morning Star, and Jesus stated: 'I am the root and the offspring of David, the bright morning star' (Revelation 22:16).

In fact, none of these propositions are accurate because the original Aztec myth says nothing about a prophecy nor that Quetzalcoatl was white. These readings emerged after the Spaniards had started to chronicle the beliefs of the Aztecs. Although Motecuhzoma was doubtless bothered by some disturbing portents presaging the arrival of the Spaniards, such as lightning striking the main temple in the Aztec capital, Tenochtitlan, neither he nor any Aztec was worried about the return of a white god from the east. Scholars now think that the massaged versions of the myth were either Spanish propaganda or else an attempt by Aztec historians after the conquest to explain the Spaniards' arrival and subsequent victory.[1] There is an intriguing aspect to the Quetzalcoatl legend. Although the myth seems to have been indigenous in Classic-era Veracruz, where the image of the god in human form apparently first appears, the art style was distinctive and unique. 'This style can be mistaken for no other in Mexico; on the contrary, its closest affinities seem to lie, for no apparent reason, across the Pacific with the Bronze and Iron Age cultures of China,' writes anthropologist Michael D. Coe, a leading authority on ancient Mexico.[2] Could it be that an encounter with outsiders from the *west*, from across the Pacific, caused the long-ago Mexican Indians to revise their iconography concerning the ancient myth of Quetzalcoatl and depict him as a man? I shall explore the background to this possibility later.

The Mayan Bible

The *Popol Vuh* is the sacred text of the Quiche Maya – its name means 'council book'. It begins by describing the creation, before which 'there was nothing brought together, nothing moving'; there was only an immense sea whose waters fell away into the abyss. But three gods existed in the primordial darkness – Tepeau, Hurakan and Gucumatz (the Quiche name for Quetzalcoatl). They got together and created the Earth and raised the sky. They created the animals and made some false starts with creating human beings. The second part of the book describes the adventures of the Hero Twins, Hunahpu and Ixbalanque, in defeating the gods of the underworld, Xibalba, and includes the story of the Twins' forebears. The mysterious pre-Columbian ballgame is a major motif in this part of the *Popol Vuh*. This segment of the book is the oldest, because scenes from it are found in Mayan art depictions dating back to Late Formative times (*c.*300BC). The final section of the text recounts the legendary history of the founding of the Quiche dynasties, and lists the lineage heads in each generation up to the Spanish era.

Among these storylines there are images that some commentators find curiously reminiscent of those found in the Judaeo-Christian texts, such as a somewhat Genesis-like opening creation scene, a great flood, the miraculous parting of waters, and the giving of divine law to priests on a mountain. So does the *Popol Vuh* reveal mysterious ancient influences of Old World religion? The answer is, again, probably not, because quite apart from the possibility of coincidental imagery, the provenance of the *Popol Vuh* as we know it may have been compromised to some extent. In the middle of the 16th century, a Mayan nobleman transcribed the work into a Romanized form of the Quiche language. He was working from an original book of hieroglyphs that has since been lost. A century and a half later, the Quiche-speaking Spanish priest, Francisco Ximenez, came across this Quiche text and translated it into Spanish. That twice-removed version of the *Popol Vuh* is the oldest we have, and there is no telling whether it contains a degree of 'European contamination'.

Travellers' Tales

A more careful approach to the possibility of 'mythic memory' was put forward by Franz Boas (1858–1942), a noted anthropologist of his day who studied American Indian societies, linguistics, legends and traditions. He specialized in the North America Indian tribes of the north-west Pacific.

Boas made a long and careful analysis of the way American Indian mythologies and folktales grew and developed. His findings were that the dissemination of myths 'was almost unlimited'.[3] They travelled from tribe to tribe, being carried in all directions. He distinguished the fact that there were some elements and motifs in myths that were effectively universal, elements that could appear independently in societies all over the world. An example he gave was the motif of a man being swallowed by an animal of some kind: so, variously, a fish (Great Lakes; Bahamas), a cow (in the Tom Thumb tale) and a whale (India; the Biblical Jonah), to name just a few. But he found that when more complex elements recur in myths in societies distant from one another, then diffusion – actual geographical transmission – was to be suspected as being the more probable agency. He analyzed mutations within a given tale where it occurred in various regions, often being able to determine which direction it had travelled in. This was not always and necessarily a smooth transmission of mythic tales. (Boas discovered that a story could 'jump' between two distant groups who each possessed it in their lore, somehow bypassing the societies between them, and he explored the reasons why this might occur.) Nevertheless, he found that, broadly speaking, groups of American Indian myths travelled over portions of the continent. He found, for instance, that diffusion of tales between Inuit peoples and Indian tribes of the western half of North America has been quite extensive.

Then, in a tentative way, Boas went much further than this. He stated that he had found 'a series of complicated tales' that were common to myths in both the Old and New Worlds. One example he gave was of a fairy tale belonging to the Samoyed-speaking tribes of north-west Siberia, just north of centre of the great Eurasian landmass. In this, two sisters were running from a pursuing cannibal witch. One girl threw a whetstone over her shoulder that transformed into a canyon, thus delaying the witch who was forced to cross it. The hag had almost caught up with the two girls again when the other sister threw a flint over her shoulder that transformed into a mountain, blocking the witch's way. For good measure, the girl then threw a comb over her shoulder, which changed into a thicket. Boas found an almost identical story among the Indians of America's North Pacific coast. In this version, the child threw a whetstone that became a mountain, a bottle of oil that became a lake and a comb that became a thicket.[4] It is salutary to note that the two regions that share this tale are roughly 8050km (5000 miles) apart.

Boas discovered more corresponding myths between Siberia and North America, as well as other startling examples. For instance, he found a series of tales belonging to the indigenous Ainu people of Japan that have 'very close analogues on the North Pacific coast'.[5] Again, he discovered 'a curious coincidence' between a myth from Pelau Island – part of the Micronesian Caroline Islands group in the western Pacific Ocean – and several American Indian tales along the American Pacific coast. Boas' comments on such strange discoveries are worth giving in full: 'Setting aside the similarity of the north-west American tales to those from Micronesia, I believe the facts justify the conclusion that transmission of tales between Asia and America has actually taken place and, what is more remarkable, that the main points of coincidence are not found around Bering Strait, but farther south; so that it would appear that diffusion of tales, if it took place along the coast line, was previous to the arrival of the Eskimo in Alaska.'[6]

If one *doesn't* exclude the Micronesian similarities, the implications are even more startling.

Does such myth-based evidence – however indistinct – tell us of Pacific contacts with the Americas in ancient times? Diffusionist ideas were more popular in Boas' time than now, and today's scholars use them only to provide limited explanations within particular contexts (usually genetic). There are good reasons why they take this approach. Nevertheless, this evidence needs to be explained. Moreover, not only do we have a vague hint of possible Pacific contacts in the art style of Late Classic Veracruz (above), but, as we shall find in the next chapter, research into American-Indian DNA and recent skeletal discoveries is tentatively pushing towards similar conclusions – this more than a century after Boas originally wrote of his findings, in 1891. Franz Boas' observations of an early south Pacific transmission of mythic information from Asia to America (revealing contact between Old and New Worlds outside of the standard Bering Strait migration theory) suggest that the apparently 'softer' science involved in the study of myth can reach conclusions ahead of 'harder' technical science.

CHAPTER THREE

SCIENCE AND THE DAWN PEOPLE OF AMERICA

One of the earliest theories concerning the origins of the American Indians was put forward in 1590 by Padre Jose de Acosta. He suggested that some part of what was then the unexplored far north of the Americas must join or closely approach the Old World, allowing migration into the New World. Of all the ideas floating around at the time, this one most closely foreshadowed the standard modern scientific theory to explain the original peopling of the Americas. This states that the initial migrants to America, the 'Palaeoindians', came across a land bridge over what is now the Bering Strait, which separates Siberia and Alaska.

Strait Talking

Until about 100,000 years ago, the sea separated Siberia and Alaska, much as it does now, but at around that time the last glaciation began. The deep, vast ice sheets that expanded out from the poles locked up vast quantities of water from the world's oceans. Consequently the sea level dropped 100 metres from its present level exposing a land bridge across the strait. This newly revealed land, known to geologists as Beringia, reached its maximum extent on two occasions during the deepest freezes or 'maxima' of the Ice Age. They occurred between c.70,000–45,000BC and again between c.25,000–12,000BC. Scholars think these provided two large 'windows of opportunity' when people from Siberia could have most readily migrated across Beringia and into America. However, on a clear day Siberia is visible from Alaska, and in severe winters the Bering Strait can freeze to the extent that people, sleds and dogs can cross the pack ice even without a land bridge.[1] (Indeed, in March 2002, a British team was planning to walk from America to Russia by this means.) So, theoretically, people could have moved between the continents at other times too. As the biological anthropologist Michael Crawford has noted, 'The Bering Strait may not ever have been an effective barrier to human migration.'[2]

Such stories conjure images of fur-wrapped, nomadic Ice Age Palaeoindian hunters following big game such as mammoth and mastodon across Beringia into North America, and perhaps also living off marine life along its shifting coastline. But what happened after they made the crossing? Huge ice sheets extended down across what is today Canada and the northern United States and presumably formed a barrier to any progress farther south into the American hinterland. Until recently, scientists

24

thought the Palaeoindians would have had some opportunities for onward travel through this Arctic barricade. It was thought that the North American glaciers were divided into two great ice sheets, known as the Cordilleran to the west, and the larger Laurentide covering central and eastern North America. Scientists assumed that at less frigid times in the Ice Age there might have been an ice-free (if still exceedingly chilly) 'corridor' between them that could potentially have allowed human and animal access to warmer lands farther south. Now, though, further geological research strongly indicates that there would never have been a passable corridor. If this is so, then there could only have been coastal travel available to the Beringian migrants. The extreme western coastal regions would have been ice-free, and there was always the option of boat travel southwards along the western coast of North America. Although no Palaeoindian boats of the era have been found by archaeologists, palaeo-peoples from Asia did conduct sea crossings to Australia at least 40,000 years ago.

If Beringia was a possible route for human migration from the Old World into America, the crucial question is: what evidence do we have that this actually took place? To answer this, scholars have compared American Indian and Siberian populations. First, they note similarities in appearance of bodily (or 'morphological') characteristics. At the superficial level, both Asians and Americans tend to exhibit straight black hair, sparse body hair, the 'mongoloid sacral spot' (an area of skin discoloration on the triangular area at the base of the spine), small brow ridges and high cheekbones. The face is relatively flat and some Indians, like most Asians, have a fold on the upper eyelid that gives a distinctive oriental appearance. Then there are the teeth: whereas Europeans have broad incisors with a single ridge, American Indians and Asians have double ridges and a shovel-like shape to the incisors. This characteristic shovel shape occurs in 50–100 per cent of north-eastern Asians and American Indians, between 20 and 40 per cent of southern Asians, and from zero to ten per cent of Africans and Europeans. There are other dental characteristics – such as the number of roots characteristically found on certain teeth – shared predominantly by north-eastern Asians and American Indians. Even the earwax of the two populations shares common qualities – dry and brittle as opposed to the sticky, wet variety usual in the rest of the world!

Second, there are cultural similarities between many north-eastern Asian and American Indian societies. Although most American Indian cultural forms developed within America, indelible Eurasian traits are traceable. Prominent among these is shamanism, an archaic tribal religious practice that involves direct, visionary contact with the spirit otherworld; its hallmark is the occurrence of ecstatic, trance states in the shaman (see Part 3). Shamanism is found throughout the Americas, yet the classical version of shamanism – and the term itself – comes from Central Asia. Associated with shamanism is a style of rock art that shows the internal structure and organs of animal and human figures, and this 'X-ray style' is found on both sides of the Bering Strait – indeed, westwards through Eurasia and eastwards into the Americas as far as modern-day Venezuela.[3] Then there are ceremonials connected with worship of the bear – the mythologist Joseph Campbell pointed out that the extent of the cultural trait of the Bear Cult was circumpolar. Animism – a belief that spirits inhabited animals, plants, places and inanimate objects such as rocks, and that they had to be placated by rituals – may also have travelled across Beringia and into America, along with its close companion, totemism. The deeply-imbued tradition of the Great Hunt was also a fellow traveller from west to east, and with it the spear and atlatl (the Aztec word for spear-thrower) – the atlatl was a sophisticated piece of technology for its era, allowing a spear to be hurled with sufficient force to kill big game such as bison and mammoth. In terms of cultural technology, both Siberian and Native American tribes possessed dwellings made of similar materials to similar designs – for example, the 'chuums' of the reindeer herders of Siberia and the 'teepees' of the Plains Indians are virtual look-alikes. Yet another piece of cultural technology that travelled from the Old to the New World was the calendar stick. This tool for astronomical, particularly lunar, observation was used on both sides of the Bering Strait, and its origin seemingly dates to the Middle Palaeolithic, the Old Stone Age, of Eurasia (the term for the entire continental mass stretching from Europe in the West to Siberia and China in the east).

A Question of Timing

The scientific case for the arrival of the Palaeoindians in America via Beringia is both powerful and multi-faceted, but the timing is a matter of some considerable debate. Archaeological finds suggest that the major migrations of Palaeoindians from the north-west down through the Americas occurred between about 14,000 and 9000 years ago as the American glaciers retreated northwards and the Ice Age came to an end. At first, archaeological evidence for human habitation of America was hard to come by, and archaeologists assumed – as many still do – that the very earliest migrants, the dawn people of the Americas, lived in small, mobile groups that left little trace.

Until 1926, most experts believed that human beings did not occupy America until about 5000 years ago, but a discovery at Wild Horse Gulch near Folsom, New Mexico, put this assumption into question. Excavators found a flint that had been artificially chipped into the shape of a large spear point deep in clay alongside the bones of an extinct species of Ice Age bison, thus implying an early date for human occupation. The artefact was removed and an excited team leader, J.D. Figgins, announced the find to his colleagues. But they didn't believe him, doubting the quality of his excavation. One advised him to leave any future finds just where they were, so that its depth in the ground (and

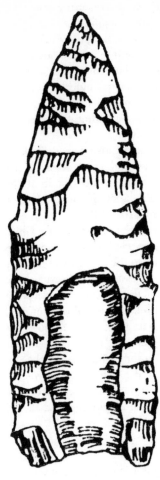

Fig. 3.1. An example of a Clovis spear point, about 13cm (5in) long, showing the fluting where the shaft was fitted to the point.

therefore age) and its context (any associated bones or artefacts) remained undisturbed, allowing confirmation by others. The following year, Figgins and his colleagues managed to do just that when they found another flint spear point wedged in the ribs of an Ice Age bison.

The date for the earliest known human occupation of North America continued to be rolled back. In 1932, a highway construction company digging a gravel pit unearthed a thin flint blade and a large animal tooth at Blackwater Draw, near Clovis, also in New Mexico. Archaeologists were alerted, and in excavations between 1936 and 1937 they found human artefacts in association with mammoth bones *below* the Folsom level in the ground. They identified a type of fluted flint spear point that was both larger and earlier than the Folsom blade, and so is now referred to as the Clovis point (Figure 3.1). It is dated to *c*.9000BC. The Folsom and Clovis flint spear points are referred to as 'fluted' because once the point was worked and shaped by percussive stone-on-flint 'knapping', a single flake was removed from the base of the point to ensure a snug fit with the haft to which it was affixed by sinew or gut. Fluted spear points do not appear in prehistoric Asia, so this technique seems to have been developed in America. These American spearheads are beautiful objects, superbly crafted, and were designed to penetrate even the thick hide of a mammoth. Being the first of its kind, the Clovis point is sometimes jokingly referred to as 'the first American invention'.

Subsequent archaeological research has located Clovis-type flint blades and other evidence of the 'Clovis culture' at find spots across North America, Central America and even into South America.[4] In 1994, archaeological investigators excavated fluted flint spear points in a region adjacent to the Bering Strait that they dated to c.10,500BC.

The Clovis culture is still regarded as the earliest in America for which there is incontrovertible evidence, and it is now clear that human beings were in the New World from at least the era when the Ice Age was drawing to its prolonged close. But there are problems in assuming that even this is early enough and questions remain. Why, for instance, are the dates for these artefacts throughout the Americas all within a thousand years or so of one another? How quickly could people migrate southwards through the two continents? Shouldn't the more southerly finds be much later and the original Bering crossing much earlier? Another problem is that as archaeologists are now increasingly prepared to dig below the Clovis level, other sites are being found that seem to date from a time well before the Clovis era. Such finds, though still controversial, are beginning to challenge the Bering land bridge migration theory.

Tangled Timelines

Challenges to the Clovis timeline representing the absolute earliest phase of human occupation of America began to emerge in the 1970s. One set of excavations began in 1973 at the Meadowcroft rock shelter not far from Pittsburgh, Pennsylvania. This had been a prehistoric campsite barely 50km (31 miles) south of the nearest edge of the Laurentide ice sheet. The site consisted of 11 distinct layers, making it one of the longest-occupied places in America (it was in use as recently as seven centuries ago). With meticulous care, James Adovasio and his team excavated the series of buried 'floors', the living surfaces that the Indians had used over periods of time. By the time they had finished, many years later, the excavators had removed well over three million objects, including the bones of over 100 different animal species, and stone tools from a surprising number of quarries. To discover their ages, a technique called radiocarbon dating was used. This method measures the amount of a naturally occurring radioactive substance called carbon-14 there is in a sample of organic material. Because carbon-14 decays very slowly but at a known rate, the amount that is left in a sample indicates the age when the material, such as a piece of wood, first formed. Radiocarbon dating can only be used on organic material, so inorganic substances such as rocks or minerals, cannot be dated by this means. Eight radiocarbon dates confirmed human presence in the Meadowcroft rock shelter in 10,800BC, but the burnt wood from one campfire yielded a date over 15,000 years old, and at the deepest level a burnt remnant of matting or basket proved to be in excess of 19,000 years of age. Just as with Figgins half a century earlier, there are some scholars who do not want to accept such a finding, claiming the dating samples were contaminated. However, Adovasio himself is in no doubt about the accuracy of the dating, and there is a broad body of opinion that now accepts that Adovasio's work was too meticulous to be dismissed so easily.

Among other North American human habitation sites yielding pre-Clovis dates are Bluefish Caves in Yukon, Alaska (13,000BC), Fort Rock Cave, Oregon (12,000BC) and a mastodon kill site near Sequim, Washington State that is 12,000 years old, or even older. There is a good scatter of other sites, such as Old Crow in the Yukon (20,000–40,000BC) and the Pendejo Cave in New Mexico which have yielded dates possibly twice as old as those of Meadowcroft, but these currently remain considerably more contentious or are as yet insufficiently investigated. But the challenge for those trying to hold to the Clovis timeline increases the farther south we go.

The best-attested pre-Clovis site in South America is currently Monte Verde, about halfway down the coast of Chile. It had been a long-term settlement comprised of two sites a few hundred feet apart alongside a stream. Shortly after its inhabitants finally left it was flooded, sealing the site beneath with what became peat, and so preserving it. After locals found large bones at the site (the bones proved to have come from a mastodon), US archaeologist Tom Dillehay was alerted to its existence and excavations began in 1976. A plethora of objects have been skilfully unearthed, including hundreds of stone, bone and wooden tools, animal bones, especially mastodon ribs (and even some mastodon flesh), bits of food, cylindrical spear points, timber poles with attached pieces of knotted reed, being the remnants of what had been hide-covered huts, fire-pits and even a child's footprint preserved in clay. All were in 'stratigraphic order' – that is, they were found in undisturbed layers of earth revealed by the excavators' trenches so their sequence and relationships with one another could be determined. A series of radiocarbon dates revealed this part of the site to be, on average, about 13,000 years old. The American archaeological establishment was forced to reconsider established assumptions, for here was a site 16,000 km (10,000 miles) from the Bering Strait that was considerably older than the North American Clovis culture timeline. The child whose footprint was found at Monte Verde had walked before Clovis people were understood to have arrived in North America. And there was another factor – the prehistoric people who had lived at the site were not simple hunters, as was assumed of the Clovis culture. A fundamentally different type of cultural behaviour had been present: the archaeological evidence showed the people to have both hunted and eaten the meat of mastodon, but they had also gathered plants for food and for medicinal and possibly ritual use.

When the inevitable uproar began from the sceptics, Dillehay invited key critics down to the site. The evidence forced some of the doubters to reconsider and even to become strong supporters of Dillehay's findings. Scepticism remains, but scholars generally now accept Monte Verde as a site revealing a pre-Clovis people. But the controversy didn't end there. Dillehay dug farther to see if he could discern the founding layer of the settlement site and, at almost 3m (10ft) down from the ground level he found more than two dozen stones clustered with three possible hearths. Radiocarbon dating indicated that the hearths were almost 30,000 years old. Despite a degree of dissension, some archaeologists think the dating will hold, and Dillehay, though cautious, has voiced similar views. Indeed, it seems he can countenance a peopling of America between 50,000 and 100,000 years ago.[5]

Boquierao da Pedra Furada ('Perforated Rock') in Brazil is a similarly controversial historical site. One of the largest rock shelters in an area of sandstone cliffs in the remote north-eastern plain of the country, in the state of Piaui, Boquierao da Pedra Furada features over 400 archaeological sites.

Brazilian archaeologist Niède Guidon's work revealed that at least 300 of them contain rock art. The first time Guidon lowered herself into Pedra Furada, in the 1970s, she was attacked by a swarm of killer bees, but managed to survive despite being stung 200 times. Undeterred, she has continued to work at Pedra Furada to the degree that limited funding allows. The site is extensively decorated with red and white prehistoric rock paintings representing human beings as lively stick figures accompanied by a variety of animals. In order to determine the age of the paintings, Guidon and co-workers began excavations at the foot of the painted rock wall panels in 1978. As they went down through successive layers of soil and clay, they encountered stone tools and the charcoal from campfires. In all, there were five such sedimentary layers. At each level, Guidon sent samples of organic material to the foremost radiocarbon dating laboratory in France, the Centre des Faibles Radioactivités, based in Gif-sur-Yvette.[6] The dates started at 6000 years old for the upper level, becoming progressively older down to the deepest level where a hearth yielded the age of 32,000 years. These dates were confirmed later by an American laboratory. Tests at other sites in the vicinity of Pedra Furada produced a similarly startling range of dates.

Pedra Furada's sandstone walls have shed some of their painted surfaces over time. Guidon and colleagues found these pieces at various levels as they dug down, enabling them to calculate minimum ages for the paintings. The fragments of painted sandstone were found variously at levels indicating ages between 10,000 and 17,000 years. The sliver of sandstone in the older, lower layer has two red lines painted on it, probably part of a figure.

Guidon's peers decried her findings and cast doubts on her excavation skills and interpretations. Some of the apparently worked, pebble tools she had found, for instance, were not human artefacts, they opined, but were simply rocks that had been damaged by falling into the shelter long ago. Another criticism was that the hearths she had dated were actually naturally occurring fires. Guidon countered that the carbon was from inside the shelters where natural fires do not occur.

Some of Guidon's supporters feel her critics are biased – partly because she is a woman, and partly because this challenging site is in South rather than North America. One scientific observer has commented that North Americans 'cannot believe that they do not have the oldest site'.[7] Unlike Monte Verde, it appears that few critics have actually visited the site, and Guidon's comment that 'Americans should excavate more and write less' therefore seems a fair rebuke.[8] The debate continues. Although skeletons are invariably destroyed by the acidic soils at the site, Guidon has managed to recover three fossilized teeth and part of a human skull. The results of dating announced in 2000 reveal them to be 15,000 years old. If this is so, Guidon's discoveries are the oldest human bones so far unearthed anywhere in the Americas. The fact that Guidon has found evidence of a human presence at Pedra Furada dating to more than 48,000 years old contends that humans existed in America 50,000 or more years ago.

Caverna da Pedra Pintada in the Brazilian Amazon, excavated in the 1990s, is another controversial example of a painted sandstone cave in South America. The cave exhibits stratified layers of Palaeoindian deposits, and 56 radiocarbon dates from burnt plant samples give ages of up to 11,000 years. This is roughly contemporary with the Clovis culture, but triangular spear points unearthed at the site show that a different culture is involved. Further dating tests, using the more variable thermoluminscent method, has yielded dates going back some 16,000 years.[9] If the Clovis people came across the Bering Strait, then where did *these* people come from?

There are other South American sites – in Argentina, Venezuela, Peru and Chile – that are also tentatively producing pre-Clovis dates. The clamour from the south for the revision of existing models for the early peopling of America is growing all the time. The view that people either migrated across Beringia much earlier than is currently supposed, or that the southern cultures took another route seems likely. Perhaps there is something in the early idea that people came to parts of South America from Australasia or Oceania–Australia or south-western Pacific islands (see Chapter One). This idea will need revisiting if it is conclusively shown that humans were in America over 40,000 years ago, because archaeologists now know that there were no peoples living in Siberia before that time who could have come across the Bering land bridge.

Points of Contention

As if these controversies were not enough, anthropologist Dennis Stanford, of the Smithsonian Institution, has rekindled debate over the contentious issue of whether or not very early Europeans may have made contact with North America. Along with a few other scholars, Stanford noticed that there were some striking similarities between Clovis projectile points and those belonging to the Solutrean peoples of north-coast Spain, whose culture existed between c.20,000–14,500BC – the later Old Stone Age, or 'Upper Palaeolithic' era. Because the Solutrean culture ended thousands of years before the emergence of the Clovis culture in the Americas, it was largely dismissed as coincidence. But Stanford was not satisfied with this conclusion. He noted the recent geological findings that an ice-free corridor had not existed between the great North American glaciers during the Ice Age, and he further noted that no animal bones have been found that date to the period when the ice-free corridor was supposed to have been open. So how had the Clovis people reached the central and eastern parts of North America from the western coast and hunted big game? Stanford also knew that this puzzle was compounded by the fact that more Clovis sites had been uncovered in the south-eastern United States than elsewhere, and that radiocarbon dating indicated that some of these pre-dated Clovis sites in the west. Stanford began to consider the unthinkable: were the ancestors of the Clovis people Stone Age Europeans?

Stanford set about making a close study of stone technology from Palaeolithic Spain, France and Portugal. His work revealed a high degree of correspondence with the Clovis stone and bone tools. The two cultures used 'nearly identical stoneworking technologies' Stanford observed. In addition to the similarities between the tools, both the Old and New World Stone Age cultures engraved limestone tablets, shaped bones similarly and stored their stone tools in caches filled with red ochre. 'The Solutrean toolkit is, with a few exceptions, nearly identical to that of Clovis,' Stanford concluded.[10] He further commented that had Solutrean stone tools been found in Siberia or north-east Asia, nobody would question their historical relationship with Clovis.

The main problem with the theory lies in establishing how Stone Age people would have crossed the Atlantic to reach America. Did Stone Age Europeans have seagoing craft? There is no direct evidence of this but, as many other Stone Age cultures around the world are known to have had them, it would be theoretically possible. Also, early Bronze Age boats have been found in Europe. One, unearthed in north-west England, is over 16m (52ft) long, constructed from massive oak planks sewn together with flexible yew branches and caulked with moss. Archaeologists estimate that it could have seated 18 oarsmen. Radiocarbon dating revealed the big boat to be 4000 years old. If such vessels could be built at such a point in prehistory, it may well have been that the knowledge of boat building went back thousands of years earlier. The Vikings, for example, are known to have reached America in timber craft powered by wind and oars. Stanford thinks the Solutreans may have worked their way across the Atlantic by sailing along the edge of the ice sheets along the north Atlantic, and living off marine life. There are also 'conveyor belt' currents active in the Atlantic just as there are in the Pacific – and the Atlantic is but a pond compared to the Pacific.

Stanford's ideas do not attract a big following, but conclusive proof that America had multiple Stone-Age contacts with the Old World by one route or another, east or west or both, looks set to come from recent research into genetics, the deep cellular memory of humanity that is only now beginning to be accessed.

Gene Genie

Among the various aspects of our genetic make-up – such as blood groups and proteins, and nuclear DNA – there are two that anthropological geneticists are increasingly focusing on when probing inside human cells. These are mitochondrial DNA (mtDNA) which is passed down from, mother to daughter, and Y-chromosomes, which are traced through the male line. These genetic pathways tend to accumulate changes or 'mutations' at a roughly predictable rate over the passage of time. Using such genetic markers allows the researchers to plot the evolution and divergence of human lineages. Further, because the mutations can be correlated with the geographic region in which they first occurred, it is possible for researchers to piece together ancient human migratory patterns. There is also the phenomenon of 'genetic drift', which is the change in gene frequencies that can occur in a people over generations owing to geographic isolation, migration, or to divisions that happen when one group leaves to found a new population (the 'founder effect').

The genetic memory has now been decoded to a point that it can be determined with a high degree of certainty that modern humanity had a common origin in Africa (as one school of scholarship has long argued) from where it radiated out, dispersing throughout the rest of the world. In trying to trace how America fits into this pattern, anthropological geneticists have begun to glimpse an unsuspected ancestral tapestry, the various genetic strands of which have not yet been fully woven together.

Work with mtDNA from living American Indian populations revealed that they consist overwhelmingly of four 'haplogroups' or lineages, designated A, B, C and D. Through world-wide sampling of mtDNA, these particular haplogroups are traceable back to Siberian and East Asian populations, with their origins indicated variously at between 25,000 and 40,000 years ago. Most anthropological geneticists feel that the presence of the four haplogroups in modern American Indians signifies three or four separate migrations, the first occurring up to 40,000 years ago. The story the genes tell therefore seems to blow the Clovis barrier asunder, and gives potential support to the archaeological work on pre-Clovis sites. But more recent research is turning that story into a riddle: another haplogroup, X, has now been found in American Indian populations.

The X and Y Files

There are a number of problems with haplogroup X from an interpretive point of view. It is found primarily in North America, whereas the other haplogroups are found throughout the Americas, and statistical analysis of the mtDNA data shows that it arrived there between c.13,000 and 28,000BC. More extraordinary still is the fact that haplogroup X is also found among Europeans but *not* Siberian peoples. It seems to turn on its head the story of the other four American-Indian lineages, and apparently re-awakens the spectre of ancient transatlantic contact with America. In particular, it could lend support to Dennis Stanford's suggestion of there having been Stone Age European contact – the dates for the purported Solutrean transatlantic adventure would fit neatly with the period indicated by the genetic information. While this is a real possibility, the mtDNA by definition can tell only half the story of humanity, and new research with Y-chromosome genetic markers has opened up other interpretations.

Research involving the Y-chromosome is relatively recent compared to work with mtDNA, but it is already yielding fascinating results. In a 1999 paper, researchers reported how a world-wide study of over 300 men revealed that the major Y-haplotype (lineage marker) present in most American Indians was traceable back to relatively recent ancestors common with Siberians. These were the Kets and Altaian peoples from the Yenissey River Basin and Altai Mountains respectively, and thence to a more ancient common ancestor in the central Eurasian region that apparently also gave rise to caucasoid or European Y chromosomes.[11] This last observation was confirmed and expanded by research published in 2001, which was based on almost 2000 men across the whole expanse of Eurasia.[12] It found that the most ancient ancestral lineage marker to which the American Indian Y-haplotype related originated in a central Eurasian population dating back 40,000–50,000 years. This ancient haplotype, identified as 'M45', was found to be also ancestral to European lineage markers – so both western European and American Indian Y-haplotypes were found to be traceable back to a common central Asian source.

The Y-chromosome trail was leading in a similar direction to the mtDNA work with the haplogroup X. However, the findings of the latter revealed that about 50,000 years ago groups of modern humans from out of Africa appear first to have settled a population in central Asia, and that subsequently elements migrated into northern Eurasia, west into Europe, and east through India to China and south-west Asia. Presumably there was eventual onward eastward migration via Australasia or Oceania to America, or north-east via Siberia to America, or both, in order to account for the Y-markers in both Old and New Worlds being traceable back to an ancestral Y-marker in central Asia. It does not necessarily rule out Stanford's suggested Solutrean visitation of America, but it offers an alternative explanation. In such a model, Columbus and those who followed him were just completing the circuit. Such thinking has yet to be confirmed, and the paper's authors readily admit that the full genetic history 'awaits further study of mitochondrial DNA and autosomal markers'. What does seem to a be a safe statement is to be found in another paper: in presenting a new human genetic tree based on Y-chromosome research, the paper's authors observe that 'Native Americans are located [on the tree] between Eurasians and east Asians indicating common ancestry with both'.[13]

It is perhaps too early to try to reconcile all the information flooding out of the new genetic research, but at first glance it seems as if it opens up all options concerning the early peopling of America. There seems to have been an ancestral population in central Asia sourcing migratory routes westwards into Europe and eastwards into south-east and north-east Asia, either or both of which could ultimately have continued on to America. In such a scenario, westwards, transatlantic European contact with America that predates the Vikings and Columbus cannot be ruled out.

These new visions of our genetic history are naturally of importance for everyone, not only American Indians. If we all can call Africa our first home, then central Asia is beginning to look as if it was our first home from home. If this presents intellectual challenges for scholars, it represents a nightmare for racists and nationalists who reject the implications of our common humanity.

On the Tip of Tongues

The timescale for the peopling of America is also of concern to linguistic scholars. It was noted in Chapter One that there were up to 2000 languages being spoken in the Americas at the time of first European contact. About 600 still survive, and these fall into nearly 200 distinct families, some containing but a single language. Earlier theories contending that all the native American languages derived from three primary language groups – the Amerind, Na-Dene and Aleut-Eskimo – that were related to three separate migrations between 12,000 and 6,000 years ago have been largely abandoned. It is now considered that the great diversity of indigenous American languages could only have come about over a very long period of time, amounting to tens of thousands of years. The 12,000 years that have supposedly elapsed since human migration into America first occurred simply would not have been sufficient for the required number of linguistic changes to have accumulated. Additionally, Crawford points out that when linguistic evidence is correlated with geologic and ecological evidence it provides 'indirect support for a pre-12,000-year presence of Amerindians in the New World'.[14]

Linguistic research indicates that the deep structural properties of American Indian languages have affinities with Old World languages spoken around the Pacific region. As I have already suggested, a possible Pacific connection appears in some form or other in the findings of almost all of the various disciplines attempting to determine who the dawn people of America were, and when they arrived. Its relevance must be revisited when the very bones of the distant American past are disinterred.

Skeletons in the Cupboard

The man from Spirit Cave stank. 'A musty, thick sweetness that clings to the back of your throat' was how one reporter put it.[15] The man's naturally mummified remains had been uncovered in a dry desert cave in Churchill County, Nevada, in 1940. He was found lying on a fur blanket, dressed in a robe made from twisted strips of rabbit pelt and hemp cords, wearing leather moccasins and with a skilfully woven twine mat sewn around his head and shoulders and another placed beneath him. Skin remained on the back and shoulders of the man, who was 1.75m (5ft 10in) tall, along with a tuft of straight, dark hair. Spirit Cave Man had been about 45 years of age when he died, and was in such a good state of preservation that it was assumed at the time that it was the body of some Indian chieftain who had been in the cave for up to 2000 years, remarkably well-preserved because of the dry conditions. But in 1996, when better techniques were available than had been the case in 1940, and when a stronger agenda to find out more about the ancestry of aboriginal Americans prevailed, he was radiocarbon dated. The results showed that Spirit Cave Man was not 2000 years old after all – he was over 7000 years old.

The year 1996 also saw the discovery of an ancient skeleton on Prince of Wales Island in Alaska, which was radiocarbon dated to 9700 years old. Yet more surprises started brewing on 28 July of the same year. On that day, two young men attending the annual hydroplane races on the Columbia River near Kennewick in Washington State found a skull in the river's shallows. One of the young men, Will Thomas, had thrust his hand into the water and pulled out what looked like a particularly smooth, round rock. As Thomas turned the brown object around in his hands, it grinned at him: 'All of a sudden, I saw teeth'. When the authorities were brought to the site, other bones were found spilling out of the riverbank. It was at first treated by police as a possible murder scene, but when archaeological experts became involved, radiocarbon dating showed that the bones, adding up to an almost complete skeleton, were those of a man who it seemed had been deliberately buried between c.6900 and 7200BC. In addition, when the man's remains were examined using a CAT scan (which produces a computer-generated X-ray image) it revealed a Clovis-era stone spear point lodged in his pelvis, a wound that had healed over.

The skeleton, by now known as 'Kennewick Man', was handed over to the Army Corps of Engineers (ACE), who had jurisdiction over the section of the river where the bones had been found. A coalition of five local Indian tribes then filed a claim for the skeleton under the Native American Graves Protection and Repatriation Act (NAGPRA), a 1990 federal law that provides for the repatriation of ancestral human remains to Indian tribes. Only one of the tribes advocated that further scientific work should be carried out on Kennewick Man, the others wanted him reburied at once. ACE was about to hand the skeleton over when scientists became extremely concerned that this could potentially mean a major loss of information about American Indian origins and so they began a legal battle to prevent the transfer. Although they allowed Indian representatives to visit the boxed remains and pray over them, ACE eventually gave Kennewick Man to the United States Department of the Interior. Scientific access was allowed, and religious ceremonies were conducted at Kennewick Man's original burial site. But, as the scientific studies got under way in December 1998, it was found that two of the leg bones had been stolen. Although there were suspicions, the person or persons who had done this deed were never identified.[16] Fortunately, the missing femurs, together with other fragments, reappeared in June 2001. The FBI took possession of them, although their investigation was later dropped.

The discovery has been plagued by bitter argument between Indians, scientists, politicians and government organizations. In one or two other instances, though, the issues raised by the discovery of a very ancient skeleton have been handled more diplomatically and productively, in that scientists and Indians have joined in co-operative attempts to investigate the origins of indigenous American humanity together.

These cases are examples of the very limited number of American skeletal remains dating back 8000 years or more – the oldest apparently being a female skeleton from central Brazil dating to c.9700BC. Though rare, these discoveries allow for overlapping ways of investigating the origins of human occupation of the New World, namely, morphological archaeology. This is the study of the overall characteristics of ancient skeletal remains, physical anthropology and characteristics in a geographical context. A related discipline is craniofacial study, which is the precise measurement and analysis of multiple skull and facial dimensions and their comparison against a world-wide database of such measurements, ancient and modern. Earlier (and cruder) manifestations of these disciplines were sometimes used to find evidence for a racist agenda, but today they are technically and technologically advanced, politically neutral forms of study that can cast light on the migratory adventures of early humanity.

Early on in the Kennewick Man saga it became apparent that the remains featured a distinctively long narrow skull, projecting nose, receding cheekbones, a high chin and square jaw – the cranial characteristics of a modern Indo-European, Polynesian, or the Ainu of Japan – rather than the broad face, prominent cheekbones and round skull of the modern American Indian and Siberian peoples. The lower bones of his arms and legs were long compared to the upper bones, traits uncommon among modern American Indians. These features were so pronounced that, until his true age became known, some thought that Kennewick Man might have been a 19th-century European trapper. Spirit Cave Man showed similar characteristics. Richard Jantz of the University of Tennessee and Douglas Owsley from the National Museum of Natural History in Washington DC have spent decades collecting and analysing measurements taken from modern American Indian populations, and they found that Spirit Cave Man and two ancient skulls from Minnesota simply did not fit into the range of modern American Indian characteristics – they had looked more like Indonesians, if not Europeans. Other work on ancient skulls in North and South America have found characteristics variously showing affinities with south Asians, north Asians and even Australian Aborigines, in the case of the Brazilian skeleton. So far, it seems that only two early skeletons show dimensions and forms that match the range of those of modern American Indians, namely Wizards Beach Man, another Nevada find dated to 7200BC, and Idaho's Buhl Woman, dating to 8700BC. These have been repatriated to Indian tribes and reburied.[17]

Some of the most recent craniofacial research available at the time of this writing offers a more finely focused view.[18] From a comparison of recent and prehistoric Old World samples and a similar sample range from America, it appears as if the first known entrants to America did not relate to any known mainland Asian population. 'Instead, they show ties to the Ainu of Hokkaido and their Jomon predecessors in prehistoric Japan and to the Polynesians of remote Oceania,' the researchers declare.[19] In turn, all these Old World peoples can be linked to Upper Palaeolithic (late Stone Age, c.33,000–8500BC) and recent inhabitants of Europe. The researchers envisage a Stone Age 'continuum of people across the northern fringe of the Old World'. In their view, these people, who became the true Palaeoindians, gave rise to most of the American Indians south of the United States–Canadian border. On the other hand, the researchers also claim that what are now considered the more recent American Indian peoples, the Inuit or Eskimo, the Aleut and the Na-Dene language groups do show similarities to the mainland populations of eastern Asia. (The Na-Dene group comprised various Indian tribes of the Pacific north-west, with a breakaway group that reached the south-west and are recognized today as the Navajo and Apache peoples.)

It is by no means clear as yet, but taking the totality of skeletal evidence to date it appears that it cannot yet be confidently claimed that all of the dawn people of America were necessarily the direct ancestors of today's American Indians. The picture seems to be one of multiple early entries into America of people from differing Old World sources, with modern American Indian ancestors representing only some of them. Why no vestiges of the other early migrants are apparent in the modern Indian skeleton could be for any number of reasons – they may have been very sporadic visitors or have arrived in small groups that did not develop to a sufficiently significant degree for their lineage to survive. (However, if that is the case it is difficult to explain why their remains are the ones most frequently discovered.). Alternatively, they may have been assimilated into – or even eliminated by – the direct American Indian ancestral populations. Whatever the reasons, the unexpected cranial characteristics of many of the early skeletal remains carries the obvious implication that modern American Indian tribes might not be on solid ground in making ancestral claims for them all. This is of course a politically delicate issue. What is certain is that scientists must approach their work relating to American Indians with sensitivity, particularly when challenging their claims to the American earth, as the indigenous American people. In truth, whatever the archaeological situation turns out to be, today's American Indians must have the strongest claim of any people now living in America. By the same token, American Indians could see the scientific determination of the origins of the most ancient human remains in the New World to be an honouring of those elders, whether or not all of them were directly their ancestors, and to become partners with scientists in that celebration of human antiquity. It is crucial, though, that when research on the remains is conducted, scholars should return them to the appropriate Indian tribe. This is necessary for the remains to be re-interred with due ceremony in the American earth that yielded them up, the very earth that these extremely ancient people were among the first to walk upon.

* * *

If the sometimes conflicting strands of evidence I have reviewed so far are to be reconciled, it would appear that a fairly inclusive view must be taken of the early peopling of America – one that allows several theories to co-exist. In summary, though, it seems that America was empty until the arrival of the first modern humans from other parts of the world. There is evidence to suggest that there were migrations of modern human beings across Beringia during the last Ice Age and towards its close, and probably at times subsequent to this, and that during the Ice Age migrations these people, who were Siberians or other north-eastern Asians, journeyed by boat down the west coast of North America, and perhaps farther south. Some may have travelled inland when they were south of the ice sheets covering what is today Canada and the northern United States. There is increasing evidence, though, that other migrants may have reached America from more southerly Asian, Australasian and Oceanic sources, reaching South and Central America at various times, some of them perhaps very early indeed, even before the first Beringia migrations. These peoples could have been, variously, south-east Asians, including Jomon and Ainu peoples from what is today Japan, and possibly Australian and Polynesian. It seems likely that all these people, by whatever route they arrived in America, ultimately harked back to a central Asian ancestral population. There is also a faint, outside chance that some Stone Age peoples from Europe made transatlantic contact with eastern North America and perhaps Central America too. Before we can build up a clear picture of how humanity first arrived in America, much more scien tific work needs to be carried out and the evidence collected so far needs to be refined – but that is for the future. The following sections of this book explore the strange or enigmatic aspects of what happened after humanity did arrive.

PART 2

LOST CIVILIZATIONS

ANCIENT AMERICA'S
MYSTIFYING LEGACY

CHAPTER FOUR

CITIES OF THE GODS

America's prehistoric settlers gradually changed from hunter-gatherer ways and began to develop more complex societies. The catalysts for this shift from a timeless form of simple, low-impact lifestyle to the more structured system of a civilized society are unclear, but such evolutionary developments occurred in the New World just as surely as they did in the Old World. Whole civilizations arose, complete with social and religious systems, calendars, accomplished artwork, sometimes writing, and often with sophisticated masonry and remarkable cities. Distinctive cultures emerged, and some of them appear to have been exceedingly strange – indeed, a few are amongst the most curious we know of anywhere in the ancient world.

Because these civilizations rose and fell over great periods of time, later pre-Columbian American Indians themselves sometimes stood in awe before the remnants of earlier American Indian achievements. The Aztecs, for instance, confronted by the vast ruins of the great prehistoric city of Teotihuacan in the Valley of Mexico, felt that such a place could only have been the dwelling of the gods themselves. They deliberately tied their own mythic history to it, as they did to the remnants of the more recent Toltec empire. This was certainly to aggrandize themselves, though there may also have been authentic links of continuity between their culture and those great builders of the past.

To give a flavour of the range of lost civilizations of the Americas, this chapter overviews a necessarily selective sample of key cultures involved, identifying a major site or city associated with each one of them, and indicating other relevant centres. The overview follows a generally chronological rather than a geographical arrangement, from earliest known cultures to the latest prior to European contact, though there are inevitable overlaps of timelines because different cultures sometimes arose in similar time periods in various parts of the Americas. The overview commences with the oldest city yet uncovered in America.

Caral, Peru: *c.*2600BC. Unknown Andean Culture

The sand-smothered ruins of this 81-hectare (200-acre) urban complex in Peru's remote Supe Valley – 22km (14 miles) inland from the arid Pacific coast and over 160km (100 miles) north of Lima – had been noticed initially in 1905, but was only rediscovered archaeologically in 1996, when Dr Ruth Shady Solis began excavating it. In 2001, radiocarbon dating of

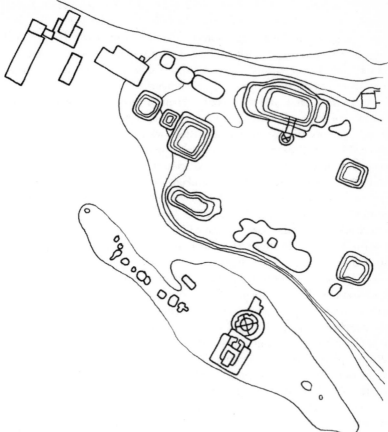

Fig. 4.1. Plan showing part of the ceremonial centre of Caral, Peru.

fibres and other organic matter uncovered in the dig gave startling results, showing the site to be over a thousand years older than any other city found in America. The dates obtained ranged between 2627 and 1977BC.

Caral is the largest of 18 ancient complexes scattered along the Supe Valley – the others have yet to be archaeologically investigated. The core area of the complex contains 32 monumental structures, of which six are terraced pyramids or 'platform mounds' (Figure 4.1). The largest of these is the substantial 'Piramide Mayor', some 20m (60ft) high. Investigation shows that these buildings were constructed in just one or at the most two phases, thus indicating the presence of complex planning and large-scale logistical organiation. Other structures include sunken circular plazas or amphitheatres, temples, and residential buildings. Many of Caral's architectural features were the forerunners of designs that were to reappear in various Andean (and Mesoamerican) civilizations over the following 3000 years.

This ancient city thrived at a time before grains were cultivated and pottery was used in South America, thus disproving the previously held archaeological belief that civilization could only take place when both those factors were present. The domesticated plants found at Caral included squash, beans, and cotton. The remains of fish were also uncovered, so it appears the city drew on both fishing and agriculture, from the coast and from the hinterland, and this may have helped turn it into a major centre – a kind of trade and cultural crossroads for its region. It developed where it did, it seems, because of the Supe River, which the inhabitants of Caral successfully used for irrigation purposes. Apart from these economic and ecological underpinnings, there was clearly a well-developed religious structure in place at Caral, for the sunken plazas appear to have been used for public ritual and ceremonial displays, in much the same way as such features were used in later Andean cities.

Warfare is another factor assumed by modern scholars to account for the rise of cities. Yet evidence of war is absent at Caral, since no defensive structures or weapons have been uncovered, and no mutilated bodies dug up. What *has* been unearthed includes flutes made from condor and pelican bones, and evidence of the use of aphrodisiacs and visionary, mind-altering drugs – a recurring feature in ancient America (see Chapter Seven). It seems the people of Caral preferred to make love rather than war. However, there is much more archaeological investigation to be carried out at Caral, and this is a particularly exciting opportunity for the investigators, because the site is pristine – it was not built over by succeeding cultures, and it was not subjected to European influence. Here is a place where civilization appears to have flowered first in the Americas, and it did so at roughly the same time that it was happening in the Old World, since the pyramids of Caral are as old as those of Egypt.[1]

It may be premature, even now, to assume that Caral is the earliest city of the Americas. But the discovery of such sophisticated architecture and religion established at Caral attests to its inhabitants being remarkably advanced for their time. And it is quite possible that under the dunes of the Andes' arid regions, or lost in the dense green gloom of the Amazon rainforest, an even earlier city lies waiting to be discovered.

La Venta, Mexico:
*c.*1200–400BC. Olmec Culture

The Olmec heartland was on the Gulf Coast of Mexico, in an area that is now included within the modern states of Tabasco and Veracruz, from where the Olmecs spread their influence over a much wider area. It is not known who the Olmecs were – the name simply comes from the Aztec word for rubber (*Olmeca)* and was bestowed upon them by modern scholars. The Olmecs as an identifiable people first appear in the archaeological record in *c*.1500BC since they were among the first Mesoamericans to transform (for unknown reasons) from a village-type society to a complex, stratified high culture. The Olmec era declined, again for reasons that are not known, during the final centuries of the first millennium BC.

La Venta (now La Venta Park) stands on an isolated, 3.2-km-wide (2-mile) sandy island rising out of surrounding swampland near the modern city of Villahermosa, and is one of the few known major Olmec sites. La Venta is comprised of ten architectural groups laid out along a north–south axis. Set on the centre line is 'Mound C', a cone-shaped clay (adobe) pyramid with curiously fluted sides standing over 30m (100ft) tall. It is thought that it is an effigy of San Martin Pajapan, a dominant and sacred volcano in the Tuxtla range, from where the Olmecs obtained their basalt for monumental sculpture (see Chapter Eight for more on this American Indian trait of venerating the natural landscape). To the south of the pyramid are a series of platforms and parallel plazas or avenues. To the north, two long, parallel earthen mounds extend from the base of the pyramid, beyond which there are rectangular plazas once bounded by basalt columns and an adobe wall. There are also earthen mounds, and mosaics made of serpentine slabs embedded in tar that, bizarrely, had been concealed beneath layers of clay. And La Venta, like other Olmec centres, boasted complex stone drainage systems.

In its heyday, La Venta must have appeared bright if not gaudy or 'psychedelic' as one archaeologist has put it, for the Olmecs painted their ceremonial architecture in solid red, pink, yellow, blue and purple colours, and carefully selected coloured clays and sands were used in geometric patterns to great effect.

The Olmecs left behind massive pieces of sculpted basalt of varying kinds. There were slab-like stelae with relief carvings showing kings or priest-chieftains in elaborate costumes accompanied by supernatural creatures, and altar-like blocks with niches in which regal figures sit clad in tall head-dresses. The most famous of the monumental sculptural items, though, are undoubtedly the 'colossal heads'. The largest are around 3m (10ft) tall and can weigh up to 20 tonnes or more (see Plate 2). The locations of the known sources of the basalt used are 80km (50 miles) or more distant. Whether the giant blocks were transported by land or water is unknown. Tests conducted for a British television documentary[2] initially showed that the volcanic rock was exceedingly hard and therefore difficult to carve, but they then found another type of basalt that was much easier to work with. So the real mystery about the heads is not so much how they were made, but rather who they portrayed. They show flat-nosed, thick-lipped faces framed by tight-fitting helmets. Scholars are fairly confident that the heads are portraits of Olmec rulers, as each face is individually depicted, but it is the facial characteristics that raise the biggest question: were the Olmecs African? Could these Olmec effigies tell of early African contact? Many scholars argue that the facial characteristics fall within the overall range found amongst Mexican Indians, but it is difficult to ignore the strong characteristics so insistently displayed by the heads.The Olmecs have left many other smaller but equally tantalizing artefacts. Natural rubber balls have been found that, along with some images in Olmec artwork, support observations about the presence at this early time of a mysterious and apparently ritualistic ball game. This required the ballcourts found at numerous later Central American and Mexican archaeological sites, and even at sites in Arizona (see Plate 3). It is probable that the tight helmets on the Colossal Heads relate to the ball game. What seems to be an Olmec magnetic compass has also been found and in 1967 a lodestone magnet carved into the shape of a grooved oblong bar was unearthed at another Olmec site, in San Lorenzo (*c.*1200–900BC), and was found to orient quite accurately to magnetic north. In addition, concave mirrors (reflective surfaces polished to 'optical specifications') made of magnetite have been unearthed.[3] Experiments conducted with them have shown that they can start fires, and can even project images onto flat surfaces in the manner of a *camera lucida* (which uses a prism to achieve the same effect). Archaeologist Michael Coe has commented, 'One can imagine the hocus-pocus which some mighty Olmec priest was able to perform with one of these.'[4] The Olmecs were particularly skilled in carving figurines, masks and decorative items in, variously, serpentine, jade, wood, iron, and basalt, and it is these that leave the most intriguing record of this strange and ancient culture. One such Olmec masterpiece is the so-called 'Wrestler', a 66-cm (26-in) figure carved out of basalt that realistically depicts a person engaged in energetic activity (see Plate 4). Perhaps more significantly, though, the figure is a *bearded* man. Bearded American Indians are uncommon, but are frequently depicted in Olmec art as well. Moreover, it has to be said that the Wrestler looks more Asian than American Indian and very different from the faces on the Colossal Heads.

As mystifying as these details are, the most extraordinary, disturbing and baffling of Olmec artefacts are those showing variations on a 'were-child' theme and a human-jaguar hybrid image, which recur throughout Olmec art. Infantile figures, chubby dwarf-like creatures, and snarling 'were-children', some revealing toothless gums and others displaying the fangs and claws of jaguars, are common images in Olmec art (see Plates 5 and 6). Another recurring motif in the sculptures is of an adult, possibly a king-like figure, cradling a 'were-child'. Many of these strange infants – and some adults – are shown with deformed, elongated head shapes. The expression of the curled-back lip, often revealing filed teeth, is a characteristic Olmec motif, sometimes referred to as the 'Olmec snarl'. Scholars have long pondered what this range of images could be about, for they were clearly important to the Olmecs. It has been suggested that beliefs concerning child-spirits still held by the present-day Indians of the Gulf Coast region may be a memory of the infantile form found in Olmec art.

While the ancient figurines clearly represent supernatural beings, the actual source of the image may be quite disturbing if the findings of two researchers, archaeologist Carolyn Tate and cardiologist Gordon Bendersky, are borne out. They realized that various characteristics of the Olmec figures were those of foetuses, in particular the oversize heads and bent knees.[5] In fact, the head-to-body ratios were 1:3 or 1:4 in the sculptures, and these are the ratios found in foetuses of 12 to 30 weeks. The poses of the figures are also characteristic of those taken up by a foetus in the womb. When the researchers sought specialist medical opinion, the experts were able to point out that finer detail on the figurines, such as incompletely formed ears, swellings and folds around the eyes, and the bony protrusion of the collar bone were all evidence of them portraying foetuses. So precise were the renditions that the experts were able to identify gestational ages represented by individual sculptures. Even the translucency of foetal skin seemed to be represented by the use of suitable materials, and the veins, clearly visible through foetal skin, were depicted on the figurines by fine vein-like engravings. Moreover, the medical experts could detect specific congenital deformities in the foetal representations, such as undersize or missing jaws (microanthia and agnathia) and unnaturally shaped large heads (macrocephaly) over and above the normal large foetal head size. Such deformities would be likely to have caused spontaneous abortion, and so the source of the figurine imagery may have been miscarried foetuses and stillborn babies.

There is preliminary archaeological support for the theory: excavations around fresh and saltwater springs at the Olmec site of El Manati, Veracruz, uncovered a ritual deposit dating back to c.1200BC. This contained about 40 wooden busts of 'baby-faced' human figures, along with a range of other objects such as jade axe-heads and stone sceptres. Scattered over this assemblage were the disarticulated leg bones and skulls of several newborn children and foetuses. One of the wooden busts covered the complete burial of a foetus or newborn.

Why would the Olmecs have been so obsessed with foetal imagery? We cannot be certain but Tate proposes a plausible theory. The Olmecs may have been fascinated by the developmental forms the foetus goes through, from an almost tadpole-like structure, through reptilian shapes to the fully-formed baby. This transformative process may have been a metaphor for, or a conceptual prototype of the visionary transformations the Olmec priest-kings or shaman-chieftains went through during a trance, when the body-image of the person experiencing the altered mind state changes into that of an animal or bird. This subjective transformation would have been controlled by powerful cultural suggestion and externalized for onlookers by costumes, masks, ceremonial imagery and sacred art.

This brings us to the human–animal hybrid images, especially the 'were-jaguars' associated with both infantile and adult sculptural figures. These figures are human forms fused with feline characteristics, specifically those of the jaguar. This magnificent animal was seen as the chief spiritual embodiment of the wild nature surrounding the Olmec and certain other American Indian societies and the jaguar spirit or god theme recurs in ancient South American cultures. Most scholars now agree that this hybrid image probably relates to the idea of visionary transformation in altered states of consciousness. Some figurines form a set that actually show the full transformation of man into jaguar in a series of 'freeze fame' depictions, much like cinematic special effects today can show us an actor in a werewolf movie apparently transforming into a wolf.[6] One such figurine gives the secret away, for it is engraved with the image of *Bufo marinus*, a species of toad whose glands secrete the hallucinogenic substance bufotine. While excavating San Lorenzo, archaeologist Michael Coe discovered a great many bones from this toad,[7] some of them deposited in ceremonial caches, adding to the theory that extensive ritual use of mind-altering substances was commonplace in La Venta.[8] (Coe made another interesting find at San Lorenzo: he and his team came to realize that the whole city had been built on a man-made earthwork 1.2km (¾ mile) long, which he suspects was created in the shape of a giant bird.[9])

In the last few centuries BC, as the Olmec culture faded away, the Maya civilization was beginning to emerge to the east and south. The Olmec civilization had a profound influence on that emerging culture and on many of the other high cultures that subsequently appeared in pre-Columbian Mexico.

Poverty Point, Louisiana, USA:
*c.*1000–500BC. Unknown Culture

This location on Macon Ridge in the Lower Mississippi Valley was occupied perhaps as early as 1800BC, but reached its zenith around 1000BC when the site had developed into a huge earthwork complex. Its remains are still visible to some extent, and consist of six artificial embankments cresting at up to 2m (6ft) and arranged in concentric arcs in a fairly uniform fashion 43m (142ft) apart. This semi-circular earthwork complex is 1.2 km (¾ mile) wide and ends on bluffs overlooking the Bayou Macon, the stream that bounds the eastern edge of the site (Figure 4.2). The concentric banks, which are intersected by four aisles, embrace an open plaza covering an area of 15 hectares (37 acres) which had been artificially levelled. A straight, built-up causeway projected out of the concentric embankments to a mound beyond. Almost immediately to the west of the outer embankment stands a gigantic earthen mound (Mound A) which is 21m (70ft) high, around 195m (650ft) wide and over 216m (700ft) long.

This mound's purpose remains a mystery, but it is a curious shape and many archaeologists think it forms the schematic representation of a bird. If so, it is the largest effigy earthwork known of in North America. To its north stands Mound B, a conical structure 6m (20ft) high. This had been constructed over a burnt area that contained human bone, so might have had funerary significance. To the south of Mound A are various other mounds and earthworks, including one that is an artificially modified natural feature.

Large postholes offer evidence that there had been giant timber structures within the complex too.

No one can say who the Poverty Point people were, but it is known they were hunter-gatherers because of the nature of the finds at the site. These included stone dart and spear points, broad, stone knife blades; stone weights for bolas (cords with weighted ends that were hurled at small game to wrap round their legs); and food residues including fish, nuts, seeds, fruits, plants, and a variety of animals such as turkey, duck, alligator, and turtle. There was no agriculture as such, and these people lived before the invention of the bow and arrow. A great many small baked clay balls that had been used for cooking were found, which would have been heated then dropped in water to bring it to the boil, or piled around food on a hearth. It is remarkable that hunter-gatherers could have shown the skill and planning required to erect a massive structure such as Poverty Point and it is totally out of character with what archaeologists and anthropologists have come to expect of hunter-gatherer societies. Massive public works are normally associated with a people who practise agriculture. It is estimated that the Poverty Point complex contains around 910,000 cubic metres (1,000,000 cubic yards) of earth, and had been built up by the use of millions of basket-loads of soil. It could only have been achieved by sophisticated central planning, even if the work was carried out over a long period of time (but much of the complex seems to be based on a single concept and so it may well have been constructed within a relatively short time).

Artefacts to do with the religious and social life of the Poverty Point people have also been unearthed. These include small, crude hand-modelled clay figurines, often depicting pregnant women, stone 'peace pipes' (calumets), and polished stone beads and pendants beautifully worked into animal or geometric shapes. The types of stone used for these decorative items were carefully selected and came from far and wide, and it is clear that this unknown Poverty Point culture had remarkably extensive trade networks.

It is not known what Poverty Point was used for. Evidence has been found showing that the terraces between the semi-circular embankments were used for dwellings. These probably took the form of shallow pits covered over by bent-pole frames topped with thatch and daub. In the wider region around the site there were smaller sites of the same culture, many linked by waterways, and so Poverty Point could have been the central 'metropolis' for the whole region. On the other hand, it may have served as a great religious focal centre for that scattering of sites, and the dwellings could have been for priests, ceremonial leaders, and their entourage. Or it could have served both purposes. It is still subject to speculation since only a small percentage of the site has been thoroughly investigated to date.

Chavin de Huantar, Peru: c.900–200BC. Chavin Culture

This profoundly mysterious place was a temple, shrine, and oracle centre. Because of this it was also a pilgrimage centre, forming the heart of a shamanistic religious cult that projected its influence over thousands of square miles of Andean highlands and coastal desert. One of the ways it expressed its nature was through an art style to which the complex gives its name: 'Chavin is a very complex, "baroque" and esoteric style, intentionally difficult to decipher, intended to disorient, and ultimately to transport the viewer into alternate realities,' writes Rebecca Stone-Miller. 'The terms "hallucinatory" and "transformational" aptly describe much Chavin subject matter and artistic effect.'[10]

The temple is situated about halfway up the Andes, midway between coast and jungle in northern Peru. It stands at the confluence of two rivers. These are all factors that made it a perfect pilgrimage location, and also why the place enjoyed an influx of trade, resources, and ideas from the varied regions. But the location was also symbolic: it was the holy place at the crux of the Andean world of its day. The temple buildings developed over time, as the religious cult became more popular. The 'Old Temple' was an east-facing U-shaped structure embracing a sunken circular court or plaza, but the south wing eventually became extended into the 'New Temple' and larger plazas were built, linking the river with the striking black and white stone entrance of the New Temple. Sculptures adorned the temple complex, and though these are now largely lost or fragmented, what has been found of them indicates a preponderance of half-human, half-feline beings. Hidden away inside the windowless Old Temple is a labyrinth of dank, unlit passageways connected by stairways and 500m (1600ft) of vents and drainage channels that exceed any discernible engineering requirements. It has been proposed that these in fact formed an impressive sound system. During experiments, in which water was passed through the drainage channels, vents in the system were opened and closed causing the sound of rushing water to be amplified.[11] The temple reverberated with thunderous 'pink noise' which the experimenting archaeologist likened to the sound of applause. 'Pink noise' is an acoustical term for a kind of wide-frequency sound that has slightly more acoustic 'colour' than 'white noise' (a static-like hiss). Pink noise is, in effect, a natural form of white noise – such as the sound of wind in foliage or rain falling on a forest canopy, etc. It can promote a relaxed-but-alert mental state, often found in meditation subjects. Apart from its potential mind-altering effects on initiates or priests within the temple's passages and rooms, this bravura acoustic display may have also been used to great effect in impressing pilgrims gathered in front of the temple, generating awe at the sound of the gods within. The secret passages and stairways would also have allowed priests to appear as if by magic on temple rooftops, and vanish in similar enigmatic ways.

Deep inside the Old Temple there is the *Lanzon*, an enigmatic 4.5m (15ft) high, carved monolithic stone monument situated tightly within a cruciform gallery, set within the building's structure (see Plate 7). This still occupies its original position, and seems to have been the focal point of the whole temple complex from the beginning. The carving shapes the standing stone into a stylized figure, a god with a head-dress made of feline heads and a smiling (or snarling) mouth baring teeth and animal fangs. The deity's hair and eyebrows end in snakes' heads, and its feet and hands have claws. In short, the *Lanzon* is an idol. The top of the monolith pokes up through the ceiling of the cruciform gallery into a secret room above. It has been suggested that a priest may have occupied this, providing the idol's voice during oracular sessions.

Over 40 sculpted stone heads that had been fixed to the outside walls of the temple by means of tenons show human features transforming, stage by stage, into exotic creatures. Again, this is thought to be an expression of the hallucinogenic experience of the body-image changing into an animal, a common theme in shamanism. Once again this process seems to have

Fig. 4.2. Drawing of the bas-relief in the sunken plaza at Chavin de Huantar depicting a supernatural being or masked priest holding the mind-altering San Pedro cactus.

been aided and abetted by the use of mind-altering drugs. That the hallucinogenic cactus, San Pedro (*Trichocereus pachanoi*), is depicted on an engraved stone panel in the wall of the circular sunken plaza further supports this theory (Figure 4.2). The long, ribbed cactus is shown being grasped by a human–animal being that has jaguar fangs – perhaps the image of a costumed shaman-priest holding the cactus as a staff of authority. It is thought that the priests of Chavin de Huantar obtained their knowledge of hallucinogenic brews and snuffs from Amazon forest peoples to the east, tribal societies who remain intensely shamanistic to this day and have great knowledge of both the visionary and medicinal potential of plants.

There have been speculations about exotic associations with Chavin de Huantar. One is that there was contact between Olmec and Chavin cultures, as the use of mind-altering drugs to effect hallucinatory animal transformations plus the deification of the jaguar are shared factors between them. Another even more speculative idea returns once more to the possibility that the Chavin culture may have come into contact with Asian influences. The Chinese art of the Shang dynasty (*c*.1750–*c*.1050BC) depicted snake eyebrows, horned cats lacking lower jaws, and scales on the tails of feline creatures, which are all similar to imagery found in Chavin art. A type of anthracite mirror associated with Chavin culture is also found in a Chinese province, both cultures bred special 'temple dogs', and there are strong similarities in decorative motifs used in both Shang China and Chavin Peru. (Strangely, if such an influence is genuine, it might explain the perceived connection between Chavin and the Olmec without there having been actual contact between the two American cultures, for there are also strong similarities between Shang and Olmec decorative motifs, a phenomenon we will explore in Chapter Six.)

The Chavin religious cult reached the zenith of its power *c*.400–200BC. After that, it faded away. But the Chavin phenomenon did establish a pan-Andean religious sensibility that was to continue in varying forms for thousands of years.

Monte Alban, Mexico: *c*.500BC–AD700. Zapotec Culture

Claimed as the first city in ancient Mexico, Monte Alban occupies the artificially levelled summit of the largest in a group of hills rising 390m (1300ft) above the floor of the broad Valley of Oaxaca. In the first millennium BC, the region was occupied by the Zapotec people, and their descendants are still there, speaking a lyrical tone language (in which pitch and intonation can determine the meaning of a word) that has been described as 'the Italian of the Americas'. Various chiefdoms developed within the valley, but then in a process not fully understood they became dominated by the political and ceremonial complex that we know as Monte

Fig. 4.3. One of the stones from Building L in Monte Alban depicting a so-called 'dancer', but in all likelihood an image of a corpse.

Alban. This started out around 500BC as a kind of citadel and it subsequently developed and changed in five major phases up to the time of European contact (1521), but by then it was just a shadow of its former self.

The complex is laid out on a north–south axis, and essentially consists of a huge rectangular central plaza almost 300m (1000ft) in length, bounded on east and west by impressive arrays of temple platforms and palatial structures. At the north end of the eastern line of buildings is a ritual ballcourt, that ubiquitous presence in ancient Mesoamerican cities and ceremonial complexes. Included on the western side is the structure known as Building L, 'The Temple of the Dancers', which was built over the oldest structure at the Monte Alban site. In its foundations were stone slabs depicting figures in a variety of unusual poses. Initially assumed to be dancers, on closer inspection the figures appear to represent corpses, probably slain captives of war (Figure 4.3). Some of the figures are shown mutilated, and it appears that some of the images represent the flayed skins of the deceased. This is just one piece of evidence found at the site showing the real power of Monte Alban at one time to have been military.

The north and south ends of the plaza are defined by massive platforms. The North Platform is thought to have been the official dwelling area of the chief and his kin – the royal family – while the South Platform supported the main temple. On the plaza floor in between, there is a row of temple platforms. These follow the axial direction of the plaza and the whole complex, but one isolated arrowhead-shaped structure known as Building J, at the southern end of the row, is set at an angle. This may have had astronomical functions.

The overall site plan echoes the layout of the valley itself,[12] providing another instance of how the American Indians viewed their natural surroundings with a curious veneration.

Ordinary Monte Alban citizens lived in huts on terraces cut into the sides of the hill and the surrounding slopes. It is probable that the main plaza was not used for normal everyday assembly, but was reserved for ceremonial and ritual activities. This is suggested by the facts that the temples around its perimeter open out onto it, presenting their backs to the main population on the terraces outside, and the ways into the plaza were limited and constricted.

The Zapotecs of Monte Alban had hieroglyphic writing carved in stone on and around their buildings, and not all of it has yet been deciphered. This means writing in ancient Mexico appeared a few centuries before even the ancient Mayans. The people of Monte Alban also had a 260-day divinatory calendar. This was the first appearance of the oldest element of a calendrical system that was to develop later throughout ancient Mexico up to the time of European contact, in which the 260-day calendar was combined with a 365-day one. The two calendar systems ran concurrently, as toothed wheels of different sizes engaged with one another in gearing systems. A given date would be expressed in terms relating to both calendars. It took 52 years for the 'meshing' to complete a full cycle. Each calendar had day and month names, but while the 365-day calendar was obviously based on the solar year, the basis of the 260-day calendar is not fully understood. It is comprised of a repeating cycle of 20 day names paired with 13 day numbers, amounting to 260 days overall. It is possible that it was devised by midwives to work out birth dates, calculating from the first missed menstrual period through to birth, in effect the approximate nine-month gestation period.[13] The logic of this was that people considered that they had completed one 260-day cycle at birth. The calendar was used as an almanac by seers when foretelling the future, for every day, name and number had its particular properties from a divinatory perspective, and some combinations had better aspects than others. Incredibly, this ancient ritual calendar survived among a group of Mayans in Guatemala until the 1940s.[14] Further, a board made from an old door was found in the 1970s by an anthropologist in Milpoleta, a remote village in Chiapas, which had on it marks made by the local shaman, linking the 20-day ritual cycle with the 365-day solar cycle. Examination with infrared techniques showed the board to have been used for over a century prior to its discovery.[15]

Archaeological investigation of tombs in the landscape around the main complex of Monte Alban has revealed murals in bright colours and a stunning array of grave goods displaying exceptional craftsmanship. In particular, there were many gold objects. In one tomb alone (Tomb 7) there were 121 items of finely wrought gold. This was centuries before metalwork became a widespread practice in Mesoamerica. The tombs also yielded silverware, onyx urns, delicately carved bones, carved rock crystal, polychrome pottery, and other items of jade, turquoise, amber, coral and shell.

In its first centuries, Monte Alban's population probably hovered around 5000, but during its prime, between c.AD500 and 700, that increased to 25,000. After that period, though, the organization of the region devolved into smaller population groups and ceremonial centres and estates. But Monte Alban appears to have been respected as a symbol of cultural unity, even to the point that the modern city of Oaxaca rose close by it.

Tiahuanaco, Peru:
c.250BC–AD1000. Unknown Andean Culture

The remains of this ceremonial city and pilgrimage centre stand close to Lake Titicaca at an altitude of 3600m (12,000ft) in the Bolivian Andes (Figure 4.4). Like Chavin de Huantar, it developed out of a religion that dominated the region as early as 1000BC. Though the site of Tiahuanaco was occupied by that date, the city proper existed from c.250BC. At its height, it covered at least four square miles and had up to 40,000 inhabitants – a population that was increased by the influx of pilgrims. The city's influence extended throughout the southern Andes by means of religion, trade and, possibly, a limited amount of military force.

Fig. 4.4. Andean ruins, probably Tiahuanaco, drawn by E.G. Squier during his 1877 expedition. (E.G. Squier)

Although the altiplano site of Tiahuanaco looks bleak and barren today, archaeological research has revealed that the little-known people of Tiahuanaco had developed a type of raised field system called 'waru waru' that extended out for 14km (9 miles) around the shores of Lake Titicaca. This consisted of 'fields' that were really earthen platforms punctuating a network of canals. In addition, the people would have herded llamas and alpacas as well as feeding on fish, birds and natural vegetation around the lake. Further, Tiahuanaco established enclaves in distant and kinder climatic areas to help the supply of food in hard times.

Both the location and design of Tiahuanaco is an expression of sacred geography. Lake Titicaca was the mythological point of creation and emergence for Andean peoples from the earliest times and the sacred islands of the Sun and Moon in the lake contain shrines that date to Tiahuanaco times. This natural situation is mimicked by the layout of the ceremonial core of Tiahuanaco in that it is surrounded by a purely symbolic, non-defensive moat, thus making it a sacred island. The major ceremonial structures on this core-island are oriented to the four cardinal directions, with the east–west axis being dominant. The sun rises over the three sacred peaks of Mount Illimani in Cordillera Real to the east, and sets over Lake Titicaca towards the west. Doorways and staircases in the temples relate to both directions, but emphasize the east–west axis.

The most dominant monument at Tiahuanaco is the Akapana temple, a 17-m (56-ft) high mound with seven stone terraces, some of which may originally have been faced with gold sheet decoration. It would have been a magnificent sight to behold. The focal point of the ceremonial complex, it was long assumed to be a natural hill. The materials comprising the mound were transported to the site from other locations. The summit of this temple mound, which had originally been covered by a distinctive green gravel taken from stream beds in the Quimsachata mountains to the south, is the only place in Tiahuanaco from where Mount Illimani and Lake Titicaca are both visible. Tiahuanaco was an expression in stone of that already-noted landscape veneration common to the American Indians – and, indeed, to many early peoples the world over.

Alan Kolata, a leading archaeological investigator at Tiahuanaco, discovered that sanctification of the land had, in fact, been taken further. The Akapana was equipped with a well-built stone drainage system that carried rainwater down through the mound to a tunnel network that fed into a sewer system beneath the entire core of Tiahuanaco, and eventually drained into Lake Titicaca itself. Kolata was puzzled because he could see that the drainage system was too over-engineered to be merely functional – a simpler system could have drained the water away, if that was all that was needed. He then realized that the considerable volume of water that would have collected during the altiplano rains in a sunken court built on the mound's summit would have entered the system and gone inside the mound only to reappear at the first terrace. At this point it would have gushed from a channel into a drain on the terraces, before disappearing inside the mound once more, only to reappear at the next, lower terrace, and so on. The rainwater therefore ran both inside and on the surface of the mound ultimately to replenish the sacred lake in the same way rainwater runs down and through the nearby mountains to feed the rivers and thus the lake. The green stream gravel reinforced this symbolism. The Akapana was therefore an artificial holy mountain providing a working model of the processes of nature. Kolata also observed that during heavy rainstorms, the roar of rushing interior water through the drainage system would have caused a rumbling sound like the thunder in the mountains.[16] This sophisticated arrangement is similar to the use of water-driven acoustic effects at Chavin de Huantar, 1288 km (800 miles) away to the north-west.

To one side of the sunken court on top of the Akapana, Kolata and his team found a series of burials in which a row of seated adults were facing a seated male figure holding a puma-shaped incense burner. It is quite possible that these were the last priests of the temple.

There are other ceremonial features immediately to the north of the Akapana. One is the 'Semi-Subterranean Temple', a sunken courtyard that originally had a 7-m (24-ft) tall, carved sandstone slab known as the Bennett Stela standing at its focal point, but which has been removed to La Paz. The carvings on this stone show a richly attired human figure holding a ritual cup and ceremonial sceptre or staff, surrounded by an array of elaborate images, including depictions of the hallucinogenic San Pedro cactus. Along with snuff trays, inhalation tubes and other paraphernalia to do with the consumption of mind-altering substances found at various Tiahuanaco sites, these carvings confirm that the religious phenomenon that provided Tiahuanaco with its power structure was a shamanistic one using plant hallucinogens.

West of the Semi-Subterranean Temple is the platform-temple known as the Kalasasaya. This has a sunken court and a monumental entrance staircase and gateway which, when viewed from the Semi-Subterranean Temple, frames a tall sculpture known as the Ponce Stela, depicting a figure carved with similar designs to the Bennett Stela. This faces east towards the Semi-Subterranean Temple where the Bennett Stela had originally been placed facing west, as if the two were exchanging glances. The line of their mutual gaze marks the alignment of the equinoctial sunrise through the two temples and forms a most elegant piece of ceremonial astronomy.

The Gateway of the Sun is undoubtedly the most famous of Tiahuanaco's monumental structures. Standing in the north-west corner of the Kalasasaya, it probably originally stood in a nearby complex. Among the carvings on it is a frieze of motifs that may be a form of calendar.

Remarkably, the 3-m (10-ft) tall gateway was carved from a single block of andesite, and most of Tiahuanaco's ceremonial structures were built either from this or from red sandstone, which had to be quarried at some distance away and brought to the site, where the dressed blocks were fitted tightly together in place using metal clamps.

Mound City, Ohio, USA: c.150BC–c.AD500. Hopewell Culture

The so-called 'Mound City' by the Scioto River near Chillicothe is actually a 5.25-hectare (13-acre) necropolis, a city of the dead that served the Hopewell people. Their heartland was today's middle Ohio Valley, but another major focus was in Illinois, and they had trade links or an exchange network that extended far afield, from Michigan in the north to Florida in the south. The Hopewell Culture was in essence a religious phenomenon based on shamanism, and rather than being a distinct tribe it was a sphere of influence that encompassed different Indian groups. The Hopewellian era seems to have been a fairly peaceful one, because signs of warfare become more abundant in the archaeological record after it came to an end.

Mound City contains 23 burial mounds enclosed within an earthen bank over 1m (more than 3ft) high forming a vast, round-cornered square (Figure 4.5). The mounds cover burials and, especially, cremated remains belonging to varying numbers of individuals, as well as a range of grave

Fig. 4.5. Nineteenth-century plan of Mound City. (After E.G. Squier & E.H. Davis, 1846)

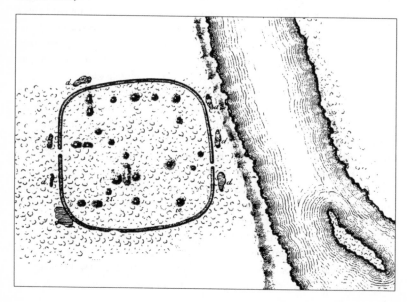

Fig. 4.6. Hopewell effigy pipe. (E.G. Squier & E.H. Davis, 1848)

goods. The mounds have been given names to indicate the nature of some of the goods they contained. Mica Grave Mound, as the name suggests, contained sheets of mica and shapes such as hands and eagle claws cut out of mica. These objects have holes and were designed to hang on ceremonial clothing. In the same grave, among numerous other types of grave goods, there were shell beads, elk and bird teeth, copper objects, spearheads made from the black volcanic glass, obsidian, bird and toad effigy clay pipes, and two copper head-dresses. One head-dress sported three pairs of copper antlers, the other represented a bear. (They were probably both shaman's gear, as bear and stag were classic shamanic animal 'familiars' – or demon attendants – in ancient Asia, and some Siberian shamans wore antler headgear during their séances). In the Mound of the Pipes, more than 200 clay effigy smoking pipes were discovered, depicting reptiles, birds and animals (Figure 4.6). Death Mask Mound contained a headpiece made of human skulls, and Mound of the Fossils intriguingly contained pieces of mammoth and mastodon tusks, while the Mound of the Pottery contained a beautiful ceremonial vessel decorated with an incised duck motif. It is clear that some of the mounds – such as Mica Grave Mound – were intended for the burial of shaman priests, and the discovery of a 0.3-m (1-ft) copper-covered wooden effigy of a hallucinogenic mushroom indicates yet again that ancient American Indian shamanism was generally underpinned by the use of mind-altering drugs (Figure 4.7).

Fig. 4.7. Wooden effigy of a 'magic' mushroom from a Hopewell mound.

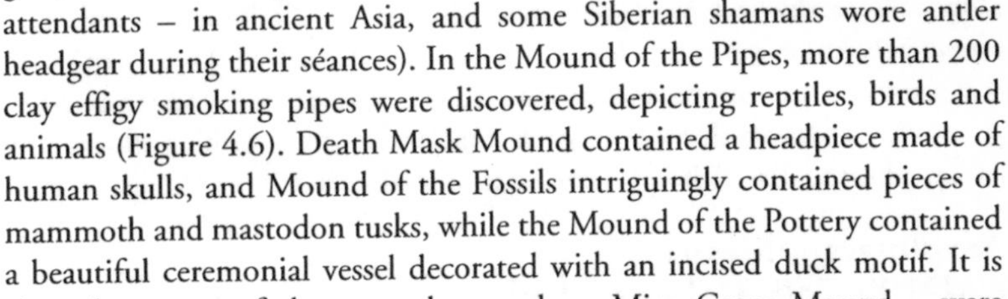

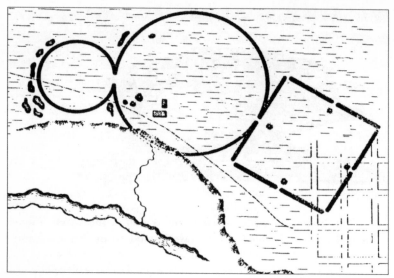

Fig. 4.8. Nineteenth-century plan of Hopewell geometric earthworks on the banks of Paint Creek near Chillicothe, Ohio. (After E.G. Squier & E.H. Davis, 1846)

The Hopewell also built extraordinary geometrical earthworks (Figure 4.8) covering many hectares (acres), earthen pyramid-like platforms, and linear features that seem to have been ceremonial roadways. Many Hopewell earthworks were destroyed during the Colonial period, but fortunately some survived. It was the Hopewell earthworks in particular that exercised the minds and imaginations of the early European settlers, prompting them to develop theories concerning the possible influence of Atlanteans, the Ten Tribes of Israel and so forth (see Chapter One).

Teotihuacan, Mexico:
c.AD100–750. Unknown Culture

The ceremonial city of Teotihuacan, situated in a side valley of the Valley of Mexico, 32km (20 miles) north-west of modern Mexico City, was a great religious and economic centre founded in the first century AD. It grew to its greatest power between AD350 and 650, during which time its population peaked at around 200,000, making it one of the largest cities in the world at that time (see Plate 8). Its 19 square km (12 square miles) contained temples, shrines, plazas, dwellings and workshops (many of them handling obsidian). In the late 8th century, it was burned and abandoned, possibly as a result of civic strife rather than invasion by outside forces.

The first significant feature at the site was a natural cave that was being used ritually in the latter centuries BC. It is a four-lobed cave, with lava tube extension, and by the first century AD artificial modifications had been made to it, so that parts of the lava tube passageway were narrowed, or lowered by the addition of slab-covered ceilings. This would have meant that anyone entering would have been forced to switch repeatedly between standing, crouching and kneeling.[17] The lava tube passage, by a remarkable coincidence, aligns to the setting point of the Pleiades. This constellation was of great symbolic import for ancient Mesoamericans because its heliacal (first pre-sunrise) annual appearance heralded one of the two times each year at the latitude of Teotihuacan when the sun passes directly overhead. Crucially, this has always been the point in the year – around 18 May – when the rainy season begins.

In what appears to have been one enormous planning episode, the city proper of Teotihuacan was superimposed on this site. Teotihuacan's main pyramid, the 63-m (210-ft) tall Pyramid of the Sun, was built directly over the cave and oriented in line with the lava tube passage, thus also aligning to the Pleiades' setting point in AD150. This founding axis of Teotihuacan appears to have been permanently marked by 'surveyor's benchmarks' consisting of pecked crosses and circles on the floors of some of the city buildings and on rocks out beyond the city's limits.[18] Set perpendicular to this line at about 15 degrees, five minutes east of north is the 'Street of the Dead', a processional way flanked by temple complexes, leading to the base of the 46m (147ft) Pyramid of the Moon at its northern end. The pyramid is framed by Cerro Gordo, the sacred mountain that provided the water source for Teotihuacan (see Plate 9). In the plaza in front of the pyramid, a 3-m (10-ft) tall, 22-tonne statue of a goddess (known to the Aztecs as Chalchiutlicue) was found, with a skirt bearing a symbol that in later Aztec times meant running water, so this is likely to have been its original meaning, too.

Later, the Street of the Dead was extended farther south, beyond the Pyramid of the Sun. Many more temples and workshops grew up around the central ceremonial core, as did *barrios* (designated apartment enclaves or wards for specific types of workers as well as immigrants, visitors and pilgrims from distant regions). Of these other temples, one of the most important was that of the Feathered Serpent, the protototype of the Mayan Kukulcan and the Aztec Quetzalcoatl (see Chapter One). Set in a vast quadrangular complex just south of the Pyramid of the Sun, known as the Ciudadela (Citadel), the temple was unearthed from its covering mound during archaeological investigations between 1917 and 1922. Its façade, comprised what are called *talud-tablero* terraces – vertical panels resting on outward-sloping walls or 'aprons' – as the hallmark style of sacred architecture at Teotihuacan. Projecting from the façade are four-ton heads of the feathered serpent, its body shown in low relief snaking along the walls.

Further work on the site has revealed disturbing new details: pits containing human foundation sacrifices have been found at each of the corners of the building, in its foundations, and inside the temple. In total, approximately 120 skeletons have been found to date, deposited in groups of recurring numbers, and distributed symmetrically to the north, east and south sides of the building, both inside its base and alongside its exterior.

The victims, who included both men and women, had their hands tied behind their backs and were accompanied by various objects, presumably offerings, including a set of small greenstone conical objects whose nature remains a mystery. The men wore metal discs identifying them as warriors. A number of victims had shell necklaces made to look like human teeth, with pectoral bones used to look like jawbones. It appears that the victims had all been sacrificed in two short periods at the beginning of the temple's construction (c.AD150) and when it was inaugurated. Tombs inside the temple contained some richly attired skeletons, one had been buried with a wooden baton, or staff of power, that had been carved into an image of the head of a plumed serpent.

Archaeologists interpret the temple as being the ceremonial power base of the ruling military elite of Teotihuacan. One of the excavating archaeologists, Ruben Cabrera Castro, has theorized that the total number of sacrificial victims may have been 260, suggesting a relationship to the ancient Mesoamerican 260-day ritual calendar.

When a percussive sound, such as clapping hands, is made in the Temple of the Feathered Serpent at a particular spot within the Ciudadela, the building answers with an echo that is acoustically close to the primary call of the quetzal bird, the sacred bird of the later Mayans. This bird's colourful feathers were used in ceremonial garb related to both the Mayan Kukulcan and the Aztec Quetzalcoatl. Although this is treated as something of an inconsequential parlour trick by most archaeologists, there are other examples of such 'acoustic symbolism' at other Mesoamerican sites.[19]

There are no sure signs of language glyphs at Teotihuacan, so its inhabitants presumably did not have a written form of their language, but inside some of the buildings – palaces or temples –sumptuous murals depicting deities and mythology can be seen (see Plate 10).

Uxmal, Mexico: c.AD750–950. Mayan Culture

Uxmal, a Mayan ceremonial city on the Yucatan Peninsula was built during the Late and Terminal Classic periods (which cover the period c.AD600–1000), though there was also Preclassic (before c.AD250) presence at the site. Uxmal has some excellent examples of the Mayan architectural style called 'Puuc'. This involved the fitting of pre-worked elaborate façades consisting of geometric patterns or repetitive masks – specially of the Mayan storm god, Chac – onto the basic structure of a building, rather than carving the building stone directly. It was a style that was to influence one of modern America's greatest architects, Frank Lloyd Wright, many centuries later.

As well as remarkable masonry skills, the Mayans used ceremonial astronomy, developed a sophisticated form of arithmetic (incorporating the concept of zero and used a vigesimal – 20-based – counting system). They also kept written records using a heiroglyphic form, writing on stone stelae and in the plaster-coated bark paper or animal skin books now referred to as Codices.

Mayans used integrated calendars based on different schemes, which provided them with an accurate dating system. One system used a 365-day (solar-based) year comprised of eighteen periods, or 'months', of 20 days (plus an unlucky period of five days) and the previously described 260-day calendar was also used. In addition the 'long count' was referred to, which related to a base date of 3113BC, long before any Mayan monuments were erected. There has been much speculation about this curiously early date, and there is an opinion among some scholars that in the Mayan cosmology it may have represented the last creation of the world. The Mayan belief was that we are now in the fifth world, there having been four previous creations. The full cycle of integration between the 260-day period and the 365-day system took 52 of our years, and is called the Calendar Round.

At its peak, the Mayan domain extended from the Yucatan Peninsula southwards into what are today Belize, Guatemala, El Salvador and Honduras. The Mayans began building stone monumental structures from c.400BC. The flowering of their culture, during the various phases of the 'Classic Period', occurred from c.AD250 to 950. In around AD950 the culture collapsed in the southern territories, causing the Mayan ceremonial cities here to be abandoned, probably because of a mix of religious and political breakdowns, possibly combined with ecological disasters. Mayan culture continued in the Yucatan, and remnants survived until the Spanish Conquest in the 16th century. Even today, there are several million Indians who still speak the Mayan language. They are now ostensibly Roman Catholic, but active Mayan shamanism has continued from ancient times to the present day.[20] Uxmal was therefore built in the latter part of the long Mayan era. The site is oriented along a north–south axis and covers 30,000 square metres (100,000 square feet). One of its most impressive structures is the so-called Temple of the Magician, 35m (115ft) in height (see Plate 11). Earlier versions of the pyramid lie concealed within the now visible exterior. Alongside is a quadrangular arrangement of four buildings enclosing a large plaza which is, curiously, subtly trapezoid, a deformity that actually corrects the perspective effects caused by the size of the plaza. This quadrangular arrangement, misnamed The Nunnery, was an elite residence and ceremonial enclosure. There is latticework surmounted by motifs depicting serpents and Kukulcan imagery decorating the façades of the buildings. It is thought that the four-sided arrangement symbolizes the Mayan cosmos.

Elsewhere in the Uxmal complex is the ubiquitous ballcourt, further temples, a major pyramid, and what is considered a masterpiece of Mayan architecture, the so-called House (or Palace) of the Governor – a huge building 100m (320ft) long and containing 24 rooms (see Plate 12). The upper register of the frontage has over 20,000 individually cut and fitted pieces creating a complex frieze containing glyphs, serpents, Chac masks, and some 350 glyphs representing Venus. The emphasis on Venus is of significance. It has been found that if a Mayan astronomer-priest had stood in the central doorway of the House of the Governor at the appropriate time, he would have seen Venus rising over the horizon at a point marked by the pyramid of Nohpat some 9.6 km (6 miles) away – an almost invisible skyline pimple unless the observer's attention is drawn to it. This was the most southerly rising point of Venus. So, in that event, the Nohpat pyramid, and the House of the Governor encrusted with Venus symbols would have stood in line. On the same alignment is an altar standing in front of the House of the Governor, and next to it, a leaning column that was once a painted and stuccoed representation of the Mayan World Tree (see Plate 13). In addition, archaeologists in the 1930s found that one of the enigmatic straight Mayan causeways ran from Nohpat to Uxmal, probably ending at the altar.[21] The straight ceremonial road would therefore have marked this significant astronomical alignment on the ground. (The Mayan causeways or *sacbeob*, 'white ways', were just one example of the bizarre American Indian trait of building straight roads, trails, and ground markings, a phenomenon that is explored further in Chapter Nine.)

Tula, Mexico:
*c.*AD950–1150. Toltec Culture

Tula, situated 80km (50 miles) north-west of today's Mexico City, was the capital of the Toltec, a people whose name is well-known but about whom there is still much archaeological confusion. They seem to have emerged from the north Mexican Chichimeca peoples who lived on the fringes of the great civilizations farther south. These Tolteca-Chichimeca came south and first settled in the Valley of Mexico at a place called Colhuacan. From this settlement there emerged a great priest-king, known as Topiltzin in later Aztec legend. He may have been a real person, and according to the myths it was he who led his people to Tula. In the Aztec legends, as told to the Spanish, Topiltzin was also, confusingly, the feathered serpent, Quetzalcoatl. He ultimately fell foul of evil sorcery perpetrated by the god Tezcatlipoca and had to flee Tula. According to one Aztec poem, when he reached the Gulf of Mexico, he set fire to himself, his ashes floated up to the sky and he became the Morning Star. In another version, he set off with his followers on a raft formed of serpents and travelled eastwards across the water (see Chapter Two).

The legends state that the city of Tula thrived until a series of droughts

1. Feathered Serpent boss on temple wall, Teotihuacan, Mexico (Chapter 2).

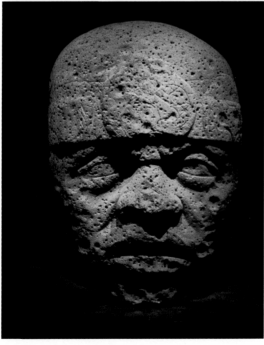

2. Olmec giant stone head (Chapter 4).

3. *Part of a ballcourt in the ancient Mayan ceremonial complex of Coba, showing the stone ring that formed an integral part of the ball game. The ritual ball players had to knock a solid rubber ball through the ring, using any part of their body except their hands (Chapter 4).*

4. *Olmec figurine of a wrestler (Chapter 4).* (Sol Devereux)

5. *An Olmec baby figurine. These curious objects often have filed teeth (Chapter 4).* (Sol Devereux)

6. *Another of the Olmec babies. Some are 'were-children' displaying half-human, half-jaguar characteristics (Chapter 4).* (Sol Devereux)

7. *The Lanzon, the carved monolith-idol in the darkened depths of the Chavin de Huantar temple, Peru (Chapter 4).* (Peruvian Embassy, London)

8. *The Pyramid of the Sun, Teotihuacan, viewed from the Pyramid of the Moon. The pyramid echoes the shape of the sacred mountain beyond (Chapters 4 and 8).*

9. *Pyramid of the Moon, Teotihuacan, looking along the Street of the Dead. As with the Pyramid of the Sun, the siting of this pyramid seems to relate to the sacred peak beyond, Cerro Gordo, where the water goddess dwelled (Chapters 4 and 8).* (Patrick Horsbrugh)

10. *Museum reproduction of one of the Teotihuacan murals.* (Sol Devereux)

11. *The Temple of the Magician in the Mayan ceremonial complex of Uxmal, Yucatan (Chapter 4).*

12. *House of the Governor, Uxmal (Chapter 4).*

13. *A view out of one of the doorways of the House of the Governor, Uxmal, along an alignment of two shrines towards the skyline pyramid of Nohpat (not visible in this view owing to haze), which marks the rising point of Venus. The alignment is marked for miles through the forest by a straight Mayan causeway or* sacbe *(Chapter 4).*

14. *A* chacmool *in Chichen Itza, Yucatan, with the Castillo stepped pyramid beyond (Chapter 4, and see also Chapter 5 for the Castillo).* (Mexican Tourist Board)

15. *An Anasazi Indian cliff-house at Mesa Verde, Colorado (Chapter 4).*

16. *Pueblo Bonito, an Anasazi ceremonial Great House in Chaco Canyon, New Mexico, and the largest prehistoric ruin in the United States. The central dividing wall visible in the picture is accurately aligned north-south (Chapter 4).*

17. *The Coricancha, Cuzco, Peru. Formerly the major Inca temple, the Spanish built a church on top of it but some of the superbly fitted dark andesite blocks of original Inca walling still show (Chapter 4).* (Peruvian Embassy, London)

18. *The extraordinary Inca walling of the Sacsahuaman citadel-temple on a mountaintop above Cuzco, Peru (Chapter 4).* (Klaus Aarsleff/Fortean Picture Library)

and factional disputes caused a Toltec diaspora. According to the legendary annals, the last ruler, Huemac, committed suicide.

Tula was known as Tollan in the legends, and it took archaeologists many years to locate the actual site. The city stands on a rocky promontory, and the area was occupied prior to the Toltec heyday, perhaps by lingering Teotihuacanos. The Toltec city covered 16 square km (5½ square miles) and its population grew to exceed 30,000. It was the centre of a larger population in the surrounding region. The original, pre-existing city on the site was oriented on a true north–south axis, but the Toltec rulers re-oriented it to 15 degrees east of north (intriguingly, approximately the same orientation as Teotihuacan). Strangely, this was in turn switched to fifteen degrees *west* of north around AD1000.

The inhabitants of Tula lived in groups of flat-roofed, single-storey dwellings of square or rectangular plan, each group separated from another by courtyards and walls. Altars have been found in these communal courtyards, and it seems that the dead were buried in pits beneath the houses. (However, some rooms were used for dumping the bodies of sacrificial victims, who had been cannibalized.) The core of the city consists of a plaza surrounded by ceremonial architecture. This includes ballcourts to the north and west, a large pyramid ('Pyramid C', currently unexcavated) on the eastern side, a building known as the Burnt Palace on the northern edge of the plaza, and a temple platform at the north-east ('Pyramid B'), fronted by now roofless colonnaded halls referred to as the Vestibule. Both the Vestibule and the Burnt Palace have low benches carved with images of cloud serpents, plumed serpents and processions of richly attired human beings. One interpretation of these is that they represent merchants engaged in ritual activity. A stairway leads from the Vestibule to the 40-m (130-ft) high summit of Pyramid B, where there are square-section carved columns and atlantean (column-like) figures of warriors wearing head-dresses. The warriors are shown standing to attention, each with a butterfly emblem on his chest, an atlatl in one hand and an incense bag in the other. These columnar features once supported a roof, which has now disappeared. Around the sides of the temple platform are relief carvings showing prowling jaguars and coyotes, and eagles eating hearts: these were references to the Toltec warrior orders.

Aside from their military activities, the Toltec seem to have been predominantly traders. They handled obsidian, like their Teotihuacan forerunners – it has been estimated that up to 40 per cent of Tula's inhabitants worked on producing obsidian blades and spear points for home use or export. They imported Tohil Plumbate, one of the few examples of glazed ware in ancient America, from Guatemala, almost 1600km (1000 miles) to the south. It was made to order. They also brought in another kind of pottery from Costa Rica.

It now appears that Toltec trade and influence also extended to the far north-west of modern-day Mexico, where goods were exchanged for turquoise with the Pueblo Indians of what is today the south-west region of the United States. A key interface point would have been the Anasazi centre of Casas Grandes in the Chihuahua desert, just south of the modern border between Mexico and the United States. This interaction – referred to by a number of archaeologists as the 'Turquoise Road' – would explain why ballcourts are to be found in some ancient centres in the south-west United States, along with other evidence of influence from the great Mexican civilizations to the south, such as the appearance of a plumed serpent in the mythology of Pueblo peoples (see Chapter Two). In short, it seems the Toltec culture acted as the conduit for much conceptual traffic between Central America and the southern United States.

The Aztec legend of the Toltec god-king Quetzalcoatl sailing across the Gulf of Mexico may refer to an actual 10th-century Toltec invasion of the Yucatan Peninsula, the territory of the Maya. The mystery of the Mayan ceremonial city of Chichen Itza lends credence to this theory since it was built in two phases, an older one forming the south of the complex that is clearly Mayan, and a later one comprising the northern part. This northern section contains Toltec-like architectural details such as warrior-columns and columnar halls, serpent temples, or Toltec-style reclining sculptures known as *chacmools*. The sculptures contain depressions into which were deposited still-beating human hearts wrenched from the chests of sacrificial victims (see Plate 14). Although there are now other theories attempting to account for these apparent Mayan–Toltec links, such as trade or religious intrusion, the fact remains that the obvious Toltec elements at Chichen Itza remain unexplained.

As for Tula, its end was sudden and violent: buildings were torched and walls toppled. A destructive rage was directed at the city, but no one knows by whom. The Aztec later robbed the place of much of its sculpture and architectural details because they held the Toltec era in high regard as a recent ancestral culture.

Mesa Verde, Colorado, USA:
c.AD550–1300. Anasazi Culture

Mesa Verde is a sandstone tableland or plateau in south-west Colorado. The Mancos River has cut a deep 300-m (1000-ft) canyon on the east and south sides of the plateau, which is also split by other canyons creating individual mesa tops. Although stone projectile points going back to 3000BC have been found at Mesa Verde, it effectively became one of the numerous Anasazi centres only from the 6th century AD when people started living on the mesa tops. They built their famous cliff dwellings in the canyon bottoms only at a much later date.

Anasazi roots probably go back several thousand years to Palaeoindian times, but they emerge into the archaeological record as a recognizable body of people in the last centuries BC, developing out of the groups of hunter-gatherers who roamed the south-west of North America. When they learned how to grow corn, they gradually adopted a more settled lifestyle, and agriculture and habitations developed. The early Anasazi lived in 'pit houses' – dwellings made of poles, brush and mud covering a circular or rectangular pit. They also wove fine baskets, which earned them the archaeological term 'Basketmaker' for this stage in their evolution. Between AD450 and 700, pottery and the bow and arrow made an appearance. By the eighth century, above-ground dwellings with connecting rooms were preferred; these were initially made of 'jacal' – 'wattle and daub' construction using upright poles laced with interwoven branches covered in mud. These buildings presaged the 'pueblo' type of community – terraces or groups of connected flat-topped buildings. Over the next one or two centuries these developed in complexity and pueblos two or three storeys high were constructed using adobe (sun-baked clay), sandstone, and eventually walls of thick, double-course stone masonry. Pottery changed, too, with distinctive black designs on a white background and polychrome styles joining the older and more everyday dull grey pots. The pit house structure was deepened to form storage places, and this development was adapted to the construction of semi-subterranean ritual and ceremonial chambers known as *kivas*.

The Anasazi people attained their cultural flowering between c.AD900 and 1300. Their primary territory was the 644-km (400-mile) wide San Juan Basin, and the area immediately around it, which is where the present-day states of New Mexico, Utah, Arizona and Colorado meet, a region known today as the Four Corners. Not only were they accomplished builders, astronomers, artists, basket-makers, potters, weavers, and jewellery-makers, but the Anasazi were also successful engineers, building irrigation canals and laying remarkable roads. These mysterious, often perfectly straight roads seem to have primarily linked ceremonial centres in the San Juan Basin. Some were as wide as modern multi-lane highways, even though the Anasazi had no beasts of burden and did not have wheeled transport (see Chapter Nine).

The Anasazi culture collapsed suddenly during the 15th century, probably dispersing into or founding what are now the various Pueblo peoples of the American Southwest, such as the Zuni and, especially, the Hopi, who see themselves as the descendants of the old culture. The reason for this sudden decline is not known, but severe drought (evidenced in tree ring records for the period) has been considered a prime candidate, and political and religious changes and unrest may also have contributed. There are signs that cannibalism took place among the Anasazi during this troubled final period of their culture. The Navajo, a Na-Dene language group people (see Chapter Three), moved into parts of the Four Corners territory a few centuries later, and it was they who called the founding pueblo culture 'Anasazi', which means 'Ancient Ones' or 'Ancient Enemy'. At Mesa Verde, the Anasazis appear relatively late, around AD550. They followed through the general Anasazi development but primarily on the mesa tops, and the Far View and Wetherill mesas on the Mesa Verde plateau became heavily populated. It was not until AD1190 that the first cliff houses appeared, when the Mesa Verde Anasazis famously built their sandstone pueblos in the great arched recesses that had been worn away at the bottom of the canyon cliffs over geological time (see Plate 15). Numerous cliff house communities appeared at Mesa Verde, but their occupation lasted for only about a century before the Anasazis left the area as part of general cultural decline. Nevertheless, during that period Anasazi art, architecture and religion flourished.

Although viewed as a collective cultural phenomenon, the Anasazis actually had numerous centres, and various regional styles of 'Anasazism' developed. Among the most powerful of these were the Anasazis based at Chaco Canyon in north-west New Mexico. This broad sandstone gorge is thought to have been a pilgrimage location, because, although people lived in the canyon, archaeologists now think that Chaco was primarily a ritual centre that attracted a much larger population from the surrounding areas at certain times of the year. Along the canyon floor are the ruins of nine 'Great Houses', multi-storied pueblo complexes that seem to have been primarily ceremonial buildings. The largest is Pueblo Bonito, covering 1.2 hectares (3 acres) and containing 800 rooms, two Great *Kivas* and 37 smaller ones (see Plate 16). It is divided by a wall that is precisely aligned to true north, a feat that requires some knowledge of astronomy. All of the Chaco Great Houses were built between AD900 and 1115. The ruins of 150 others have been located in the surrounding area. Another major feature within the canyon is Casa Rinconada, a Great *Kiva* 19.2m (63ft) in diameter. Like Pueblo Bonito, it is set on a precise north–south axis, its doors aligned due north with a Great House called Pueblo Alto. Pueblo Alto lies on the northern rim of the canyon at the point where one of the major mystery roads of Chaco, the 'Great North Road' as it has been nicknamed, begins (or ends). This road stretches for tens of miles in a perfectly straight line across the arid scrub to the north of the canyon.

This north–south obsession evinced by the Anasazis takes on particular significance in the light of recent research. Another important Anasazi centre was Aztec in northern New Mexico, which shows both Mesa Verde and Chaco Canyon influences. Archaeologist Stephen Lekson has made the observation that Aztec is about 80 km (50 miles) due north of Chaco Canyon, and that the two centres were connected by the Great North

Road. Using the satellite-based Global Positioning System, Lekson has calculated that this north–south alignment can be precisely extended almost 644 km (400 miles) farther south to Casas Grandes (Paquime) in the Chiahuaha desert, south of the modern United States–Mexico border.[22] Casas Grandes was the major centre of the south-west until c.AD1500, displaying a mix of Anasazi and Mesoamerican influences – it has already been noted that the Toltec apparently traded here. Lekson suggests that this is where the Chacoan Anasazis ultimately ended up, and that their astronomical skills allowed them to plan out this vast and doubtless symbolic terrestrial alignment.

Cahokia, Illinois, USA: c.AD700–1500. Mississippian Culture

After the close of the Hopwellian era, another broad coalition of Indian peoples – known collectively to archaeologists as the Mississippian culture – gradually emerged across what is now the north-central United States. They had a highly organized social system, and their religion, like the earlier Hopewell, seems to have been shamanistically based, which is doubtless what bound them together (Figure 4.9). They were farmers, astronomers, traders and mound builders noted in particular for their effigy mounds, probably being responsible for Ohio's famous Serpent

Fig. 4.9. Shaman's wooden deer mask dating to the Mississippian culture.

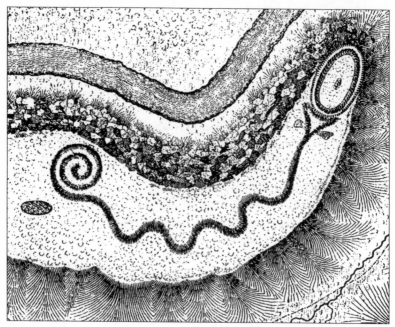

Fig. 4.10. Nineteenth-century plan of Serpent Mound, Ohio; the gape of its jaws is 23m (75ft). A Mississippian effigy mound. (E.G. Squier & E.H. Davis, 1846)

Mound, formerly thought to date to earlier Adena or Hopewell times (Figure 4.10). This huge terrestrial feature, about 0.5km (¼ mile) in length and 1.5m (5ft) high, did not contain burials and so presumably belonged to some religious symbolic system we know nothing about. Radiocarbon testing of material in the mound dated it at AD1070.

The major centre of the Mississippian culture was Cahokia, a city and ritual complex. The site was inhabited by 'Late Woodland' people from about AD700, but the city started to take shape c.AD850 during the emergent Mississippian era, and grew to its greatest form between c.AD1000 and 1400, when it covered some 9.6 square km (6 square miles) and had a population of 20,000 – the largest community of its time in North America. Its central feature was Monks Mound, the tallest prehistoric earthwork north of Mexico. This rises in four terraces to over 30m (100ft) in height, covering 5.6 hectares (14 acres) at its base. The mound was the hub of the sacred geography of Cahokia's ceremonial landscape, the centre point of the 'Four Directions' – a fundamental concept in the cosmologies of many ancient American Indian cultures.

Three types of mound are found at Cahokia: platform mounds for temples, charnel houses and dwellings for the elite; conical mounds for burials of important people and eight mysterious ridge-topped mounds.

While they cover burials, the primary role of the ridge mounds seems to have been that of symbolic geographical markers – five of them define the extreme limits of the ceremonial area around the mound, and three of them align with Monks Mound to form a meridian – Cahokia was laid out to the compass points. The remains of a temple were uncovered on the south-west corner of the first terrace of Monks Mound, a position which lies precisely on the course of the north–south line running through the Cahokia complex. The shrine would have acted as a marker silhouetted against the sky when viewed by anyone walking along the meridian. Running south from this position on Monks Mound, the meridian passes through a ridge-top mound (mound 49 in the archaeological notation used at Cahokia), between a great platform and conical mound pair nicknamed 'Twin Mounds', on through ridge mound 72, and terminating at the massive southernmost ridge mound 66, known as Rattlesnake Mound (Figure 4.11).

On the summit of Monks Mound there once stood a timber building over 30m (100ft) in length, and perhaps 15m (50ft) high. It is thought this was the chieftain's house, which was itself probably a ceremonial structure. A great timber post was erected outside the building, forming a highly visible landmark. The Cahokian chieftain or king may well have symbolized the sun to his people, as is known to have been the case in other Indian tribes, and there were astronomical features at Cahokia that would have reinforced this symbolism (see Chapter Five).

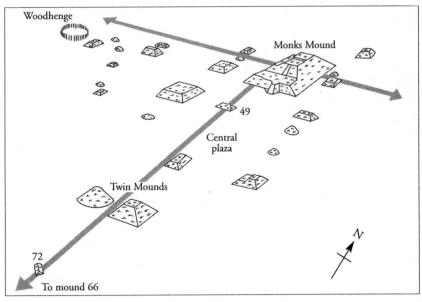

Fig. 4.11. Sketch overview of central Cahokia.

Tenochtitlan, Mexico:
AD1345–1521 (Spanish conquest). Aztec Culture

'During the morning we arrived at a broad causeway... and when we saw so many cities and villages built in the water and other great towns on dry land and that straight and level Causeway going towards Mexico, we were amazed and said that it was like the enchantments they tell of in the legend of Amadis, on account of the great towers and temples rising from the water...' wrote Bernal Díaz del Castillo in 1519, when, as part of the band of Spanish conquistadors, he first set eyes on the Aztec capital of Tenochtitlán, where today's Mexico City stands. He and his comrades wondered if they were dreaming.

The Mexica Indians (who were called the Aztec only after the Spanish conquest) emerged from tribes that inhabited central Mexico after the collapse of the Toltec empire. They supposedly started on a great migration in the 12th century that eventually led them to the Valley of Mexico, where they founded Tenochtitlan in AD1345 on a lake island site found by means of divination. By the 15th century, the city had become an independent state and ruled the whole valley along with Texococo and Tlacopan, a triple alliance of which the city of the Mexicas was the dominant partner. Tenochtitlan developed into a mighty imperial city with a population of over 200,000, requiring tribute from the provinces the Triple Alliance had conquered. This great island city containing palaces, plazas and pyramids was laid out according to the compass points, the 'Four Directions' – a cosmological design still discernible in the street grid of modern Mexico City that overlays it – and was connected to the shores of the (now largely drained) lake by means of three main causeways (Figure 4.12). These major routes focused on higher ground at the centre of Tenochtitlan, which was the administrative and spiritual heart of the Aztec empire. Dominating this sacred centre of the city was the Great Temple (Templo Mayor), a twin-shrined pyramid dedicated to the solar war god, Huitzilopochtli, and the storm god, Tlaloc. This huge temple stood on the divined spot, the very foundation point, of the city, and as archaeologists discovered when they excavated its remains, had been built and overbuilt seven times over two centuries. The full extent of these remains were found by accident beneath a corner of the zocalo, main plaza, of Mexico City, alongside the cathedral.

Aztec society came to have a hierarchical structure, with nobility, priests, administrators, and professional warriors forming class tiers above the commoners. Aztec religion made sophisticated use of a wide range of plant hallucinogens for sacramental purposes. The Aztecs were adequate astronomers, fine masons and craftsmen, powerful traders, effective agriculturists, had a rudimentary form of pictorial writing and used the intermeshed 365-day/260-day Mesoamerican calendar. Aztec Mexico may have been the only place in the world at the time to have universal education

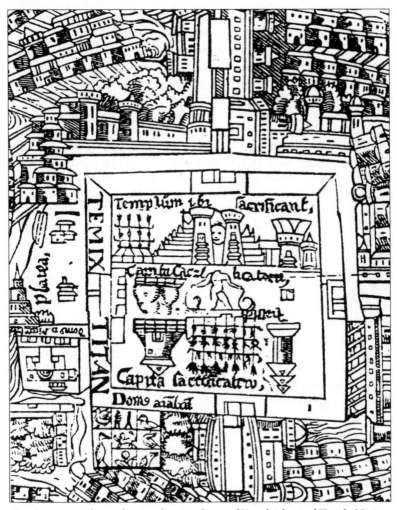

Fig. 4.12. A 1524 map showing the central area of Tenochtitlan and Templo Mayor. (Note that the sun is shown between the temple's shrines.) The four great avenues or causeways come into the centre zone from the cardinal points. (From L. Biart, 1886)

for boys and girls, and women had equal rights in divorce. There was slavery, but it was as humane as it is possible for slavery to be, and was well-regulated in law with slaves having specific rights – indeed they could become wealthy and influential in certain circumstances. However, the overriding characteristic of Aztec culture was its warlike nature. This was essentially because the major Aztec god Huitzilopochtli (or his priests!) had an insatiable appetite for human blood, requiring the Aztecs to engage in almost constant warfare in order to maintain a steady supply of captives for use as sacrificial victims.

Cuzco, Peru:
c.AD1440–1532 (Spanish conquest). Inca Culture

Situated in the valley of the Vilcanota River in the high Andes, Cuzco was an old, obscure village that was transformed relatively quickly into the capital of the Inca empire. The Inca, who began to emerge as an identifiable culture around AD1200, called their empire Tahuantinsuyu – 'Land of the Four Quarters'. Cuzco was the conceptual centre of that empire and was also a microcosm of it, so people visiting from distant parts had to live in the quarter of the holy capital city that represented the direction of the region from where they came. Cuzco's symbolic ordering was instigated in AD1440 by the emperor Yupanqui (who took the name Pachacuti, meaning 'transformer of the earth'). He canalized the Huatanay and Tullumayo rivers through the city, and divided the Cuzco into upper (*Hanan*) and lower (*Hurin*) halves, for the dominant and subordinate members of society respectively. The main buildings were laid out to a grid pattern, which was oriented intercardinally (south-west–north-east, north-west–south-east); the resulting unequal quarters were called *suyus*. The intercardinal directional system that was, and is, prevalent among Andean Indians derives from their observation of the behaviour of the Milky Way, a striking feature of the Andean night sky, which seems to 'swing' intercardinally across the sky one way then another over successive nights.

At the heart of Cuzco itself was the Coricancha ('Golden Enclosure'), the so-called Inca temple of the sun, a place of ancestor worship. According to Inca belief, the spot for this most sacred of all Inca temples was found by Manco Capac, the mythical first Inca, who was sent to Earth to bring civilization. He used a golden rod to seek out the correct location, and he knew he had found it when the rod disappeared into the ground. The Coricancha was oriented towards the sunrise at the winter solstice (June at this latitude). On that day, the divine Inca, the son of the sun, would sit in a recess faced with gold plates set with precious stones. The sunbeams would strike the recess causing it to shimmer, reflecting glory onto the Inca. Below the temple was a symbolic garden created with chunks of gold representing the earth, from which sprouted carefully fashioned golden corn stalks. It is said that there were additionally pots of gold and jewels. Shortly after they occupied Cuzco, the Spaniards founded the monastery of Santo Domingo on the spot, destroying much of the Coricancha's structure in the process, though some of its superbly worked and fitted andesite block walling still survives (see Plate 17).

The Coricancha formed the centre of a system of 41 alignments called *ceques*. These radiated out into the landscape surrounding Cuzco through sacred places (*huacas*), which were natural features such as unusual rocks, bends in rivers and sacred peaks, or buildings such as temples or shrines, or even places where important events had occurred. There were between three and 13 of these sacred points along any one *ceque*, adding up to 328 in the entire system – the number of days in the lunar-based Inca year. This system in effect represented a giant terrestrial lunar calendar. People living along a particular *ceque* would have to prepare and organize the appropriate ceremonies when the time of year implicated their *ceque*: the ceremonial year rotated, as it were, through the alignment system. The *ceques*, which seem to have been either conceptual or line-of-sight alignments, or a mixture of both, were used for pilgrimages, ancestor worship, the organization of kinship groupings, and other ceremonies.

The Great Plaza in Cuzco (now much reduced in size) was also the focal point for another landscape system radiating out from Cuzco – the remarkable Inca roads. This system has been estimated to have contained 40,230km (25,000 miles) of roads stretching through much of the Andes. Some sections are paved, while others, especially in desert areas, are marked simply by edgings made of loose rocks. The roads had shrines along them, and also wayside stations (*tampu*) for use by runners who carried messages and special goods. The roads usually ran straight between any two points (although they did occasionally bend to avoid insurmountable obstacles). At ridges the roads turned into rock-hewn staircases. Archaeological investigation has revealed that many sections of Inca road were based on pre-Inca track systems.

The Inca empire came to cover one million square km (386,000 square miles) and encompassed a hundred different societies and strikingly varied ecological domains. The Inca had no writing, but had a sophisticated notational, numbering and mnemonic system effected through bundles of knotted cords call *quipu*.

The Incas had a hierarchical social order underpinned by a complex kinship-based system. They were a militaristic people, but also diplomats, and employed feasting, gift-giving and various organizational techniques to stabilize local rule in subjugated regions. The creator-god of the Incas was Viracocha who was deemed the ancestor of the royal lineage; thus the emperors were considered divine, and when they died their bodies were mummified and cared for.

The Incas were superb masons. Although they built with adobe, field rocks, and mud, they are noted for their fine cut stone walls. No better example can be seen than the huge citadel, or temple, of Sacsahuaman on a mountaintop overlooking Cuzco (see Plate 18). The stones used in the cyclopean walling there, for instance, weigh up to 200 tonnes apiece and are 5m (16ft) in height. They were fitted together without mortar, yet so tightly that a knife cannot slide between them. Even more incredibly, they have been cut into complex shapes so that they interlock: it is common for a stone to have up to six corners, and some Inca stones have as many as twelve. So overwhelming is this stone-working skill to modern eyes that some observers have been tempted to invoke levitation, stone-softening chemicals, and even ancient astronauts to explain it.

In fact, the stones have markings on them where they have been hammered into shape by rock cobbles. The interlocking nature of the stonework is also explainable – it was an excellent way of constructing walls and buildings that could withstand the shock of the earthquakes that are so common across the Inca domain (during the space of one year, for example, Cuzco experienced 1,500 tectonic shocks). That massive Inca walls have stood for centuries is a testament to the brilliant effectiveness of the technique.

The Incas left many cities and structures behind them, perhaps none more famous today than Machu Picchu, a 'city of the clouds' that clings to a ridge 2500m (8000ft) high in the Andes. Its precise nature is not understood, and archaeologists consider three possibilities: it was a citadel, a summer retreat for the elite, or a temple complex. There were 173 burials at the site, including one of a high-status woman. The value of Machu Picchu to archaeologists is that the Spanish never found it, so certain details were not obliterated by their actions, as was the case at most other sites. The discovery of another such untouched site was announced in March 2002, by an expedition that had penetrated remote and difficult terrain in the south-eastern mountains of Peru. It is a well developed and sophisticated Inca settlement called Corihuayrachina by the local Indians; initial investigations indicate that it could yield a record of Inca civilization from the very beginning to the very end. First reports say that it possesses a 'spectacular' ceremonial platform and traces of very early Inca presence that might necessitate the dates of the first Inca expansion of their empire being revised backwards.

This amazing culture came to an effective end in the first half of the 16th century as a result of its conquest by the Spanish, a process that was facilitated by a smallpox epidemic predating the arrival of the Europeans, and civil war amongst Inca factions.

Old Oraibi, Arizona, USA:
c.AD100 to the Present Time. Hopi Culture

There are approximately 9000 surviving Hopi. Their language belongs to the Uto-Aztecan family, which contains dozens of tongues spoken from the north-western United States to as far south as Panama. The Hopi reservation covers some 6,440 square km (4000 square miles) near the heart of the much larger Navajo reservation in north-east Arizona, where Hopi villages have arisen over centuries on three dramatic, 200-m (600-ft) high mesas or escarpments. Situated on the vertiginous promontory of the Third Mesa is Old Oraibi, the oldest continuously inhabited settlement in the United States. Radiocarbon dating indicates that the still-occupied village goes back to at least AD1100. This is when the Anasazi culture was at its peak, and this may not be without significance, for the Hopi consider themselves to have been the first inhabitants of America. While this may be an exaggeration, it is probably at least true that they have descended from the lost Anasazi and Sinagua peoples. In the 1930s, Hopi pilgrims on the way to the sacred San Francisco Peaks stopped to pray at Elden Pueblo, a ruined Sinagua site, near Flagstaff, Arizona. In the 1990s, Hopis have been noticed quietly visiting little-known Anasazi sites in Utah, perhaps as part of a spiritual process of ancestral reclamation. And the Hopis have a rich body of living lore, tradition and ritual that originated in ancient times, perhaps providing a window onto the lost world of the Anasazis.

* * *

This journey through the time and space of ancient America has allowed only a glimpse of some of the many cultures that rose and fell in the New World, and is not by any means a complete view. Nevertheless, it is enough to show the rich and complex nature of the lost civilizations of America, and to note some of the themes seeming to unite them. It is further noteworthy that most of the oldest, and all of the more materially sophisticated civilizations, do not belong to North America – it is even possible to discern a general south-to-north flow of influence if not direct chronology. Mystifying indeed, if the standard north-to-south view of the peopling of America is to be accepted.

CHAPTER FIVE

SKY TEMPLES

Astronomy conducted with the naked eye was widely practised in ancient America, and was an important aspect of the religious life of American Indians. It ranged from simple sun and moon observations that acted as celestial calendars to more structured and sophisticated developments using astronomical phenomena for enhancing or framing ceremonial, symbolic, or ritual activities, or even for displaying a kind of cosmological showmanship with which priests and theocracies could impress the common people. The actual forms and procedures involved in these ancient astronomies varied enormously, and sometimes the challenge for modern scholars of ancient astronomy – 'archaeoastronomers' or ethno-astronomers – is simply to recognize how and where it took place. But in whatever form it took, ancient American Indian astronomy was not 'scientific' in the way we now understand that term: it was used in the service of what we would better understand as astrology or, perhaps more accurately, cosmology. With regard to the Incas, the depth of this process has been persuasively argued by William Sullivan.[1]

The study of ancient astronomy is a world-wide research activity involving many ancient cultures. In western Europe, notably Britain, the discipline has evolved in technique and approach over the last century. In the Old World, the sites studied for astronomical orientations and alignments usually belong to totally lost Stone Age peoples. But in America some ancient societies such as the Andean cultures, the Pueblo Indians of the south-western United States, or the Maya of Mexico still survive, and although their cultures have been strongly affected by historical changes, it is possible to find vestiges of ancient lore, ceremonial and religious survivals, and ethnological information that can help understanding. Indeed, Anthony Aveni, one of the major figures of American archaeoastronomy (see Plate 19), has urged his colleagues to make even more use of ethnology combined with a study of the orientations of sites in the field. In his view, such combined approaches have led to significant discoveries relating to the axial alignment of certain ancient American Indian cities, the importance of the Milky Way and the Pleiades constellation to Andean and some Mesoamerican peoples, and could lead to other astronomical factors being realized.[2]

It is now accepted that the idea of ancient Americans using astronomy is not some figment of the modern scholarly imagination imposed on the past. Quite apart from alignment evidence garnered at the sites themselves,

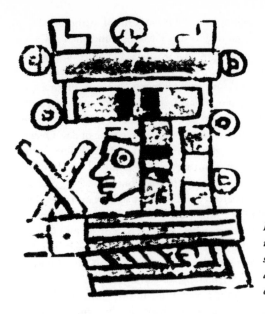

Fig. 5.1. Drawing of an image in the Bodley Codex showing an astronomer in an Aztec sky temple using cross-sticks for observation.

and the gathering of snippets of ethnological information, there is in some cases direct documentary evidence. Illustrations in Mayan Codices give many clues, for example. A recurring image is of a figure with a pair of crossed sticks, often looking out of a building shown to which eye-symbols had been fixed– symbols that were typically used by ancient Mayan illustrators when depicting the night sky (Figure 5.1). It is thought that the crossed sticks were used as a sighting device for marking the rise or set point of an astronomical body on the horizon. Tests have shown that the device can work surprisingly well if used in conjunction with another set of crossed sticks as a foresight, or if the sticks are used as a backsight with a distant horizon foresight like a hilltop, pyramid or other feature. In some Codices, this image is modified into a stick-and-eye symbol, and the Mendoza Codex, produced shortly after the Spanish Conquest, shows a Mayan astronomer at work looking up at the night sky. Also, the Spanish chroniclers themselves confirmed the existence of American Indian astronomers in Mexico and the Andes regions, and noted what astronomical phenomena was of most importance to them.[3]

Here Comes the Sun

The essential function of astronomy for American Indians was to provide calendrical information for agricultural purposes such as planting times and for ceremonial activities that had to be held at specific times of year. Nomadic and semi-nomadic societies also had to know seasonal information with some accuracy so that the movement of animal herds could be predicted. Sun-watching was the basic form of astronomy for all these purposes, and this took varying forms. The most fundamental was the noting of the sun's annual progress along a skyline – the 'horizon calendar'.

Living with the Hopis in the 1930s, anthropologist Alexander Stephen found that such a 'sun-watcher' role was still being observed. From a given location in or around the pueblo (village), a designated sun priest would observe the position of the solar disc through the day, relative to specific horizon features, such as peaks and notches, to tell the time of day. Over the year, the setting or rising of the sun over such identified skyline features indicated the times of year for planting or harvesting. The Hopis also erected sun shrines not only around their pueblos but also at the places on the horizon where the sun appeared to rise or set at significant times. These shrines could be up to 24km (15 miles) away from the pueblo observation point, but at the appropriate times, when the sun rose or set over a shrine, runners would be sent from the pueblo to plant prayer sticks within it. 'The young Hopi initiates run in as straight a line as possible to the shrines and back ... They follow, as it were, literally, the straight road of a beam of sunlight,' writes archaeoastronomer Ray Williamson.[4] This fixation with 'the sanctity of the straight' is a recurring theme in the American Indian mentality and will be discussed in more detail in Chapter Nine.

Sunbeams were also used for similar calendrical purposes by the Hopi and other Pueblo peoples. Hopi elder, Abbott Sekaquaptewa, told ethnologists that there are still houses at Hopi that track the sun's annual procession by means of marks on an inside wall. At Oraibi, he commented, one such location made use of a small recessed chamber in an interior west-facing wall at the time of solstice (whether he meant midsummer or midwinter is not specified) when late afternoon sunlight entering the room through an opening in the outer west wall would illuminate this chamber. Sekaquaptewa said that Hopi sun-watchers had for centuries used holes in the walls of clan houses through which shafts of sunlight struck markings on opposite walls or ceiling beams to measure the progress of the sun.[5] Similar arrangements were noted elsewhere. For example, in the 19th century, anthropologist J.G. Bourke visited Zuni Pueblo. He reported being taken to the upper storey of one of the tallest houses in the village and shown an old blue china plate fixed on a wall. This, he was told, had been put in place 'in the time of the Spaniards' to conceal a painting of the sun that faced a small rectangular aperture in the eastern wall. The sun shone through the aperture when the time of spring planting had arrived.[6]

The Zunis and Hopis are inheritors of the traditions of the ancient Anasazis, if not their direct successors, so it is no surprise to learn that archaeoastronomers have been investigating Anasazi sites seeking evidence of earlier sun-watching and other astronomical practices. A piece of rock art has confirmed that the people of Chaco Canyon had been sky-watchers: the painted panel consisted of three images – a many-rayed star, a crescent shape, and a handprint denoting sanctity. Archaeologists learned from archaeoastronomers that what would have been the brilliant supernova that subsequently formed the Crab Nebula appeared on 4 July, 1054, flaring into visibility alongside the waning crescent moon. This was during the time when the Anasazi were highly active at Chaco, and there can be little doubt that the rock panel depicts this exceptional celestial event. Another piece of rock art revealed the sun-watching activities of the Chacoans. In the eastern reach of the canyon, near the ruined Great House known as Wijiji Pueblo, archaeologists found the image of a sun disc with four feathers protruding from it painted in white on a rock wall. Standing at this location a sharp break in a mesa profile could be seen that framed the top of a naturally eroded sandstone pillar. It turned out that the winter solstice (21 December) sun rises in this notch, its light flooding out on either side of the stone pillar. However, Williamson has noted that crouching down directly in front of the painted sun symbol would have allowed the Anasazi sun priest to observe the sun rising in the notch 16 days prior to the solstice. This is important, as a major function of the sun priest's role was to be able to *warn* of the actual solstice, equinox or other key dates in the year where the ceremonial calendar was concerned because there had to be time to alert the community in order to prepare for a ceremonial session. This included manufacture of prayer sticks and costumes, fasting, abstinence from sexual relations, and dance and song practice. At the Hopi village of Walpi, on First Mesa, Soyal, the winter solstice ceremony on 10 or 11 December, is warned of by the sun priest on 6 December when preparatory activities begin.[7]

Archaeoastronomer Michael Zeilik has noted what appears to be an interesting combination of natural and artificial sun-watching arrangements at Chaco Canyon. Viewing the eastern horizon from the great ruined structure of Pueblo Bonito, he observed that the skyline has enough features on it to serve as a horizon calendar at sunrise for most of the year, but that it flattens out so as to make it unworkable after October. However, just when this skyline change causes the horizon calendar to fail, sunlight begins to appear in one of the curious corner apertures that occur in certain rooms within Pueblo Bonito. 'It may be surmised that the failure of the horizon calendar to predict and confirm the winter solstice may have led the Chacoans to incorporate the special openings in Pueblo Bonito,' Zeilik concludes.[8] Other man-made structures in Chaco Canyon thought to have possible astronomical significance include the Great Kiva of Casa Rinconada, across the canyon from Pueblo Bonito, which is oriented on the four compass directions and has an aperture that lets in the rays of the summer solstice (21 June) morning sun. However, there are structural reasons why this may not have worked in Anasazi times when the kiva was complete, and so it remains contentious.

81

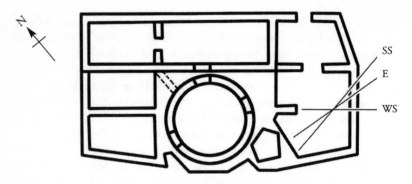

Key: SS = Summer Solstice; E = Spring and Fall Equinox; WS = Winter Solstice.
Fig. 5.2. Plan of Unit-Type House, Hovenweep. (After the Mesa Verde Museum
Association, Inc.)

Buildings at another Anasazi site, the Hovenweep complex, on the
Utah-Colorado border, may also have had astronomical significance. One
of them, a partly ruined group consisting of a D-shaped tower and
attached rooms known as Hovenweep Castle, has small apertures in its
western and southern walls that Williamson has found align, respectively,
towards the summer and winter solstitial sunsets (see Plate 20). The outer
and inner doors of two rooms in the structure additionally align to the
equinoctial sunsets (21 March and 21 September). Williamson feels that
sunbeams entering the building through the openings at these key solar
times may have played on wall and lintel markers in the manner of the
Hopi and Zuni houses. Unfortunately, there is insufficient surviving
plasterwork inside to confirm this. Also within the Hovenweep complex
are the remains of the structure known as Unit-Type House (Figure 5.2),
which has slits in the wall of the east room that are variously aligned to
the solstices and the equinoxes. Additionally at Hovenweep, at a site
known as Cajon Ruins, shadows cast at sunrise and sunset through the
year between a tower structure and a nearby room block have been found
to work as a kind of solar calendar. The towers of Hovenweep are
mysterious, and perhaps astronomical usage is the most constructive way
to go about explaining them.

The Hohokams (a name that means 'those who have gone' – we do not
know what they actually called themselves) were another ancient people of
the south-west who used solar-based astronomy. They appeared in the
southern Arizona area around 300BC and were active up until the 15th
century AD, when their culture disappeared for unknown reasons. They
were fine jewellers and accomplished canal engineers (a skill which allowed
them to farm in the desert), and they seem to have lived peacefully. As with
the Anasazis and their successors, their solar astronomy could be both basic

(using natural features), and sophisticated (using constructed buildings).

A significant naturally occurring phenomenon in terms of the calendear is Hole-in-the-Rock, a sandstone butte (rocky hillock) in Papago Park, Phoenix. The 'hole' is formed by two large overhanging rock shelters that face in opposite directions, one north-east and the other south-west, coming together in such a way as to form a gap big enough for several people to pass through (see Plate 21). The easterly-facing shelter has a small hole in its roof, and it is this that provides the astronomical significance. It is so positioned that a sunbeam can shine through it, casting a brilliant spot of light on the shelter's wall and floor, moving from west to east as the sun progresses through the sky. The sunspot also moves north to south and back again over the year as the sun changes the height of its course through the heavens. The west-to-east motion can be used to establish a daily clock, and the north-to-south shift can function as a seasonal calendar.[9] On the summer solstice and equinoxes, the sunspot strikes *metates* (grinding bowls) – deep depressions or cupules that were carved into the rock by the ancient Indians – while on the winter solstice the sunbeam breaks up into small slivers of light, owing to the sun's angle and irregularities in the rock. As they move, one sliver 'jumps' to the floor of the shelter, almost instantly filling a natural cup-like hollow with light. As the midwinter sun rolls westwards, the light spot continues to move across the shelter floor and down the side of the butte, striking a group of boulders that become bathed in the sunlight – where it is possible that a sun priest sat. Hole-in-the-Rock may have also served double value as the observation point for a horizon calendar, for sightlines from it to the solstitial and equinoctial sunset points, and to the equinoctial sunrise point, pass through ancient Indian mounds in the surrounding district. These sightlines were statistically evaluated, and it seems 'the claim may be made, now, that the observed distribution of sight-lines from the "Hole-in-the-Rock" is indeed non-random'.[10] This butte may today be littered with cigarette butts and broken beer bottles, but to the Hohokam it was more likely to have been venerated as a holy rock.

A key example of the more artificially structured aspect of Hohokam astronomy is to be found in the remarkable Casa Grande, or Big House – a mysterious four-storey adobe structure left standing in an otherwise almost vanished prehistoric Indian village in southern Arizona near Coolidge. Although now in something of a ruinous state (it has a protective metal roof over it), enough survives for its basic structure to be discernible. It is 11m (35ft) high, with a base 18 x 12m (60 x 40ft). Its walls, which have deeply entrenched foundations and contain nearly 3000 tonnes of sun-baked caliche mud, are 1.65m (5ft 6in) thick at their bases, tapering to 0.6m (2ft) thick at full height. It had over 600 timber roof beams, which had to have been imported from over 80 km (50 miles) away. The building

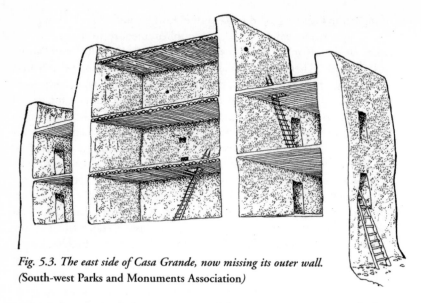

Fig. 5.3. The east side of Casa Grande, now missing its outer wall.
(South-west Parks and Monuments Association)

as a whole contained eleven rooms, and the top storey is comprised of just one of those rooms, rising as a smaller unit above the lower storeys (Figure 5.3). This odd building clearly had special importance, judging by the effort that went into its construction. The most intriguing aspects of this Big House are two apertures on each of the upper corners of its west wall, one circular, the other square (see Plate 22). It has been found that the southerly of these two, the square opening, sights to an extreme setting point of the moon during its 18.61-year cycle, while the round aperture orients to the summer solstice sunset. Because of these factors, it is generally agreed that the Big House was some kind of Hohokam observatory.

A clue to the Big House's deeper significance may lie in an 1887 observation by Frank Hamilton Cushing, a flamboyant Smithsonian anthropologist who lived with the Zuni Pueblo Indians for several years. Hamilton Cushing recognized that the floor-plan of the Big House was similar to the pattern created during the ceremonies in which Hopi cornfields were consecrated. Anthropologist David Wilcox has subsequently endorsed Cushing's view, and sees the astronomy of the site as possibly fitting in with concepts enshrined in cornfield consecration ceremonies. Interpreted in this way, Casa Grande is a three-dimensional concretization of the annual ceremonial pattern in which the central area of a cornfield represents the 'Hill of the Middle', with the surrounding areas of the field representing the 'Hills' of the four cardinal directions (Figure 5.4). Wilcox suggests that at Casa Grande the central tier of rooms represent the two vertical directions of up and down (zenith and nadir), forming the 'Middle' or 'Centre Place' of the Pueblo Indians, with the rooms around representing the Four Directions.

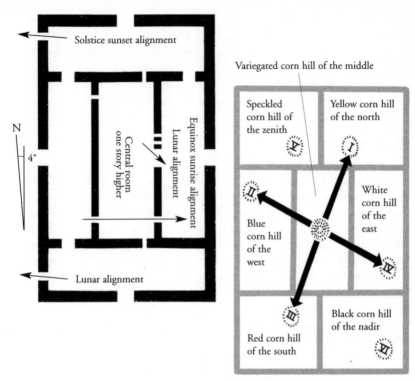

Fig. 5.4. Comparison of plan of Casa Grande, with astronomical alignments indicated (left), and the consecration scheme of a Hopi cornfield (right). (After David Wilcox, 1983)

Sun-watching activities such as those of the Indians of North America's south-western quadrant were widespread throughout the Americas. The Quinaults of coastal Washington State, like some other Indian peoples of North America's Pacific north-west region, tracked the solstices. The elders would have 'seats' (a rock or a tree stump) in various villages from where they could observe sunrises and sunsets. They usually sighted from the seat to a pole placed in the ground or to a designated tree.[11] It was the winter solstice that was the most important for the Quinaults, for that was when there were exceptionally high tides, and was deemed the time when Quinault whalers could make contact with the supernatural powers. Diametrically across the continent in Florida, prehistoric shell mounds alongside Crystal River near Tampa have been found to be solar-oriented, in that paired mounds within the group are clearly aligned towards summer and winter solstice sunrise and sunset points. These mounds contained burials and some exotic grave goods including mica sheets, copper ornaments, and shell and stone objects. Also on the site are two crude ceremonial stones or stelae, one of them incised, which seem to have been associated with the basic solar alignments. (Some archaeologists see this as an influence from Mexico during the fourth century AD). Finally, to give an example demonstrating that solar astronomy was employed in South and well as North America, it can be noted that special stone towers were built by the Incas so as to be visible on the skyline marking key solar positions when viewed from the Usnu, a stone pillar in the main plaza in Cuzco.

Shadowland

Where there is sunlight there are shadows, and they also played their part in ancient American Indian solar astronomy. In the Quinault case, for instance, the solar sightings were in some places accomplished by noting where on a marked, horizontal stick the shadow of a special, sacred tree fell at the moment of sunrise. One such mark indicated 15 days until the winter solstice. Again, Cushing noted during his time with the Zunis that the sun priest not only observed a horizon calendar, but also watched for a particular day in mid-February when the shadows of a natural feature on Corn Mountain (the Zuni sacred mountain) and a man-made pillar lined up at sunrise. This indicated that it was time to prepare the fields for planting.

Elsewhere, and certainly with the Anasazis in the south-west, astronomically significant shadows were sometimes combined with rock art. At Hovenweep, Williamson discovered a petroglyph (incised or pecked rock image) on boulders forming a roughly east–west line along an edge of Holly Canyon. The rock panel's main imagery consisted of two spirals, three concentric circles with a central dot (a Pueblo Indian symbol for the sun), a wavy line apparently representing a plumed serpent, and two circles, each with a central dot connected by a curved line. Williamson recognized all these symbols as occurring in Hopi tradition. A rock ledge overhanging the boulders formed a natural protection for the rock carvings. It was observed that just after it rises, the summer solstice sun gleams through two cracks in boulders that otherwise shade the one carved with the images, and over a seven-minute period, two slivers of light like gleaming serpents move across the surface of the boulder containing the petroglyphs. One cuts through the two spirals while the other sliver slices the sun symbol. The two streaks of light merge at a point between the sun symbol and the spirals. As Williamson noted, the boulders were placed by nature but used by humans.[12]

The best-known Anasazi example of such usage of light and shade is on Fajada Butte in Chaco Canyon. On a ledge near the top of this 130-m (430-ft) sandstone outcrop, three great slabs of rock lean against a rock wall. In 1977, artist Anna Sofaer discovered that at the summer solstice a sliver of light (or 'dagger' of light as Sofaer called it) projects through a crack in the slabs onto the shaded rock face behind them. On this rock face are carved a large spiral and one smaller one, and the 'sun dagger' cleaves

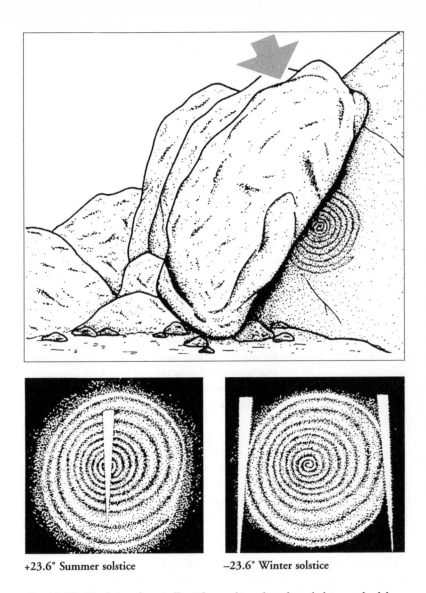

+23.6° Summer solstice   −23.6° Winter solstice

Fig. 5.5. The Fajada 'sun dagger' effect. The sun shines through cracks between the slabs casting slivers of light onto spiral rock carvings: left, summer solstice; right, winter solstice.

through the centre of the larger one. It was later found that at noon on the winter solstice two slivers of sunlight project between the slabs, perfectly framing the large spiral (Figure 5.5). During equinoxes, a long sliver of sunlight cuts through the larger spiral, while a shorter shaft bisects the smaller one. It was originally felt that is was a deliberately constructed sun-watching station for an Anasazi sun priest, but detailed study has shown that the slabs of rock had fallen against the rock face quite naturally, so it appears to be more a case of the Anasazis having carved petroglyphs to fit the fortuitous light play that resulted, just as was the case at Holly Canyon.[13] Even then, this ledge would never have been suitable for year-round solar observations, its access being so difficult, and, in icy conditions, probably totally impossible. So it is now generally thought to have been a celebratory site, a sun shrine, probably visited only at certain times by a sun priest to make offerings or conduct a vision quest. It is known that the Hopis made vaguely similar shrines, at least up to the end of the 19th century.

In some American Indian societies, shadows took on great significance in their own right. For instance, even today Andean Indians try to avoid walking along the edge of shadows, as Maria Reiche noticed when working with Indian helpers out on the pampa studying the Nazca lines (see Chapter Nine).

A particularly dramatic example of shadow veneration occurred in the Fall River Valley of northern California with the Ajumawi people. This society marked its solstices and equinoxes by watching the shadow of Soldier Mountain, which they called Simloki, on the western side of the valley. In late afternoon, an hour or two before sunset, the shadow of this 1500-m (5000-ft) conical mountain creeps across the valley floor to the Big Valley Mountains on the other, eastern, side. At the winter solstice, the apex of the shadow points directly to Little Hot Springs at the foot of the Big Valley Mountains and to the horizon point where the summer solstice sunrise occurs. This place was important in Ajumawi mythology, being where events of religious significance took place and where Coyote-man left his footprints in the rocks. At the summer solstice sunset, Simloki's shadow stretches out towards the horizon point on the Big Valley Mountains where the winter solstice sunrise occurs. There are hot springs at this location, but no known legends attached to them. At the spring and autumn equinoctial sunsets, Simloki's shadow is cast due east, directly to the point where the sun rose that morning, and where there is a sacred spring inhabited by many spirit beings. Simloki itself was viewed by the Ajumawis as a male power place, and its shadow was considered to be a spirit being that every year reminded them of the sacred places in their territory. At certain times of the year, but especially at the solstices and the equinoxes, Ajumawi braves who felt so inclined would try to race Simloki's shadow as it moved across the valley floor.[14] They believed that if they beat the shadow, they would win *denahui* – supernatural power that would imbue them with the qualities of leadership and with good fortune. Because the shadow was a powerful spirit being, it was also believed that anyone who looked back while they were running to see how they were doing would be killed on the spot. The last man known to have outrun Simloki's shadow was Hastings Lowe, who died in the 1950s.[15]

Moonlight and Starshine

Naturally, the sun was a major astronomical body studied by ancient American Indians, but other celestial features were also important, and more so in some societies. The moon was, of course, deeply significant, and it has already been noted that one window at Casa Grande was aligned to the moon, and that the Incas had a lunar calendar, as did many other Indian societies. The Patwins of California, for instance, who form part of the Wintun linguistic family, had a moon count in which they fitted two lunations (the interval between two moons) into each of six seasonal periods through the year. Elders would hang a string of 12 sticks, each about the length of the palm of the hand, in the sweat lodge, where calendrical matters were discussed, and remove one with the passing of each moon. A lunar eclipse was known as *sila'i sana'r tseru't t'ilo'kibes*, meaning 'grizzly-bear moon eating makes-it-dark'.[16] The Aztecs had a lunar eclipse table based on a count of lunations.

Stars could be of great import to some societies as well. This was revealed in the case of ancient North American peoples by study of some of the so-called 'medicine wheels'. These are prehistoric stone circles with spokes, similar to giant cartwheels made of large boulders lying on the ground. There are about three dozen of them and they are located along the Rocky Mountains of Canada and the northern United States. They are found only on or near mountaintops and typically have a cairn (stone pile) at their hubs and along their spokes or circumferences. Big Horn Medicine Wheel in Wyoming was subjected to archaeoastronomical scrutiny by John Eddy in the 1970s. This site has a central cairn and six others set irregularly on the circle's perimeter. By sighting to the peripheral cairns from the central, hub cairn, and from selected peripheral cairns to other selected peripheral cairns, Eddy discovered that along with summer solstice sunrise and sunset, the heliacal rising positions (first annual pre-dawn appearances) of three major stars, red-tinted Aldebaran, blue-tinted Rigel, and Sirius, the brightest star in the sky, were indicated. The heliacal risings of these stars occur only in the pre-dawn skies of the summer months, at one-month intervals. This fits in with what would have to have been the usage of the medicine wheels, which, because of their altitude, are inaccessible owing to snow and ice all year except summertime. Taken in turn, the star risings cover the three 'warmest moons' after the summer solstice. Sirius, the last of the three to make its pre-dawn appearance, was viewed as a warning to the people to leave the mountain, as it heralded the last moon before the onset of winter. The Big Horn Medicine Wheel has 28 spokes, the number of visible moons in a lunar month. Later research at Moose Mountain Medicine Wheel in south-eastern Saskatchewan confirmed that it marks the same astronomical events as does the Big Horn site.

In North America, some societies viewed the Pole Star, Polaris, as significant – and with good reason, for it is the point around which the heavens appear to revolve: it is the fixed point marking north. To the Chumash of California, Polaris was Sky Coyote, who played a game with Sun and Morning Star (Venus), on the outcome of which depended the order of the cosmos. Being the star that defines north, Polaris had an important role to play in the powerful American Indian concept of the Four Directions and Centre Place. The Omahas of the North American plains had a legend about a tree at the centre of four trails (the Four Directions), and had a ceremony related to it in which a pole was set up on a forked support at an angle of about 45 degrees. The Pole Star's angle above the horizon matches the degrees of latitude from which it is observed, and the old Omaha territory fell at the latitude of 45 degrees north.

The Pleiades was an important star cluster to many ancient American societies. Although it is small and fairly faint, this 'Seven Sisters' constellation is distinctive, and its first annual appearance was linked to the rainy season. Indeed, some American Indian societies believed that it actually caused rain. To the Navajos of Arizona, the Pleiades symbolized the creator, while the Pueblo Indians began a sacred nocturnal ritual at first rise of the Pleiades. The constellation was, for thousands of years, even more important in central Mexico. Not only was Teotihuacan laid out according to its setting point (see Chapter Four), but the Aztecs and probably other Mesoamerican civilizations prior to them would only commence the ceremony known as the Binding of the Years – the 'Calendar Round' point every 52 years when the 365-day and 260-day calendars meshed together – when the Pleiades crossed the zenith point of the sky at midnight (which occurred in mid-November). As the time approached, the priests watched the movement of the Pleiades attentively, and when the constellation continued its heavenly cycle through the zenith, they knew the world had not come to an end (a great fear at the close of each 52-year cycle) and that a new cycle could begin. Farther south, the Andean mind also placed great store by the rising and setting points of the Pleiades.

The Milky Way was also of huge significance in the sky-lore of more southerly American Indians. It registered strongly with the Mayans – their glyph for the Cosmic Monster is a representation of the Milky Way, which lies east–west in the first few hours after sunset on the winter solstice. This link is displayed at the Mayan ceremonial complex of Copan, where the Cosmic Monster is carved over a doorway of Temple 22 and the doorjambs cast no shadows at noon on the winter solstice.[17] When the Milky Way, during its various perambulations across the night sky, is lying flat on the horizon, the sky overhead is very dark. This was known to the ancient Mayans as *Ek'-Way* ('Black Dream-place') and was considered a portal to the 'other-world' through which shamans can pass when in a trance and from out of which spirits can come forth.[18]

The Milky Way is also a prime celestial feature for Andean Indians, offering them the equivalent of our constellations. For, when the Milky

Way is as brilliant as it is in the Andean sky, dark shapes can be readily discerned among its star fields (these are caused by clouds of interstellar dust that block out the starlight beyond). The Andeans see these shapes as we perceive patterns among the stars, and each dark shape had its name and meanings.[19] Furthermore, to the Andeans the Milky Way was (and is) *Mayu* – the celestial river, a reflection or a continuation of earthly rivers. The Milky Way also left its mark on Earth: it was envisaged as swinging on an invisible axis, and this and its intercardinal orientations provided the template for road and building layouts, and even the channelling of rivers and streams, in Andean communities large and small.

The planet Venus as the Evening or Morning Star figured large in the sky-lore of many ancient American societies, and especially so in the Mayan civilisation, where it was perceived as the heavenly manifestation of the Plumed Serpent, Kukulcan. The Mayan Venus was associated with warfare and death. Its symbolic colour was blue, and sacrificial victims were sometimes painted blue prior to being put to death. Aveni has suggested that the Mayan fixation with Venus may have come about not merely because the planet is the brightest object in the sky, apart from the sun and moon, but because of the interest the Mayans had in magical numbers. The numbers that can be associated with the cycles of Venus really are quite remarkable: Mayan priests had almanacs recording these cycles, which were keyed with their overall intermeshed 365-day solar and 260-day ritual calendars, so that they could identify the propitious times for ritual, combat and sacrifice. Five 584-day Venus cycles fortuitously equal eight 365-day solar cycles or years, so an eight-year Venus-based system was devised. But that in turn had to mesh with the 260-day system, and by yet another remarkable coincidence the actual appearance interval of Venus as morning and evening star is close to 260 days. A 104-year Great Venus Almanac was created which incorporated 65 of the 584-day Venus cycles. This period is, of course, the equivalent of two Calendar Round cycles.

Naturally, there were other key stars and constellations in the cosmological mythology of ancient America. One was *Ursa Major* (The Big Dipper, The Great Bear or The Plough), a large and easily recognizable constellation in the northern night sky. In Aztec lore it was represented by the god Texcatlipoca (lord of the night) whose realm was the north. He is shown holding an obsidian mirror (a 'smoking mirror', the meaning of his name and symbol of the black night-time sky) with his left leg severed at the ankle. This was a reference to the constellation's loss of stars at the times when its tail or handle swings below the northern horizon.[20] Again, as another example, the setting position of the constellation of Scorpio had strong meaning for Andean Indians. But the list could go on: the fact is that the movements of the heavens were well charted by ancient American Indians, at least in the more structured civilizations.

Sky Cities

The cycles of heaven, and their associations with deep cosmological beliefs, were so important to ancient Americans that many of their major cities and complexes had astronomical aspects of one kind or another. The classic example of this is Teotihuacan, with its city grid organized around the setting point of the Pleiades.

It was noted in the previous chapter that the curious arrow-headed structure known as 'Building J' in the Zapotec city of Monte Alban may have had astronomical significance, owing to the fact that its orientation deviates strongly from the other buildings. The entrance stairway of the building (not the point of its arrow-head shape, as we might expect) does actually point to the place on the horizon where the bright star Capella had is first heliacal or dawn rising in Monte Alban times. Moreover, this would have been on the very day when the sun at this latitude passed through the point directly overhead in the sky. This zenith passage occurs twice at locations in the tropics, and in southern Mesoamerica both days (in April and in August) foretell of rains. It was thought that the sun god descended to Earth at noon on these days when the shadows disappeared. The likelihood that this orientation of Building J (often referred to as 'the Observatory') is deliberate is strengthened by the presence of a zenith solar tube in 'Building P' on the east side of the main plaza at Monte Alban. This artificial vertical shaft would have – and in fact still does – let in a powerful ray of sunlight as the sun reached the zenith. Similar features have been noted elsewhere. A further feature is the sightline to Capella from Building J – the Observatory – which passes through a doorway atop Building P.

There are various astronomical features in the remarkable Mayan ceremonial centre of Chichen Itza, but the building there that seems to have been an actual observatory is the Caracol. This is a two-tiered structure with an internal winding staircase. It has eroded in such a way that it just happens to look very much like the sort of shape we associate with modern observatories (see Plate 23). At the top of the structure are three surviving 'windows', which are actually long rectangular shafts cut horizontally through the thick walls. Squinting through these shafts from an inner edge to a diagonally opposite outer one gives you a 'gun-sight' method of pinpointing two horizon locations per shaft. Experiments prove that this technique allows accurate sighting to various astronomical events on the level and distant skyline, including the maximum northern and southern setting points of Venus and the equinoctial sunsets. Furthermore, the Caracol stands on a platform, one diagonal of which aligns to the Sun's midwinter (solstitial) setting point in one direction and its midsummer rising point in the other. And a niche framed by a pair of columns in the platform's main stairway is skewed at an angle to the upper platform itself, and orients to the northern Venus extreme.

The twin-shrined Great Temple (Templo Mayor) dedicated to the war and storm gods, Huitzilopochtli and Tlaloc, that stood on the foundation point of the Aztec capital of Tenochtitlan (see Chapter Four), has been found to have solar significance, in keeping with the fact that the main god, Huitzilopochtli, was a solar deity. The edifice was carefully aligned so that the sun would rise on the equinoxes between the two summit shrines when viewed from a circular tower structure that had once stood in the plaza in front of the temple.

In South America, the Inca capital, Cuzco, had its primary axis oriented towards the western horizon at just over 13 degrees north of west. The significance of this orientation was lost on researchers for some time, until it was realized that it is the sunset point on the day when the sun reaches its nadir position, that is, when the sun passes through a point on the far side of the Earth directly beneath Cuzco. In other words, it is the opposite, the complement, of the zenith passage. These 'anti-zenith' days were viewed as special.

The ridge-top Inca citadel of Machu Picchu also boasts features of astronomical interest. One is the building known as the Torreon, a now roofless rectangular building with a curved eastern wall and a window facing the north-east and so towards the midwinter sunrise position. Below the window inside the Torreon is an altar-like rock with a cleft cut through it at right angles to the window. Researchers have observed that when the winter solstice sun rises over the San Gabriel peak to the north-east, its light causes a shadow of one edge of the Torreon's window to be cast across the altar-like rock parallel with the cleft. Astronomer David Dearborn has suggested that a frame may have been hung on the knobs that still protrude from an otherwise featureless wall in the Torreon, supporting a plumb line that would have thrown its shadow along the cleft or groove at the solstice. Interestingly, this window also opens to the rising Pleiades, while another window in the south-east of the Torreon aligns to the part of the horizon over which the stars of Scorpio rise. Another, more remarkable, astronomical feature at Machu Picchu is the *intihuana* (see Plate 24). Situated on the top of a rock spur, this strange object is carved out of a single block of granite. It consists of a stubby stone post, about a foot in height, fashioned from an irregularly shaped platform composed of a variety of planes, recesses and projections. The post is a gnomon, a shadow-throwing device like that on a sundial. Astronomer Gerald Hawkins found that its shadow could be read to within 1.25cm (½in), the equivalent of a quarter of a degree. He also observed that the solstices and equinoxes, and even variations in the lunar cycle, could all be detected by means of this device. The name 'initihuana' means literally 'for tying the sun' but is usually given as 'the hitching post of the sun'. Post-Conquest literature makes references to other such features having existed elsewhere in the Inca empire, but the devices were destroyed as they were seen as being the paraphernalia of pagan idolatry. The Machu Picchu *intihuana* is the only one known to have survived. It is thought that such features were used in solstial ceremonies to 'rein in the sun' – to stop it going on beyond its rise and leaving the Earth behind in icy darkness – but the details are neither conclusive nor well understood.

In North America, it has been noticed that a giant octagonal mound close to the Poverty Point site in Louisiana (see Chapter Four) has the unusual axial orientation of 8 degrees west of north, remarkably close to that of the principal Olmec ruin at La Venta. This has again fuelled suspicion that Olmec cultural influences somehow crossed the Gulf of Mexico at an early date. In the same vein, it has also been suggested that the clay figurines found at Poverty Point are crude copies of similar objects found at Olmec sites, as both sets of figurines display similar postures, distinctive clefts in hairstyles, and slits for eyes and mouths.

Celestial Show-time

It seems that the astronomical effects of such complex constructions were sometimes deliberately employed by the astronomer-priests to impress and awe an uninitiated audience. The classic case in this regard is at Chichen Itza in the Yucatan, where there is an equinoctial light-and-shadow display on the Castillo, a 23-m (73-ft) terraced pyramid supporting a temple dedicated to the Feathered Serpent god, Kukulcan. The structure is nominally oriented to the four compass points and seems to encode a reference to the 365-day calendar. Stairways on each of the pyramid's four faces have 91 steps, which totals 364; when this figure is added to the top platform (common to each stairway) it gives a total of 365. Between 4.30 p.m. and 5.00 p.m. on the two equinoctial days of the year, as the sun starts to sink, the serrated shadow of the pyramid's terraced north-west corner creates a pattern of seven triangles of light and dark on the western balustrade of the northern staircase. This pattern resembles the markings of the local diamondback rattlesnake and joins up to the carved stone serpent head at the foot of the balustrade, presenting a remarkable symbolic image of Kukulcan temporarily leaving his temple. If the measurements of the Castillo were not exactly as they are, this effect would not be produced – or at least, not on the equinoctial dates.[21] A somewhat similar effect occurs on the south side of the pyramid at around 7.30 on the mornings of the equinoxes, and the full range of light and shadow symbolism at the Castillo may be more complex than just this one effect.[22]

Uaxactun, in Guatemala, is another Mayan complex, and is older than Chichen Itza. There, Aveni found that a north–south line of three temples, built as a group, gives a symbolic solar display when viewed from the top platform of a pyramid to the west of the group. The equinox sun is seen to rise over the top of the central temple, the midsummer sunrise occurs along the edge of the northern temple, and the midwinter sunrise would appear from behind the southern temple. The celestial spheres choreographed to make a statement.

A similar statement was made at Cahokia in North America. In addition to the great central mound, Monk's Mound, and the ridge mounds marking out the meridian from it, archaeologists uncovered the postholes of what turned out to have been an astronomically aligned timber circle, a 'Woodhenge' as it was nicknamed, to the west of Monk's Mound. Remnants of timbers in the holes radiocarbon dated to *c*.AD1000. There had been a series of circles erected and re-erected on the site, and one of those versions has now been reconstructed. The circle was over 125m (400ft) in diameter and had poles on its eastern circumference that were markers for the four solar dates and the three solar directions – the two solstices and the shared equinoxes direction. To work, sightings to these poles had to be made from a slightly off-centre post within the timber ring. Not only was this a ceremonial astronomical circle, it had social-symbolic aspects as well, for looming on the nearby eastern skyline is Monk's Mound, the ceremonial dwelling place of the chieftain who ruled Cahokia (see Plate 25). Viewed from the circle, the equinoctial sun would appear to rise right out of the mound, and therefore out of the chieftain's temple or palace, reinforcing with the immutable power of astronomy his status as a divine or semi-divine sun-king.[23]

CHAPTER SIX

RIDDLES AND RELICS

In the dusty drawers of museum back rooms there are often, anomalous objects hidden away that don't quite fit in with accepted chronologies and theories about prehistory. This chapter looks at some features that are a little like that.

Mystery of the Stone Mounds

Hundreds of unexplained piles of stone can be found in the eastern parts of North America, ranging from the Carolinas in the south to Canada in the north. Many were robbed to provide convenient sources of building stone by early settlers, but a good number still survive, although they are largely seen as not being worthy of archaeological study. Many stone mounds of varying sizes and shapes can be found in the extensive woodland areas of New England (see Plate 26). The smallest tend to be conical and are no more than 1m (3ft) across. Next come oval mounds, up to 1.2m (4ft) tall, and from 3 to 9m (10 to 30ft) long. It was noticed by researchers in the 1970s that the long axes of these types of mound were aligned east–west in the New England states, but north–south in southern New York State.[1] The largest of these features tend to be circular mounds of rocks and small boulders, up to 18m (60ft) across and rising to 1–2.5m (3–8ft) at the centre. All classes of stone piles are of dry stone construction.

Stone piles tend to be dismissed as merely collections of rocks that had been accumulated during field clearances in Colonial times. The smaller stone piles are probably just that, but this does not explain the larger mounds, which were clearly built with considerable care and precision. Other dismissive explanations have included claims that the stone mounds were made by loggers, by 19th-century charcoal burners, or even that they were built as band platforms! None of these notions address the thinking behind many of the larger stone piles. Other more probable 18th- and 19th-century suggestions – all of which could be true – included claims that the piles were Indian route markers, and burial or memorial mounds.

In the 1880s, the Smithsonian Institution excavated an earthen mound near Patterson, North Carolina. Beneath the soil they found several stone piles accompanying skeletons (Figure 6.1). The rock structures and the dead had been interred at the same time beneath the earthen mound. Were the stone piles simply missing their coverings of earth? Fifty years were to pass before any of the stone mounds were archaeologically investigated. When they were finally examined no evidence of burials was unearthed.

After these investigations, general archaeological interest declined until

Fig. 6.1.
An 1894 depiction
of stone mounds
and skeletons
found beneath
the T.F. Nelson
earthen mound,
Caldwell County,
North Carolina.
(Smithsonian
Institution,
Twelfth Annual
Report)

the 1970s, when archaeological researcher Salvatore Trento decided that there was a need to assess such features independently. He organized a thoroughgoing field survey and literature search concerning stone piles and other neglected, anomalous stone features in a seven-state, 18-month operation. Called MARC (Middletown Archaeological Research Centre), a core team of Trento's research assistants co-ordinated the work of more than 200 volunteers. A little-known, 20-year-old archaeological report on the excavation of two stone mounds in Connecticut came to light. Although this confirmed that no burials were found, it did contain interesting information. The report stated that at the bottom of one stone pile were found pottery fragments. These dated to the Woodland period (a category in American archaeology spanning *c.*1000BC–*c.*AD1000, though varying from region to region). Even more intriguingly, they were found along with stone tools dating to the Late Archaic period (*c.*7000–1000BC). It seemed the stone pile may have been a cooking platform for shellfish (or used as such), as there was also evidence of repeated fires and clam and oyster shells at different levels. Trento notes that the Woodland people are something of a mystery themselves, since they appear suddenly in the archaeological record yet we do not know their origins. He notes that their pottery bears closest parallels with examples dating to the same era in Siberia and western Europe – which invites speculation about the cultural influence of Europe on the Woodland people. Trento further observes that stone piles, at least one of them used for burial, have been found much farther north, in Labrador, and these are thousands of years older than the Woodland culture. He warns that stone piles may have been erected for differing purposes, and that a single explanation for them is unlikely: '[T]he problem remains to plague us: *Who* erected the eastern American stone piles and for what purposes?'[2]

The Puzzle of the Stone Chambers

Another class of anomalous sites in eastern North America, and especially in New England, are stone chambers (see Plate 27). These are dry-mortared and tend to be roofed with slabs that are either laid flat or corbelled (forming a stepped dome-like roof) and covered by earthen mounds or built into hillsides. It is not known for certain who built them or why. Trento's team catalogued a range of theories that had been offered at various times to explain what the chambers were, including:

- Slave quarters
- Hermits' shelters
- Farmstead outbuildings
- Colonial root cellars (for storing vegetables and dairy produce)
- Colonial ice houses (for storage of ice blocks)
- Colonial temporary morgues
- Indian huts

Trento's team found that there was very little documentation from the Colonial era – up to the late 18th century – referring to the chambers and their function (and that rather vague, using terms such as 'man-works'). The team found it puzzling that over the whole period from the 17th to 19th centuries there were no specific references to the functions of these features nor descriptions of their construction, since Colonial structures were often recorded by colonialists. However, this could have been because the features were considered so mundane and unimportant that they were simply forgotten about. Early in the 19th century, there had been large-scale emigration westwards by New England settlers, owing to poor crop yields at that time, which could have augmented such amnesia. It does leave a nagging sense of uncertainty, however, especially as accounts do exist in the records of constructing homes and other buildings – but always with *timber*. This is to be expected, as timber was readily available, and, more importantly, was much easier to handle than large chunks of rock. If settlers built their outhouses in stone, whether for slaves, vegetable storage, or other purposes, then they built them more permanently than their own dwellings, which in many cases have now vanished. The argument against the chambers being root cellars or other outbuildings is subtler than this, though. The British settlers, whose preference was for hardwood housing, settled largely east of the Hudson River, where the greatest concentration of stone chambers exists; to the west of the Hudson (where more Dutch originally settled) there are fewer examples, despite the Dutch (and German) preference for stone constructions.[3]

Trento and colleagues found various technical reasons to put against the root cellar and ice house hypotheses, including the sizes of these chambers. In their view, the sizes of the largest chambers would either have been far too large for the needs of any known settlement, or would have served more people per local region than ever existed in Colonial times. And the chambers were not Indian huts, or at least didn't belong to any known Indians, since they did not build in stone.

There is evidence that one of the stone chambers was built as a burial vault, which fits in with a New England settler tradition of building family morgues. This was necessary because in winter the ground becomes too frozen for graves to be dug, so the settlers built stone vaults to house their dead. But the burial vaults that have survived are quite different from the stone chambers in most cases, and featured doors, which the stone chambers seem not to have had. In any case, some of the chambers are too large for them to have been designed as morgues, and are clustered together, which is unusual for settlers' vaults. Moreover, if this was the function of the stone chambers, why should there be so many more of them east of the Hudson River than to the west of it? [4]

The idea that the chambers were built by freed slaves does not hold, on account that there are far too many surviving chambers, and in any case the ex-slaves would surely have used timber for building dwellings just like the settlers. And as for hermits… well, there would have to have been a large number of hermits to account for all the hundreds of these curious chambers, some of which no single man could have built by himself – and solitariness is surely the defining characteristic of a hermit.

All of this negative evidence does not necessarily prove that the chambers were not Colonial utilitarian structures of some kind, but the vacuum of scholarly knowledge in this field gives rise to more obscure theories to account for the stone structure. These notions have included:

- Viking winter quarters
- Irish churches (based on a belief that tenth-century Irish Culdee monks came to New England)
- Astronomical megalithic temples, perhaps contemporary with the Stone Age cultures of western Europe

Trento has complained that ideas like these come from the ranks of romantic and untrained antiquarian enthusiasts and have sometimes helped create an atmosphere that is non-conducive to objective investigation.[5] The chambers are unlikely to have been Viking, as they do not look like the structures built by the Norse who are known to have reached America (see Introduction). The 'Irish monks' belief has no basis in historical fact, although that does not deter sime people from being enamoured of the notion, perhaps out of a wish to bolster Irish claims to first settlement of the region.

There is, however, some superficial evidence that certain chambers were deliberately astronomically aligned. The late Byron Dix, an electronics engineer, found two Vermont chamber sites, 'Calendar I' and 'Calendar II', that displayed solar alignment attributes. From the entrance of the Calendar I site, Dix found that some of the sun's rising or setting positions on the skyline at solstices and equinoxes appeared to be marked by stone structures in the surrounding terrain. At Calendar II not only were there outlying stone features that could have marked significant solar risings and settings when viewed from the chamber's opening, but also that the long axis of the nearly 6-m (20-ft) rectangular chamber was accurately aligned to a horizon notch coinciding with the midwinter sunrise position. This means that an observer positioned at the rear centre of the chamber looking out of the entrance would see the midwinter sun rising from a notch on the eastern horizon.[6] Subsequently, claims of astronomical orientation at various other chambers have been made by other investigators.

The astronomical claims are persuasive but not conclusive. The fact that only a relatively small number of chambers have been identified so far as being 'astronomically aligned' could suggest that their orientation is simply one of chance. Furthermore, the supposed outlying markers have not been verified as unquestionably ancient, deliberately placed features – there are myriad bits of Colonial or later stone walling, outcropping rocks, stone posts and similar features in the woodlands of New England. Also, the chambers do not look quite the same as the European Neolithic megalithic monuments (certain of which do indeed display reliable evidence of astronomical orientations), nor do they have the appearance of such great antiquity.

So what archaeological investigations of these sites have there been? In 1895, Franz Boas and a colleague from the Canadian Institute at Toronto were invited to investigate slab-roofed chambers in the Charles River Valley of eastern Massachusetts. The men came to the conclusion that the structures 'were neither the work of the Eskimo nor of the Canadian Indians'. Following this preliminary investigation, researchers from the Bureau of Ethnology at the Smithsonian Institution spent more than a month studying the chambers. They reported that they differed from anything else they had investigated, and that they, 'could not be classed with the works of any race [known to them]'. It is difficult to believe that these eminent researchers would not have known about Colonial root cellars or similar, if such is the true explanation for the chambers.

Much later, in 1977, British archaeologist Peter Reynolds and Celtic scholar Anne Ross, were invited to examine some Vermont chamber sites in the field. Reynolds and Ross were highly sceptical about the sites possessing any significant antiquity. They noted that the chambers were extremely divergent in size and structural detail, thus arguing against any specific, identifiable tradition such as is found with European prehistoric stone monuments, where constructional methods and designs lasted for centuries, thus forming distinct styles for different periods of pre-history. They also pointed out that people building structures using blocks and slabs of stone in any period of time, ancient or modern, would produce edifices of superficial similarity, as there are only a limited number of ways one can put large stones together: 'Because a structure appears to be simple, even primitive, it is quite wrong to regard it as ancient.'[7] They further remarked that though one popular belief was that the chambers were 'Celtic', there was simply no body of evidence to support this view. They did admit, however, that there was still no adequate proof that they were Colonial.

Apparently, the Calendar II site was later excavated by Reynolds but, apart from a Colonial button, nothing of interest was found. Vermont state archaeologist Giovanna Neudorfer examined approximately 50 chambers and found indications that most of them could be dated to the late 18th and early 19th centuries. On the other hand, a chamber in South Royalton, Vermont, yielded no European artefacts when it was excavated in the 1980s, but American Indian tools were found.[8] That the radiocarbon testing of a fire pit within a large stone pile near another chamber structure at Thompson, Connecticut, yielded a date of AD1245 adds to the inconclusive nature of these mounds.

The picture concerning these enigmatic stone chambers remains unclear, though more weight has to be put on the likelihood of them being Colonial and post-Colonial structures rather than features from some pre-Columbian period. Exotic theories of the latter kind require stronger evidence than has currently come to light. But questions undoubtedly remain.

Inscribed Stones

The number of stone tablets and rocks found in the Americas that have been inscribed with strange markings are legion. Many are hoaxes while others are subject to misinterpretations. Some rocks, for example, have markings identified by enthusiastic investigators as being ogham, a form of ancient, engraved Celtic writing that uses short lines in a slanting or right-angle direction either side of a 'spine' provided by a long straight line or corner (Figure 6.2) but many of these are so identified because their examiners are not properly conversant with what real ogham looks like. For instance, I have seen 'ogham' rocks in New England which simply display machine marks where they have been disturbed by ploughs or earth moving equipment, or else sport grooves scratched out of them during glacial motion. During their invited field study in Vermont, Peter Reynolds and Anne Ross made a detailed technical analysis of the grooves on one of the claimed 'Celtic ogham' stones, and convincingly demonstrated that the markings could have been made by a Colonial plough, which typically had a single metal share (blade). The angle at which the blade would have gone

Fig. 6.2. Schematic representation of ogham alphabet with modern letter equivalents.

over the rock surface could even be deduced. But Reynolds and Ross did acknowledge that some stones displayed 'organized markings' and should not be dismissed. They thought a type of chequer-board carving found on some stones – including a few associated with the stone chambers – to be the most significant of what they had seen.[9] This type of marking they described as a 'sun-net', a well-known check design carved on a rock face from which it is possible to calculate the sun positions at different seasons of the year. But it is quite possible that these could have been carved by early settlers rather than an unknown ancient group of people.

Some anomalous stones, though, have been engraved with what appear to be ancient characters. A few examples will give a flavour of the research problems such features present.

One of the more infamous artefacts of the type is the Kensington Stone, found entangled in the roots of a tree on a farm near Kensington, Minnesota, in 1898. The 90-kg (200-lb) slab was inscribed with runic characters (a form of ancient Scandinavian writing). When translated, the runes told of a 14th-century Viking expedition to America. Although accepted as a display item by the Smithsonian Institution, some scholars suspected right from the outset that it was fake and the debate continues. But over the course of the 1950s and 1960s, it slowly emerged that Olof Ohman, neighbour of the farmer who discovered the slab in 1898, was something of a history buff. Books and documents were found that showed Ohman to have had close Swedish friends, and one man, Fogelblad, a graduate of the University of Uppsala in Sweden, had boarded with him for some time. A book with a runic alphabet was found in the Ohman library, and a sheet of paper that appears to have been a preliminary draft of what was later to be carved on the stone was also discovered. Books and papers on the affair were published that effectively took the whole hoax apart. In 1974, in an apparent *coup de grace*, the reported confession of one of Ohman's children, that it had been his father who had perpetrated the hoax, was publicized in a television programme. It is hard to tell if the account of this confession was genuine or was itself a hoax, but, whatever, the stone is no longer in the Smithsonian. Despite these contentions, there are still people who consider the Kensington Stone to be an authentic artefact.

Then there are the three Spirit Pond rune stones, uncovered in 1971 on a beach near Bath, Maine. They were inscribed with runic script, and one even had a map of the locality, a unique feature. In due course, the stones were taken to the state museum. Ole Landsverk, a physicist who felt that there was a secret message in the form of a cryptogram hidden within the runic engravings of the Kensington Stone, also claimed to be able to detect cryptograms among the Spirit Stones' inscriptions, which he declared to be genuine. Although a specialist in Old Norse at Harvard, Einar Haugen, pronounced them as forgeries, opinion remains divided about the objects.

Fig. 6.3. Markings on the Bat Creek stone. (Smithsonian Institution, Twelfth Annual Report)

The full stories behind such inscribed stones are difficult to establish, and just how remarkably convoluted they can be is well illustrated by the case of the Bat Creek stone. Less than 13 cm (5in) long, the Bat Creek stone is inscribed with seven strange characters (Figure 6.3). The simple version of the story is that it was found in 1889 during archaeological excavation within an Indian burial mound at Bat Creek, Tennessee, by John Emmert, then working for the Smithsonian Institution's Bureau of Ethnology. Emmert sent it to his bosses at the Smithsonian, where the inscriptions were identified as Cherokee by Cyrus Thomas, the Director of the Smithsonian's Mound Project. This project was set up to determine who the Moundbuilders really were – Hebrews (in the form of the Lost Tribes, as many wanted to believe) or American Indians. Thomas, who was a long-time friend of Emmert's, published his report, with a photograph, in 1894. The artefact was then mothballed until the 1960s, when it was noted that if it were turned upside down, the engraved characters looked more like Phoenician and Canaanite glyphs similar to ones found on 4th-century BC letter scrolls. They were translated as meaning in English: 'But for the Judeans', or, perhaps making more sense, 'A comet for the Judeans'. The claimed palaeo-Hebraic inscription was thought to date to the 2nd century AD.

This find seemed to signal a genuine discovery of enormous implications, and some scholars and enthusiasts saw it as validating the belief that Semitic tribes who had early contact with America were responsible for constructing the earthen mounds. It was – and is – also used to support Joseph Smith's Mormon history. Of course, there are scholars who are confident that the inscriptions on the piece of rock are bogus, and suspicion has fallen on the now long-dead Emmert as the culprit, even though no one can explain what he would have gained from perpetrating such a fraud. The matter would doubtless have remained stalemated, as it has with so many of the other inscribed stones, were it not for the intensive, decade-long enquiries of a Bat Creek history lecturer, Lowell Kirk.[10] His detailed research reveals that local political intrigue and personal enmities were pertinent to the matter.

One of the factors about the Bat Creek stone that its champions emphasize is that when Emmert excavated the earthen mound he found the stone *in situ*, beneath the head of a skeleton and in association with artefacts now radiocarbon-dated to the early first millennium AD. This, they argue, rules out the possibility of it being a hoax. Unfortunately for this view, Kirk's investigations reveal a crucially different situation: Emmert was disabled at the time of the actual digging of the mound, which was accomplished by local teenagers he employed. It was they who found the stone and handed it to Emmert. Though he claimed credit for finding the object, his report of its context relied largely on what the boys had told him. Kirk realized that if there had been a fraud, then Emmert was more the victim than the perpetrator. The pressing questions were, therefore, who did it, and why?

Kirk's investigations led him to Luther Blackman, who was there when the stone was discovered. Blackman was a stone-cutter, and Kirk came to suspect a link between the Bat Creek engraved stone, and Bat Creek's stone engraver. Blackman was highly educated and had also been a Civil War officer. He was a prominent Republican involved with the local party machine, and between 1870 and 1890 he worked as a Pension Claims agent while still running his stone-cutting and engraving business. He loathed Rebels and Democrats. The less well-educated Emmert, on the other hand, was a lifelong Democrat and had served as a private in the Confederate army. He had been appointed to his field archaeological post in 1885, when President Grover Cleveland and the Democrats came to power. Cleveland was keen to clear out corruption in the US postal service and the pension claims offices, and most Republicans who held posts under Federal patronage were let go and replaced by Democrats. 'Republicans in East Tennessee were out to get all Democrats fired from Federal jobs,' Kirk reports.[11] In 1888, the republicans fired Emmert, but after an investigation ordered by President Cleveland, Emmert was re-instated.

Emmert almost immediately began his field investigations at the mouth of Bat Creek – Luther Blackman's 'back yard'. While the evidence can only be circumstantial, Kirk is satisfied that Blackman set Emmert up to get him fired from his job once more by fooling him into submitting a fake inscribed stone. Kirk states that the 'actual chart which Blackman used to copy the letters [engraved on the stone] had been published in a book in 1882'.[12] Kirk also suspects that Blackman's son was one of the young men who dug the mound, but he can't prove it; it is a fact, though, that Jim Lawson, the son of Blackman's neighbour, was in the party of diggers.

When the stone was 'found' in February 1899, the local Republicans tried to get Emmert to send it to the nearby town of Knoxville for examination (and, presumably, its denouncement), but instead he sent it immediately to his boss and friend, Cyrus Thomas. By now, the Republicans were back in power under President Benjamin Harrison (inaugurated in March 1899), and the Republicans were anxious to reverse the Federal job dismissals that had gone on under the previous administration. Emmert was dismissed, and Kirk speculates that Cyrus Thomas, being a Democrat, would have known perfectly well that the stone was a forgery, but also knew he would put his own position in jeopardy if he started an inquiry. So he simply said 'Cherokee' and put it in a drawer to gather dust.

It is not often that such a detailed study concerning the provenance of an inscribed stone is conducted, but it is at least salutary than when it is, findings of this sort are made. While not all the inscribed stones found in America have by any means been proven to be forgeries, this is probably by default because of the reluctance of scholars to invest time and effort in sifting back through the evidence and conducting further detective work. That the stone inscriptions – even after significant investigation – have been shown to be extremely doubtful, means that only unquestioning believers can remain confident that such 'evidence' proves pre-Columbian contact by people from the Old World.

Out-of-place Artefacts

Although ideas of ascribing stone chambers and dubious inscriptions to pre-Columbian Norse visitors may seem fanciful, an authentic Norse coin minted between AD1065 and 1080 was found near the mouth of Penobscot Bay, Maine, in the late 1970s. The coin had been perforated, probably for use as a pendant, and it was found in association with American Indian deposits dating to around the 13th century AD. Archaeologists think it had probably travelled from the far north through American Indian trade networks, over considerable periods of time, perhaps starting out originally from the vicinity of the L'Anse aux Meadows Viking settlement site in Newfoundland (see Introduction). The coin has come to be known as 'The Maine Penny'.

More startling artefacts have been turned up over the years. A clay object at first thought to be part of a peace pipe was unearthed during the excavation of an old Indian campsite in Clinton, Connecticut.[13] It was sent away to Cambridge University in England, where it was identified as a terracotta lamp from either Crete or Cyprus, and was dated to the 4th century AD. Unfortunately the site was spoiled before further investigation of the context could be made. Some commentators speculated that a Roman ship may have travelled across the Atlantic bearing trade goods, but there could be other explanations, such as the artefact having been a treasured item brought over by a settler, or being lost from some museum crate. Nevertheless, its presence on the American eastern seaboard does raise questions, especially as what were seemingly Roman amphorae (ceramic container vessels) have been found by a diver in shallow water just off the Maine coast in 1971.[14]

Mexico has yielded similarly puzzling archaeological anomalies. It has already been noted (see Chapter Two) that strong similarities with art motifs on relics from Bronze and Iron Ages China have been noted in the Classic era (first millennium AD) of Gulf Coast Mexico. In fact, such similarities seem to go even further back, to the time of the Olmec culture which, as we have seen, also flowered on the Gulf Coast in the last millennium BC. First, do the

Olmec Colossal Heads really depict Africans? Perhaps attention really ought to be directed westwards across the Pacific, because the great stone features can also be seen as resembling Polynesian characteristics. It is also the case that southern China and south-east Asia had many black inhabitants as late as the Chou (Zhou) dynasty (c.1027–c.725BC) – these have been portrayed in Cambodian carvings. Second, strong evidence that the Olmecs were in receipt of Asian influences comes from the work of Michael Xu, a linguist and professor of Chinese Studies in the United States. He has closely studied forms, motifs and writing characters found in the jade, stone, and pottery artefacts that have been unearthed during excavations in Olmec ceremonial centres, and found the markings on them to be astoundingly similar to those found on Chinese bone inscriptions from the Shang Dynasty (c.1750–c.1050BC). In fact, when Xu took Olmec artefact samples to show scholars in China, they initially thought he had simply brought unfamiliar sources of Shang writing. These similarities between Olmec and Shang hieroglyphs are striking and compelling. For instance, at the Olmec site of La Venta, an artefact known as 'Offering No.4' was found, which consists of a group of figurines standing amongst upright jade celts (stone axe-heads) forming a little scene, like people standing amidst standing stones. Motifs are incised on these celts, and Xu has compared them with Shang writings. Figure 6.4 shows some of these comparisons, and the profound similarities are obvious. These are not isolated examples – there are many more such correspondences, too numerous and too striking to be dismissed as mere coincidence.

Apart from what appear to be linguistic motifs, there are also many other clues suggesting trans-Pacific influences in the artwork of artefacts left by the Olmecs and other cultures from the same general Gulf Coast region of Mexico. These span from the pre-Classic era (c.1800BC–c.AD150) to the Classic period (c.AD150–1000). Many figurines clearly depict the 'mongoloid eye', for example, giving them a distinctive oriental appearance, and there are other figurines in similar poses to those found in comparable artefacts in ancient China. Again, virtually identical motifs, such as four dots with a diamond shape in the middle, recur on ritual objects on both sides of the Pacific. Then there are terracotta cylindrical tripod vessels that are incredibly similar in appearance to Chinese tripod cauldrons. Although ancient American Indian societies did not use the wheel, archaeologists have uncovered small Classic-era clay toys of dogs or deer that have wheels on their feet. Their design could have been derived from wheeled miniature birds known in China from the time of the Han Dynasty (206BC–AD220) onwards. Other comparisons include water-lily friezes in Chichen Itza that bear some detailed similarities with lotus-friezes carved in the 2nd century AD on India's east coast.

Evidence for a trans-Pacific influence has also emerged from Ecuador, in South America. There, pioneering work by Betty Meggars, a research archaeologist for the Smithsonian Institution, Meggars uncovered pottery at the fishing village of Valdivia on the Ecuador coast that dated back some 5000 years. When she made her initial discovery of Valdivia ware in the 1960s, it was the oldest known in the Americas. It was sophisticated pottery and yet appeared in the archaeological record with no contextual explanation. There seemed to be no developmental stage, so where had it come from? Meggars recognized that the style of the pottery was virtually identical to that of the Jomon tradition, yet while the Jomon culture belonged to a similar prehistoric era as the Valdivian pottery, it existed in Stone Age Japan…

Fig. 6.4. Examples of Olmec markings from the 'Offering No. 4' artefact compared with Shang writing, along with the meaning given to the modern Chinese characters that have developed from the Shang characters. (After Michael Xu)

Olmec Motifs	Shang Writing	Meaning of Modern Character
	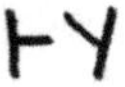	Divine
		Spirit, worship
	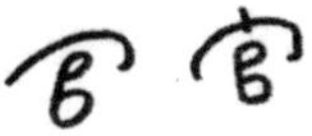	Temple, building
	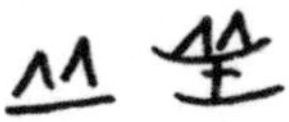	Mound, grave, hill
		Container
		Offer, contribute
		Three
		Small

There was much consternation among numerous archaeologists at the implications of this theory, and in the 1970s Meggars' critics felt able to refute her findings when Valdivia pottery was discovered that was earlier than that found by Meggars, and other find spots were located elsewhere in the region than at Valdivia. The argument was that the ceramics could now be placed in a South American context, specifically an Ecuadorian one. But, in a sense, this does not explain Meggars' observations – the Valdivian and Jomon pottery traditions are so alike it is difficult to explain it all away as purely coincidental development. For example, a Valdivian red-clay pot decorated with incised markings and having a castellated rim is a type of vessel that is found in abundance at Jomon sites, but would have been rare anywhere else in the world during the period in question.

In the course of the preceding chapters we have seen that there are shreds of evidence of many different kinds – mythic, linguistic, genetic, skeletal, artistic, and now ceramic – that hint at a trans-Pacific influence having reached the western side of the Americas. It is an influence that seemingly occurred in a sporadic fashion, perhaps from different trans-Pacific sources over thousands of years.

Would ancient trans-Pacific contact with the Americas have been feasible? There is no conclusive evidence. Both Xu and Meggars point out that there are in fact powerful currents flowing back and forth across the Pacific. Eastwards, towards the Americas, are the Kuroshio and North Pacific currents to Mexico and the west coast of North America, plus the Equatorial Counter Current to Ecuador and Peru. Westwards, homeward bound for Asian visitors, whether deliberate or accidental, there are the North and South Equatorial currents plus the trade winds. The late Norwegian anthropologist Thor Heyerdahl famously showed that both Atlantic and Pacific can be crossed in the sort of craft that would have been available to prehistoric peoples, even if he didn't conclusively prove the specific theories he conducted his expeditions for. Betty Meggars has been reported as saying that ancient people 'saw the ocean as a superhighway and not as a barrier'.[15] Michael Xu feels that Chinese expeditions to the Americas did not engage in colonization – though this does not necessarily mean that some did not stay and try to settle.

An account by the Chinese historian Li Yen in the 7th century AD tells of the voyages of Hui-Shen, a Buddhist priest who sailed eastwards from China two centuries earlier to a land called Fu-Sang. There has been scholarly controversy as to whether Fu-San is America. Orientalist Robert Heine-Geldern has argued that the Chinese started to engage in a maritime expansion from about 700BC, with deliberate voyages to the Americas – a process he suggests may have continued until the 10th century AD. We simply do not yet *know* for sure if there was early contact between American Indians and visitors from across the Pacific, but the question must be asked and seems increasingly to be acquiring an answer in the affirmative.

PART 3

SUPERNATURAL ANCIENT AMERICA

THE INNER WORLD OF
THE NEW WORLD

CHAPTER SEVEN

SHAMANS AND SORCERERS

American Indian religion was based on spirits, visions and the perceived powers of nature. The ways in which these concepts manifested themselves in what is, in essence, an earth religion varied greatly throughout the whole of the Americas, but in most of the prehistoric societies of America the key element was that of *shamanism*. We will now look at a few examples.

Shamanism

The shaman was a person who was able to travel to the spirit 'otherworld' for various purposes. On this journey he could, for example, retrieve the souls of tribal members who were ill. He could guide the dying, muster supernatural support in magical battles with rival shamans or, during tribal wars, gain supernatural potency for healing, cursing, or power in invoking rain. He also had a gift for prophetic vision, and was able to return to the mythic time of creation to learn the history of the tribe, the world and the cosmos. This journey to the otherworld was visualized as the flight of the shaman's spirit while in a trance – an altered mind state akin to what we might nowadays call an 'out-of-body experience'. It was this flight of the soul that distinguished shamans from mere ceremonialists or priests.

Such an ecstatic flight would be accompanied by animal familiars – spirits in animal form who helped guide and protect the shaman in his or her adventures in the non-material realms. Quite often, the shaman's own body was thought able to transform into a power animal, such as a jaguar or an eagle, or some other magical form – even a ball of fire. Within the social fabric, the shaman was likely to be the healer, trickster, entertainer, weatherman, astronomer, historian, diviner and general knowledge-holder all rolled into one. He or she might sometimes be a transvestite or even a trans-sexual, a kind of physical embodiment of the shamanic role as being 'betwixt-and-between' this world and the invisible otherworld. In some societies the shaman was a feared and isolated individual who could be consulted only in times of greatest need. In other societies he was lauded and respected as a wise person. The male shaman might be a chieftain, too, a kind of divine king, while in highly stratified cultures there might be a ruling shamanic priesthood, or theocracy.

In most American Indian societies, the shamanic experience was confined to particular gifted individuals. The role might even be divided up among specialists, each having specific tasks. These included rain (weather control) shamans; rattlesnake shamans, who dealt with snake bites; medical shamans who specialized in curing certain illnesses; and bear shamans who wore bear skins and were thought literally to transform into the animal and destroy tribal enemies. In some other societies, however, techniques such as the 'vision quest' (see page 113) allowed general members of the tribe to experience shamanic visionary states and powers. These were usually on a much more limited scale than those available to the shaman proper, and then often only at certain times in their lives, such as during rites of passage.

The use of ecstatic, trance states in magico-religious and healing contexts is a spiritual phenomenon found in ancient and traditional societies in many parts of the world. Therefore anthropologists generally use 'shamanism' as a portmanteau term for such healing or religious practices wherever they occur. The 'classic' form of shamanism is found in Central Asia, but the term has been used in an American Indian context for a century or more.[1]

It has already been noted (see Chapter Three) that shamanism is thought to have crossed the Bering land bridge from Siberia with the Palaeoindians, who arrived by that route. If, as seems likely, other early peoples arrived by different routes, shamanism probably travelled with them as well, owing to the almost universal nature of the phenomenon in the ancient world.

Acquiring Shamanic Power

There were various ways a person could become a shaman. Some were born with a propensity for having ecstatic, visionary experiences – in today's psychological terminology, they were inherently prone to dissociated states. An example of this is the east Californian Paiute Indian Jack Stewart (Hoavadunuki). He was 100 years old when he was interviewed by an anthropologist in the 1930s, so he came to his maturity before he had even encountered the white man.[2] The old Indian remembered having had two calls to be a 'doctor' (shaman) in his lifetime. In early manhood his power source, Birch Mountain, spoke to him in a dream or vision and asked him to become a doctor. (This perception of physical mountains acting as sentient spiritual entities is bizarre to modern thinking, but was deeply embedded in American Indian sensibility. We will encounter it again in telling contexts in the following two chapters.) The mountain explained in some detail how to carry out cures, but Jack confessed that 'my soul refused this power' because of the dangers involved in being a doctor/shaman. He later had another vision in which he saw blood on a rock. He took this to mean that he would be killed if he were to become a shaman, so once again he refused, knowing that he had the option to do so. Although Jack never became a shaman officially, he had visionary episodes throughout his life. For example, he said he conversed with the Morning Star (Venus), and had a near-death experience in which he flew in spirit and was able to look down upon the ground as he passed over it. He had countless other visionary exchanges with Birch Mountain, which conferred supernatural power on him that aided him in hunting, fighting and gambling, and in healing himself in times of illness.

There is evidence that members of at least some American Indian societies are more susceptible than white western populations to epilepsy and hysteria, and thus prone to dissociative conditions, including hallucinations. This susceptibility is mainly due to social and environmental factors.[3] What is perceived as pathology in one culture, such as our own, could be seen as a gift in another, such as an American Indian one. (Even to the ancient Greeks, the founders of modern Western culture, epilepsy was known as the 'sacred disease'.)

Severe illness in childhood could act as the trigger for the development of shamanistic tendencies, again something that modern thinking might interpret as pathological. For instance, a child in a fever might experience near-death visions and later have a change of personality, which might mark him out as 'a shaman'. A well-known example of this is the case of an Oglala Sioux shaman, Black Elk, who as a young child intermittently heard disembodied voices.[4] At the age of nine the boy came down with an illness that caused his legs and arms to swell and prevented him from walking. While lying in his parent's tepee in this condition, he had a remarkable, complex hallucinatory experience (later referred to as his 'Great Vision') in which he was taken up into the clouds by visionary beings. He looked down and saw his parents far below him, and felt sorry to be leaving them. He met the 'Grandfathers' or 'Powers' of the 'Four Directions and of the Sky and of the Earth'. After a series of awesome encounters, he had great supernatural power bestowed upon him and was given specific information. In his vision, the boy returned to his village, all the time being guarded by a visionary spotted eagle. As he approached his tepee he saw his parents bending over a sick child, who turned out to be himself. Black Elk entered the tepee and heard someone say: 'The boy is coming to; you had better give him some water.' The boy then sat up and was sad because his mother and father did not seem to know he had been so far away. He had been lying in a coma for twelve days. Afterwards, his friends noted that he seemed more like an old man than a young boy. Black Elk was homesick for the place he had visited in his vision. His father felt he was not the same boy anymore. In time, Black Elk had more visions and became a warrior and a medicine or holy man.

In other cases, the acquisition of shamanic power followed a more ordered course. A bizarre example of this was a tradition practised in northern Californian tribes such as the Yuroks. The shaman-to-be would have a dream in which a spirit – often an ancestor who had possessed shamanic powers – placed 'disease objects' into the dreamer's body. These objects or 'pains' were perceived as being animate, physical entities, albeit minute. The dreamer then became ill, and his condition was diagnosed by recognized shamans within the tribe. A long and rigorous training followed in which the novice was shown how to withstand the disease objects, which would be fatal to ordinary persons. Fasting was involved, along with a procedure known as the 'doctor's dance'.[5] Once the initiation had been accomplished, the new shaman would go on to acquire healing powers.

A quite different process was observed by Frank Hamilton Cushing during his time living with the Zunis of New Mexico. He noted how divination was carried out some days after a child's birth. Sets of sticks were painted the colours associated with each of the Four Directions, and each set was placed upright in balls of clay facing their appropriate cardinal point. Every stick had a bird feather attached to its top. The sticks were left like this until it was observed which of the feathers moved the most in the winds (or breaths) coming from the different directions. 'From this, the spiritual relation, so to say, or the source or totemic origin of the child is divined, and he will be named, and to a certain extent the course of his life will be determined upon according to this divination,' Cushing noted.[6] Each direction had its totem god. For the Zuni tribe, this was the grey wolf in the east, the puma in the north, the black bear in the west, and the badger in the south. There was a shamanic society or Lodge for each of the directional deities. So, for instance, a boy whose feathered sticks indicated the east, would be destined for membership of the Shamanic Lodge of the Grey Wolf. At puberty, he was required to go through a range of ordeals 'such as a period of vigorous fasting and purification (by means of emetics and purgatives); and retire to some lonely spot and there keep, day and night, lengthy vigils, whereby it is sought to… "still his heart" and quicken his spiritual perception and hearing of the meaning of the "Silent Surpassing Ones".'[7]

This was known as the 'vision quest'. The aim was for the fasting, sleep-deprived quester to retire to a remote spot (often a specified place) for a given period of days or nights in order to gain a vision of his spirit animal, to see signs that might guide him on his spiritual path, or, especially, to hear spirit voices (quite often giving him a unique song that he could use for the rest of his life). As he sought to gain a vision, the quester collected physical items such as stones (especially crystals), oddly perforated bones, feathers, animal hair and other objects that he felt were imbued with supernatural power. These he would keep in his 'medicine bundle'. While vision questing would only be an occasional or one-off activity for normal (and often male) members of the tribe, dedicated or specialist shamans often used the procedure as part of their normal duties.

Menomini Indians of Wisconsin were taught from the age of four years to blacken their faces, to fast, and to dream in order to gain supernatural power, seen as an immaterial luminous force. The Apaches called this power *diyu*, but there were many other terms for it among other American Indian peoples.

Though the vision quest was the cornerstone of many American Indian spiritual practices, other ordeals could release ecstatic visionary states as well. Notable among these was the ceremonial torture known as the Sun Dance, which was widespread among northern American tribes, especially those of the Plains, such as the Sioux. At the outset of this ceremony, the participating braves danced in a lodge and built an altar there; at its culmination, they danced or circled around a specially erected sun pole staring into the sun. Then they would lean back, pulling against thongs from the pole that were connected to hooks piercing the flesh of their chests, until the pain sent them into a trance in which they felt they had accrued supernatural power. A white American performance artist experimented with this type of self-torture in the 1970s, and he said it caused him to have a full-blown ecstatic (out-of-body) experience leading to a transcendental moment of illumination.

Religious Lodges

The Zuni practice of having shamanic lodges was typical of many American Indian peoples. Indeed, the early American anthropologist Kroeber commented that any Indian religious society or lodge was 'never wholly divorced from shamanism'.[8] The sweat lodge, the form of this institution that is best known to non-Indians, was used widely in North America, especially by the Plains Indians, and at least as far south as the Aztecs in the Valley of Mexico and the more ancient and southerly Mayans. Small rooms in the three temples of the Temple Group at the Mayan ceremonial city of Palenque were sweat houses, and reference to the *temascal*, sweat house, occurs in Mayan creation myths.[9] From inscriptions on the temple, it seems the sweat houses were deemed to have represented the cosmic sweat baths in which the gods were born in mythic time.[10]

The Lakota Sioux constructed the frame of a sweat lodge by arching 12 to 16 willow poles over to form a dome, and covering this with animal skins or other material. The opening was to the east, or directed towards some sacred feature in the landscape, or sometimes in a direction indicated in a dream that was experienced by the person erecting the lodge. A circular basin was dug in the lodge floor and the excavated earth was deposited as a small mound outside the lodge, linked to the entrance by a straight earthen 'sacred path'. Heated stones were carried along this path to be placed in the basin and then sprinkled with water in order to create steam. To the Winnebagoes of the Lake Michigan region, the stones are 'grandmother', the heat and steam is 'grandfather', the poles of the lodge are 'boys', and the lodge as a whole is envisaged as a bear. In effect, the participants taking part in 'the sweat' are inside a spirit animal. The sweat lodge was also symbolic of the womb: 'It is the mother's womb,' Arval Looking Horse, hereditary keeper of the sacred Lakota Buffalo Calf Pipe, has observed. 'They always say when they come out of the sweat lodge, it's like being born again or coming out of the mother's womb.'[11] The use of the sweat lodge was not so much a religious observance in itself, but 'a preparation for an encounter with the sacred'.[12] In other words, it was a purification prior to a vision quest. The sweat itself, though, can cause altered mind states in its own right.

Sacramental Drugs

By whatever method or circumstance a person acquired shamanic power, and however shamanism was integrated into a particular culture, special techniques were used to send the dedicated, specialist shaman into the ecstatic trance state 'on demand'. These included drumming, chanting, dancing and fasting, and rattles and bull-roarers were also sometimes used. In ancient America, mind-altering, hallucinogenic, drugs – usually derived from plants – were commonly employed as well. In the Americas, about one hundred and thirty species of plant were used for their visionary properties, compared with just twenty in the Old World.[13] The venerable anthropologist Weston La Barre even went so far as to call such usage a 'New World narcotic complex'. There is evidence that the ritual use of hallucinogenic substances in America goes back at least 7000 years, because the remains of a hallucinogenic cactus, peyote, along with psychoactive Texas buckeye seeds, dating to that period have been found in a rock shelter in Texas. Further, the red or mescal bean (the seed of *Sophora secundiflora*, not related to the distilled Mexican liquor called mescal), which can produce a delirium causing visionary effects, has been found in archaeological contexts in southernmost Texas dating to over 10,000 years ago. This plant was used for ritual purposes by Indians of the south-west United States up to the 19th century.

Archaeology and anthropology have revealed evidence of the usage of hallucinogenic substances in ancient and traditional indigenous societies throughout the Americas. 'Magic' mushrooms are another example. In the Great Lakes region, the Ojibwa made ritual use of *Wajashk-wedo*, the white-spotted, red-capped *Amanita muscaria* or Fly Agaric, the 'fairy toadstool' of nursery tales and the hallucinogen characteristically used by shamans in Central Asia.[14] It also figured in some Ojibwa legends. In Ohio, the Hopewell seem to have used magic mushrooms, too, as a 0.3-m (1-ft) long wooden effigy of a mushroom was found in the burial mound of a shaman there (see Chapter Four). In Oaxaca, Mexico, the secret ritual use of psilocybin mushrooms by Mazatec Indians has remained intact from at least Aztec times to the present day, and in highland Guatemala stone effigies depicting such mushrooms have been found that date back 3000 years. Depictions of similar mushrooms have been found in the goldwork of the ancient Taironas culture of Colombia.

Many other mind-altering substances were employed by American Indian peoples. The use of peyote, as noted above, goes back into the mists of time in the southern United States and in northern Mexico, where the Huichol Indians still make their annual pilgrimage to the Wirikuta plateau in San Luis Potosi to collect the small, rounded cactus for ritual use throughout the year. Of untold antiquity, this 480-km (300-mile) journey is loaded with Huichol mythology and is crucially linked to their shamanism; certain scholars have even detected hints of the Stone Age theme of the Great Hunt in some of the mythic imagery involved.[15] The Spanish conquistadores reported the religious use of peyote among the Aztecs, and the cactus is depicted on a ceramic snuffing pipe from Monte Alban dating back to 500BC. The favoured sacramental hallucinogen of some of the Indians of the territories now known as southern California, the south-western United States, and the Chihuahua Desert region of extreme northern Mexico was jimson weed (*Datura*), often used in an infused form known as *toloache*. The Chumash of the southern California coast used jimson weed for puberty rites and shamanic work. The Navajos thought that visions seen under its influence showed the causes of disease and revealed animals possessing special significance. In Zuni tradition, the plant could only be collected by rain shamans, who applied the powdered root to their eyes, enabling them to see at night, to perceive spirits and to commune with birds. The ancient Zuni Kuaua *kiva* near Albuquerque in New Mexico has a pre-Columbian wall painting of a shaman holding a *Datura* plant. It has already been noted (see Chapter Four) that the Olmec of Gulf Coast Mexico made use of the mind-altering bufotenine, secreted by a species of toad (showing that it was not always plants that provided visionary possibilities).

One of the chief hallucinogens used in the Andes region of South America was the San Pedro cactus, which, like peyote, contains mescaline. In Chapter Four it was noted that the great cult of Chavin de Huantar employed this cactus, and evidence of its ceremonial use along with other hallucinogens has been found at the ancient ruined city of Tiahuanaco. When cut across its stem, the San Pedro cactus presents a distinctive star shape, and this motif has been found on pottery belonging to the later Moche and Nazca cultures, sometimes along with depictions of airborne figures (flight being one of the characteristic sensations engendered by some hallucinogens). Species of *Brugmansia*, sometimes known as 'tree datura' because it contains the same psychoactive alkaloids as jimson weed (namely, scopolamine, hyoscyamine and atropine), was used for thousands of years in the Andes from Colombia to Chile and along the Pacific Coast. Still employed in remote parts, *Brugmansia* preparations are taken by shamans in strong doses for powerful visions, and in lesser strengths for divinatory purposes.

A considerable variety of hallucinogens were (and are) employed in the Amazon basin, perhaps not surprisingly considering the richness of the flora in the great rain forest. One of the most important used by Amazonian tribes today is the 'soul vine' *Banisteriopsis caapi*, which is used in combination with a range of other psychoactive plants to produce various types of drugs called *ayahuasca* or *yagé*. Although most hallucinogens tend to promote a sense of ecstasy – of the mind or spirit leaving the body – ayahuasca is especially noted as a 'drug for flying'. No one knows how far back its usage goes, but botanical and anthropological evidence suggests a considerable antiquity. Mind-altering snuffs were also used in parts of the Amazon, in the Caribbean islands and in Mexico. Snuffing trays and nose pipes have been found in all these regions, in Mexico going back to *c*.1200BC, and it is thought by some experts that jade 'spoons', used even earlier by the Olmec, were probably for the purpose of snuffing. A bone snuffing tray and nose tubes dating to *c*.1600BC have been discovered in Peru. Hallucinogenic snuffs were derived from various sources such as the bark resin of *Virola* trees and the beans of *Anadenanthera peregrina*. Birds, serpents and the jaguar – the main symbol of shamanism in tropical America – occur in the iconographic imagery found on ancient snuffing paraphernalia. Peter Furst, an expert on ancient hallucinogen usage in America, has commented that the bird motif 'seems to stand for the power of flight that is the shaman's special gift and that is activated by the hallucinogen'.[16] A great number of other hallucinogenic plants, beans, vines, barks, seeds, leaves, saps and mushrooms have been used for sacramental purposes by American Indian peoples throughout the New World, more than can be summarized here.[17]

Tobacco is still widely used throughout the Americas as a religious tool – as an offering, as an adjunct to prayer, or in formal, ceremonial contexts – and it is thought it was first cultivated in South America 6000 to 8000 years ago. Although not strictly a hallucinogen, tobacco can produce visionary effects in sufficiently high doses and there still exist specialist tobacco shamans in South America. In Guiana, shamans' novices are force-fed litres of tobacco juice, which brings them to the brink of death. Among the Tupinamba Indians of Brazil, shamanic candidates ingest tobacco juice to the point of vomiting blood and passing out. In a single session, some shamans can smoke up to five 1-m (3-ft) long cigars in succession while simultaneously chewing tobacco. It seems tobacco's visionary qualities may actually come about as part of near-death experiences caused by taking such massive quantitites. Tobacco shamans also display physical changes: their voices take on a deep, hoarse quality and, because of cellular changes in the retina, their eyesight becomes especially keen in twilight conditions – just like the jaguar. Also, due to increased perspiration and the release of chemicals causing a drop in skin temperature, they can perform heat-defying tricks with fire, thus demonstrating their elemental mastery.

Witchcraft and Magic

Shamanism and sorcery form an ambiguous relationship. Indians of the Algonkian family of Canada and the Great Lakes region considered that all shamans were potential witches, and elders might possess a 'witch bag': 'The feared powers of witchcraft, and powers of curing illness and insuring good fortune in hunting might be resident in one person'.[18] Nevertheless, it seems these people also identified a specific class of witch shaman, the *Wa'beno*. It was believed that these powerful old men emitted a foul odour as they went about their wicked ways, flying around, or following special, invisible paths through the woods and along river beds, or transforming themselves into animals. It was further thought that such practitioners of evil forces associated in special societies that had eight members. The Athapaskan-speaking Kaska Indians of British Columbia and the Yukon drew a distinction between a shaman and a witch, though both operated by affecting a person's 'wind' or soul. In Inuit culture, witches might be either male or female, and might or might not be shamans, though unlike shamans the practitioners of witchcraft kept their involvement secret.[19] The Apaches saw both shamans and sorcerers as manipulators of the supernatural agency *diyu*, the former for good purposes, the latter for evildoing. In practice, though, the 'two categories are not necessarily mutually exclusive'.[20] The Paiute, Shoshone, Ute and Comanches do not distinguish between shaman and witch, using the same term – meaning 'one who uses power' – for both. The Hopis, however, do make a linguistic distinction. Anthropologist Benson Saler noted that generally the Quiche Mayans of Guatemala referred to both shamans and witches as *brujo* (sorcerer), though shamans protested about this to him, saying such lack of distinction was due to ignorance.[21]

The Zunis made a strong distinction, and frowned upon witchcraft – as Frank Hamilton Cushing found out when tribal enforcers broke in on his quarters at Zuni Pueblo one night and hauled him before a council of elders to answer accusations of sorcery.[22] Witchcraft could earn the death penalty in Zuni society, and Cushing got out of a dangerous situation only when he sarcastically reminded the Zuni chiefs that yes, he must be evil, considering all the ways he had helped the Zunis resist the machinations of the government and the actions of other predatory groups (which indeed he had). In this way he shamed them into dropping the false accusations that had been made against him. Generally, Zuni shamanic lodges or medicine societies have counter-witchcraft as one of their functions, and the shamans would wear only breechcloths when using bowls of water or crystals to divine evidence of witchcraft. While engaged in this activity they smeared their foreheads with ashes for protection, and this prophylactic measure could be used by anyone, specially children, who had to venture out at night.

The nature and effects of witchcraft in American Indian societies varied. Pueblo witches were thought to be able to cause wind storms, destroy crops and cause illness. The Inuit witch created an evil spirit called a *tupilak* to do his or her bidding. In various Inuit societies this spirit could take different forms: one was a bear shape made out of snow and brought to life by having bear's teeth placed in its mouth. It could then go off in invisible form and spread sickness, cause game to vanish and bring about other misfortune. A good shaman might fight a *tupilak* during his séance by wielding a walrus-tusk knife in his left hand. In Menomini society owners of 'witch bags' were obliged to kill one person each year. This was accomplished by going to bed with the bag resting against the bare skin; the killer would fall asleep and then leave his or her body and wander around ghost-like in the local vicinity until the opportunity arose to discharge the obligation. In Iroquois tradition, the witch might use a 'charm' to cause illness or bad luck: this would be buried in the vicinity of the victim's dwelling, or else magically inserted in the victim's body. Anyone suspecting that witchcraft was being used against them could consult a fortune-teller. To effect a cure, special 'doctors' could be hired who would extract the charm from a victim's body by means of sucking, blowing, or the use of potions and emetics. If the charm was particularly deep-seated, then a knife point might be used but without breaking the skin.[23]

As a rule, Apache sorcerers pass on their secrets to close blood relations only. Apaches are said to hold nocturnal 'witch dances' in remote locations in which pieces of recently exhumed corpses might be held aloft. They use various forms of magical 'poison' in their witchcraft, including the powdered skin of corpses, menstrual blood, timber chips from lightning-blasted trees, or rattlesnake skin. Kept in small buckskin pouches hidden beneath the sorcerer's clothing, the poison is mixed with the victim's food and then thrown through the door of a dwelling, or else dropped into the mouth or nostrils of a sleeping victim. Spells are repeated four times, and include the victim's name and a line from a ceremonial chant recited backwards. The chants are uttered while the sorcerer is circling the victim or his dwelling, or while burying an object near the dwelling.

The Akawaio sorcerers of Guyana use ritual blowing ('taling'), and this is considered the cause of much sickness and death; yet again expressing the ambiguity between shamanism and sorcery, the procedure can also be used for curing illness. The blowing takes the form of a sharp discharge of air issued through the sorcerer's mouth or nostrils at the same time as a spell is uttered in a low voice or recited silently. If a person is to be harmed by the method, the spell and the blast of breath accompanying it is issued towards the direction in which the victim lives.[24] In Navajo society, 'frenzy witchcraft' produces 'moth madness'– what appear to be a form of epileptic seizure.[25] These conditions are akin to what the ancient Greeks referred to as *enthusiasmos*. Young women are considered particularly vulnerable to sorcerers out to seduce them. Typically, the girl is likely to utter a brief cry, and run around tearing off her clothes before sinking into unconsciousness.

Flying Sorcerers

In modern America, a number of locations are reportedly haunted by what are called 'spooklights'. Many of these simply appear to be images of distant vehicle lights distorted by the effect of the atmosphere, which acts as a kind of lens. But some sightings do seem genuinely to represent anomalous luminosities of some kind, perhaps ball lightning or, more probably, lights produced by geophysical causes, such as tectonic stress (natural underground forces).[26] Examples of these include the 'Marfa lights' situated in the Big Bend country of Texas. In fact, this whole region has been the subject of reports of light phenomena for over a century. The Chisos Mountains on the Rio Grande, 128km (80 miles) from the small town of Marfa, have been significant in this regard. This author himself has witnessed an unexplained light deep within the mountains while taking part in a field study of the Marfa lights phenomenon.[27] Because of their proximity to the natural world, American Indians would certainly have seen such luminosities in the pristine atmospheric conditions they enjoyed, free of light pollution. By and large they seem to have interpreted them in the contexts of shamanism or witchcraft. The Iroquois *Wa'beno* was said to be able to fly along rapidly at night in the form of a ball of fire, or a pair of fiery spirits 'like the eyes of some monstrous beast'.[28] Zuni witches were likewise said to be able to travel as swift-moving fireballs – in some Pueblo Indian areas this was considered to be their most common form of manifestation. 'Fire balls in the Taos area [New Mexico] roll off roofs or bounce through the fields,' notes anthropologist Florence Ellis.[29] In certain cases, especially with the Zunis and Hopis, it was felt that some lights were not so much transformed witches, but rather the big, flaming bowls that many witches flew around in. These vehicles do not proceed steadily, but rather jumped for a distance of 5–6km (around 3–4 miles) in one go and then descend to earth before making the next hop.[30] The Penobscot Indians of Maine considered mysterious nocturnal lights in the skies to be shamans flying off to do magical battle with rival shamans.

Such ideas were doubtless very common throughout the Americas, and they still survive. Mysterious sightings in central Mexico led to a 'UFO flap' in the 1990s. People in and around Mexico City saw strange lights in the sky and, in the modern manner, regarded them as extra-terrestrial spaceships.[31] These sightings coincided with the start of eruptions of the long dormant volcano, Popocatapetl, sacred to Indians in ancient times and still venerated by rural Indians in its vicinity. The volcano is quite close to Mexico City and the renewed activity was (and is) generating many earth tremors each day. Indians living around the volcano's base interpreted the flitting lights they saw as flying witches transformed into fireballs.

CHAPTER EIGHT

SACRED LANDSCAPES

Ancient American Indian spirituality was strongly linked to nature and the surrounding natural world was perceived as having three basic levels: it had symbolic or cosmological properties, it was populated by spirits (ancestral, animal and nature), and it contained certain topographical features that were considered to be inherently sacred. In this chapter, for simplicity, I have attempted to separate out these three aspects as far as is possible and give a range of examples relating to each. However, as will become apparent, quite often all these levels or aspects tended to overlap within the Indian mind.

Symbolic Geography

Traditional American Indians are always oriented in their native landscapes. In the case of the Pueblo Indians of the south-western United States, Hamilton Tyler has observed that this knowledge or awareness of directions is 'ingrained... almost instinctive... the whole community orients itself around a centre with a rigidity which would be called compulsive if it were a question of individual behaviour'.[1] One or other version of the notion of the Centre and the Four Directions was a standard concept almost everywhere in ancient America. It was often conceived of as the Six Directions – north, south, east and west, plus up (the sky) and down (the Earth). This directionality was not based on the compass points as such, but on the four extreme rising and setting points of the sun during the year – eastwards, the most northerly sunrise at the summer solstice and the most southerly sunrise at the winter solstice, and westwards – the sun's corresponding solstitial setting points. Mapped on the ground, this would actually form a square rather than a cross – the Four Directions being the four corners. The cardinal directions of north, south, east and west are the halfway points between these corners, and so the 'Directions' can be visualized as a cross within a square. Nowadays, the American Indian Four Directions approximate to the modern compass points (Figure 8.1) rather than the corners of the solstitial square, and Tyler wondered if this emphasis results from influence by or adoption of the white man's compass-ordered directionality.[2] 'Up' relates to the sun high in the sky at noon, and 'down' to the sun's nocturnal passage beneath the feet, on the other side of the Earth – effectively, the underworld. This up-and-down, vertical axis can be seen as the centre point of the Four Directions square and the crossing point of the cardinal directions cross. It is Centre Place.

In the deepest sense, this cosmogram underpinning the Directions

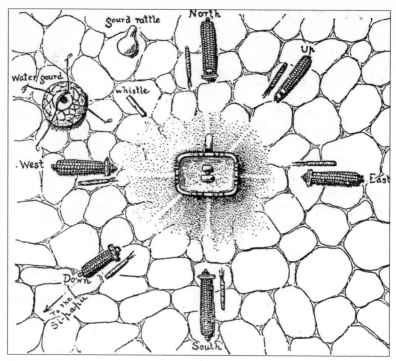

Fig. 8.1. A Hopi Six Directions altar. (J. Walter Fewkes, Smithsonian Report, 1926)

relates to an idea of 'emergence' that is held by many if not all ancient Indian societies. They all identify somewhere where their First People emerged from the ground or a body of water in mythic time, translating from an earlier 'World', 'Sun' or 'Earth' into this one. This point of emergence gives a deeper significance to the concept of 'down', and is symbolized by a small hole known as the *sipapu* in the floors of ceremonial *kivas*. Typically, after emergence the First People meet and are helped by creator beings during a migration to their present home. This is well illustrated by the Zuni emergence myth. According to this legend, the first Zuni, Havasupai and Hualapai peoples emerged as a group 'thousands of years ago' (in mythic time) from a sacred place deep within the Grand Canyon near Ribbon Falls (see Plate 28). They left the canyon, noting in their prayers all the things they saw. They wandered in search of *Idiwana'a*, 'Middle Place' – a permanent home. They made many stops as they journeyed up the Colorado River, building villages and shrines, making offerings and burying their dead. At certain places they encountered spirit beings who imparted sacred information to the Indians. These places are still remembered in the religious narratives of the tribe. At the junction of the Little Colorado and Zuni rivers, the wanderers 'had important interaction' with spiritual beings, and the spot became the place all Zunis go to after

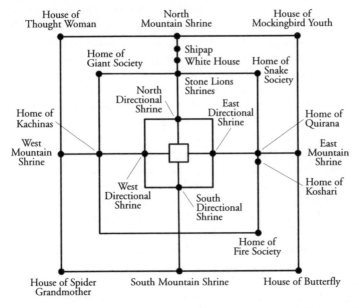

Fig. 8.2. A schematic diagram of the symbolic geography around a Keres Indian pueblo or village, made up of natural features and shrines. The central square represents the village plaza. (After James Snead and Robert Preucel)

death – 'Zuni Heaven'.[3] Eventually, Middle Place was located near the source of the Zuni River and was settled. This is the current location of Zuni Pueblo (south of Gallup in New Mexico). Every four years, a group of Zunis make a pilgrimage of over 160km (100 miles) to Zuni Heaven, retracing the course of the migratory route, making offerings, saying prayers and gathering sacred paint pigments. 'The Zuni trail itself is sacred, with every geologic and natural feature having special meaning,' states Andrew Gulliford.[4]

The Keres people use natural features, augmented by the placing of artificial shrines, to symbolically mark out the Four Directions cosmogram on the landscape around their pueblos.[5] The Keres live in a scatter of pueblo villages on the Rio Grande and the Rio Jemez between present-day Albuquerque and Santa Fe in New Mexico.[6] Although related to the neighbouring Tewa and Tiwa Pueblo peoples, the Keres form a distinct linguistic and cultural group, and their pueblos all share a common migration myth, which says that the Keres emerged from an opening in the ground called *shipap* to the north of their present territory. Powerful supernatural beings are placed at the corners of the terrestrial cosmogram (Figure 8.2) inhabiting the rim of the Keres' world – male deities on the east, female on the west. 'Thought Woman' in the north-west corner is the deity who 'thought' the people into being, and is an aspect of the Corn-Mother, an Earth goddess figure. In the cardinal directions there are the four sacred mountains, on each of which it is conceived live deities responsible for the weather and the seasons. Each mountain is also associated with its own colour, animal and tree. Although the mountains are of shared sanctity among the Keres, the symbolism of their positions can vary depending on the location of a pueblo. So, to the residents of one pueblo, Mount Taylor can be, say, the sacred mountain of the west, and to another the holy peak of the north. The venerated mountains are further sanctified by having shrines on their summits: the one on Mount Taylor takes the form of a shallow pit over 1m (3ft) across. There are special trails associated with the mountains, as each one is visited by shamans at various times.

Closer in from the edges of the terrestrial cosmogram towards the pueblos are the 'houses' of other supernatural beings, often located in caves or at springs. Pilgrimages are made to them. Perhaps the best-known of these holy sites are the two Stone Lion shrines. The northernmost of these is called *Yapashi* and is now situated within the boundaries of the Bandelier National Monument (an approximately eight-hour round-trip on foot from the visitor centre). It consists of a large circle of loosely assembled stones with an opening to the south-east and encloses two reclining lion figures carved from volcanic tuff. The southernmost of the two lion shrines is situated on a mesa in the vicinity of Kuapa, an ancestral Cochiti (Keres) village. This shrine is of similar design, but one of the couchant lions has disappeared.

Just outside each village there are directional shrines placed in the four cardinal directions and marking the pueblo boundaries. They are typically keyhole-shaped structures with their openings facing north and can be visited by ordinary villagers wishing to make offerings or to pray. Finally, there are sets of shrines within the villages themselves, the key ones being those belonging to the plazas. Traditionally, offerings of maize and tobacco were made at them and they were thought to protect the villagers against witchcraft and disease.

This Keresan scheme is just one example of symbolic geography. This was a widespread phenomenon in ancient America, although its forms could vary widely. The Incas, for instance, identified certain natural rocks and boulders, in addition to set stones and other features, as *huacas* – sacred or significant sites. 'Rocks and other landscape features… functioned as markers of kin, gender, or personal identity,' explains archaeologist Maarten van de Guchte. 'Other landscape features were reportedly exclusively affiliated with women, with young male nobles, with the health of the Inca king, or with the cult of the Earth Goddess, the Pachamama.' Rocks, both carved and uncarved, also served as 'markers of places of ancestral origin, of sites where legendary feats of culture-heroes took place, and of spots where humans and animals were turned into stone… rocks acted as lithic testimony to the involvement of metaphysical beings with the world of humans'.[7] The Incas apparently covered their *huacas* with richly coloured textiles. This practice seems to have related to Inca emergence myths, which stated that the First People emerged from caves, mountains, lakes, springs and even trees; subsequent ancestors made *huacas* in those places in commemoration. From the chronicles of the conquering Spanish, it seems Inca kinship groups decorated their clothing with designs identifying their lineage with certain places of emergence, and the textiles they placed on the associated *huacas* carried the same patterns and colours.

Spirit Haunts

Spirits of many kinds haunted the ancient American landscape and the Indian mind. While it was generally believed that ghosts could appear at certain locales, some Indians of the North American south-west associated them particularly with dust-devils – small whirlwinds. The Yavapais of central Arizona referred to whirlwinds as *matsikwita*, and they were considered ominous. If a Yavapai encountered one, then he or she was advised to make a special gesture with the hands and to pray that the whirlwind passing by did not contain a ghost. If a person was actually struck by a whirlwind, then it was assumed that a witch had sent it, and it was necessary to seek a shaman for remedy. It was said that the ghosts in whirlwinds were never of a newly dead person.

Ghosts were often distinguished from other categories of spirits. Those spirits that were more spiritual than spooky were perceived as inhabiting specific features and places in the landscape, conferring an aura of holiness on such locations. The Indians of the Algonkian family of languages in Canada called the spirits *manitous*. Humans shared the landscape with the *manitous*, and they could each enter the others' realms, especially in places such as deep lakes, whirlpools, caves and crevices, where it was felt the worlds of man and of the spirits of water and the underworld converged. The base of a lakeside cliff face was considered to be an especially powerful spot.[8] Algonkian shamans would be trained to walk into the spot on the cliff face where a magical opening was deemed to be. The shaman would bring an offering, usually of tobacco, for the *manitou* dwelling behind the cliff face, and in exchange obtain medicine power; if the shaman handled the interaction badly, or mistimed it, he would not be able to return and so remained trapped inside the cliff forever. (Such episodes presumably took place as visionary experiences in trance states.) Cliffs where especially powerful *manitous* dwelt were sometimes marked with daubs of red paint or more sophisticated forms of rock art.

This concept of spirits inhabiting specified locations in the natural environment was shared by the Sto:lo Indians, a small tribal group of the Coast Salish Indians living along the Fraser River in south-western British Columbia, Canada, among whom such beliefs continue to the present day. They recognize a whole range of varying kinds of sacred sites, but the ones they refer to as *stl'itl'aqem*, meaning a 'spirited spot', are those places with a resident spirit. This could be a named spirit, a water-baby spirit, Thunderbird, a serpent – or even a ghost. Alternatively, such a location can simply possess a generalized, non-anthropomorphic, supernatural power. Such spirit spots were fairly evenly distributed in the landscape and were most likely to be small upland lakes. However, some other features such as small river pools, stagnant ponds, certain caves, knolls and rock formations were also recognized in this category.[9] One had to be careful at these places to avoid succumbing to their power, which made one 'strange' or ill.

Places inhabited by spirits were not always small or intimate locations – they could sometimes be major features of the landscape. A classic example is the range known as the San Francisco Peak near Flagstaff, Arizona (see Plate 29). This was the Pueblo Indians' sacred mountain of the west, the home of those important but ill-defined Pueblo spirits the Hopi call *kachinas*. These supernatural beings seem poised somewhere between gods and ancestral spirits, and have various functions, although are primarily associated with rainmaking. They are represented by masked dancers and effigies in Pueblo rituals and ceremonies (Figure 8.3).

Most sacred mountains in ancient America were considered to be the homes of spirits or deities and, indeed, it is often difficult to separate spirit haunts from more generalized American Indian concepts of sacred places.

Fig. 8.3. Hopi kachina *altar. The* kachinas *are the taller figures with the head-dresses at either side of the altar. (J. Walter Fewkes,* Smithsonian Report, *1926)*

Venerated Places

There were many categories of sacred place in ancient America, and examples of all these types are still venerated by American Indians today. Although there are giant earthworks, temples and other monumental sacred places, some of the closer-to-nature spiritual sites can be very subtle. A holy spot can simply be a lightly tamped area of desert pavement marking a dance ground or sleeping circle, perhaps partially edged with a few small stone cobbles, or it might be just a couple of boulders indistinguishable from others around them to the uninformed eye. 'I can't begin to tell you about the heritage sites you've missed,' one Indian informant admonished a field archaeologist trying to compile a list of sacred sites.[10] Again, archaeologist David Carmichael acknowledges that sites belonging to the Mescalero Apaches of New Mexico and Texas can have 'very low archaeological visibility'.[11] As an example of just how subtle venerated sites can be, some Inca *huacas* are merely stones known (to those who know) as *chanca*, 'resting place', that acted as seats from which individuals could contemplate a specific sacred peak. Another example of a subtle site is the massive natural outcrop known as Indian Burial Rock, in El Paso county, Colorado. It is not a burial place at all, but a sacred altar that had offerings laid about its base and has eagles living around it. It is in a prime position that allowed earlier Indians to spot herds of buffalo.

Similarly, areas providing sacred resources can be almost invisible to people who are not members of the society to whom they are significant, who are not 'in on the secret'. An example of a sacred resource area would be the ancient pipestone quarries of southern Minnesota (Pipestone National Monument) where Indians for unknown centuries removed a beautiful soft, red soapstone from beneath layers of quartzite. It was prized as material from which sacred pipes (calumets) could be fashioned and was widely traded. Another such example is a cave in Colorado that contains every clay colour needed to provide pigments for Ute Indian religious ceremonies. Other sacred paint mines in the general region include one near Calhan, also in Colorado, and ones near Sunrise and at Rawlins in Wyoming.

Plants for use in healing and religious ceremonies are often collected on the slopes of holy mountains as well as other areas. For example, the Hopis used to make pilgrimages to the San Francisco Peak to gather certain plants (now they have to obtain a special federal permit to allow them to do so). And no one would know of the sanctity of the Wirikuta plateau in Mexico were it not for the continuance of the Huichol tradition of pilgrimage to collect the sacramental peyote cactus: the Huichols consider Wirikuta to be their place of origin, where the divine ancestors, the *Kakauyarixi*, dwell. Resource areas were not only venerated for the plants and minerals to be found there for use in sacred observances, they were also the sites of important ceremonial and ritual practices – for things were not taken from the ground without due religious observance. Furthermore, they were essentially places of pilgrimage and, often, supernatural beings were thought to inhabit them.

Vision quest sites – or dream beds or prayer platforms – are further instances of sacred spots that have minimal markings. An inconspicuous horsehoe or circle of small rocks can mark a vision quest location in a desert area, for example. In the Rockies, vision quest beds can take the form of small stone-walled enclosures just big enough for a person to sit or lie in, as well as small cairns of rocks or platforms of flat flagstones. Occasionally, a buffalo skull that had been used as a 'pillow' might be found at them. Lichen encrustation reveals many of these sites to be hundreds or even thousands of years old, although others are more recent and some still in use.[12] These features can be in precipitous locations as high as 3000m (10,000ft) up in the mountains. Vision quest spots constructed as wooden tree platforms also exist in deep canyons or on mountain ridges.[13] In the bare tablerock areas of Whiteshell Provincial Park in Manitoba, vision quest sites tend to be marked by small stones laid out in the shape of turtles (Figure 8.4). On a ridge of low hills at Three Rivers near Tularosa in New Mexico, 1000-year-old vision quest sites are merely cleared areas within rock outcrops – their only distinguishing feature being the visionary carvings on the rock surfaces facing onto the cleared patches of ground. These spots face out onto the vastness of the Tularosa Basin, and it is a characteristic of most vision quest sites that they are so placed as to provide panoramic views.

Views, visions, spirits, plants and minerals could all account for a place

Fig. 8.4. Plan of a vision quest site in a turtle-shaped arrangement of rocks, Bannock Point, Whiteshell Provincial Park, Manitoba.

19. *Anthony Aveni, one of the leading American archaeoastronomers (Chapter 5).*

20. *The summer solstice sun setting behind the Anasazi ruins known as Hovenweep Castle, Utah (Chapter 5).*

21. *Hole-in-the-Rock, Arizona, believed to be an ancient American Indian solar calendar and sun-watching site (Chapter 5).*

22. *The remains of Casa Grande, Arizona, a Hohokam solar-lunar 'observatory'; the square window, top right, is aligned to the moon, the round window, top left, is aligned to the sun (Chapter 5).*

23. *The Caracol, Chichen Itza, in Mexico's Yucatan Peninsula. An observatory or sky-watching temple used by Mayan priests to observe the movements of Venus. The aperture of one of the horizontal sighting shafts is visible in the top turret (Chapter 5).*

24. *The Intihuana at Machu Picchu, Peru. This curious pillar and complex plinth carved from a granite outcrop appears to have been associated with solar rituals (Chapter 5).* (Peruvian Embassy, London)

25. *The reconstructed 'Woodhenge' sun-watching circle at the Mississippian Indian ceremonial complex of Cahokia, Illinois. The flat-topped bulk of Monks Mound is visible in the background, and the post in the foreground marks the spot where the sun-watcher priest would have stood to make his observations. The white marking on a pole in the ring identifies it as the one that indicates the equinoctial sunrise (Chapter 5).*

26. *One of the mysterious stone piles in New England (Chapter 6).*

27. *The Calendar II stone chamber in Vermont (Chapter 6).*

28. *The Grand Canyon, believed by the Zuni, Havasupai, and Hualapai people to be their place of emergence (Chapter 8).*

29. *The San Francisco Mountains, Arizona, sacred to the Pueblo Indians and the home of the kachinas (Chapter 8). It is also one of the sacred peaks believed to be connected by mystical strings or spider's webs that the shamans travelled along during their out-of-body trance journeys or 'dreams' (Chapter 9).*

30. *Offering censors and containers to catch sacred water from the stalactites in the Mayan ritual cave of Balankanche, Yucatan (Chapter 8).*

31. *Animal and symbol petroglyphs on a rock at the remote Three Rivers site, New Mexico (Chapter 9).*

32. *A petroglyph of a bighorn or mountain sheep at Three Rivers. Further west, in the Coso Mountains of California, the bighorn was the animal spirit or 'familiar' of rain shamans, and it probably has the same meaning here. A depiction showing the killing of a bighorn was a metaphor for rainmaking. Complex markings of the kind shown here, inside the animal's body, are thought by some to be 'entoptic patterns' generated automatically in the brain during entranced states (Chapter 9).*

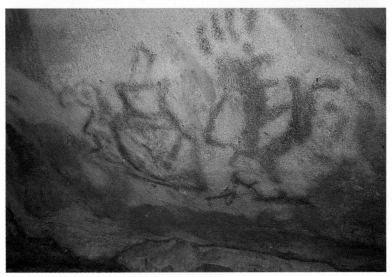

33. *Rock paintings in the Mayan ritual cave of Loltun (Chapter 9).*

34. *An ancient ritual way formed by the clearance of volcanic debris. Death Valley, California (Chapter 9).*

35. *A mysterious prehistoric line of rocks, a 'petroform', snakes across the wastes of Death Valley (Chapter 9).*

36. *A close-up of a 'Nazca Line', Peru. Difficult to make out at close quarters, the dead-straight line can be seen going up the side of a small hill in the middle distance (Chapter 9).* (Gary Urton)

becoming venerated. Another reason was if a natural feature had some strange property, such as an unusual acoustic effect. A case in point is the phenomenon of 'ringing rocks' – boulders that issue a gong- or bell-like sound when struck with a small rock or a piece of wood. Several are known of in southern California. One is a granite rock about 1m (3ft) across that is naturally perched on a giant boulder in the Menifee Valley in Riverside County, California. When lightly struck the rock chimes clearly, and a range of tones can be produced by striking it in different places; the surface of the rock is indented with deep hollows or 'cupules' testifying to centuries of percussion. There are ancient rock carvings scattered throughout the length of the valley. Another example of a ringing rock in the region is Bell Rock, now in the courtyard of the Bowers Museum in Santa Ana but formerly located in the Santa Ana Mountains of Orange County. Little is known about the use made of this kind of musical rock, but there is some ethnography to indicate they were used in rituals such as girls' puberty rites when the elders would sing in accompaniment with the sounds produced by the rock.[14] Other musical boulders are known in California, and also near Virginia City, Nevada, at Cocoraque Butte in southern Arizona, a place associated with the lost Hohokam people, and at Fort Ransom in the Cheyenne River Valley in North Dakota. There, a white granite boulder indented with cupules and incised with markings is known as the Writing Rock. It is close to a spring and has panoramic views – quite possibly a vision quest location. Writing Rock is set within a natural amphitheatre with exceptional acoustics, and the pounding of the rock would probably have been heard all over the valley.[15]

Visual peculiarities could also mark out a natural site as containing supernatural power, or being inhabited by a spirit. Referring to Inca *huacas*, Maarten van de Guchte explains, 'A stone is marked for its resemblance to a human being, and another for a shape in the manner of a falcon.' This is the phenomenon of 'simulacra' in which the shapes of some natural objects happen to resemble anthropomorphic, zoomorphic or other forms.[16] The Spanish priest Bernabe Cobo had similarly observed as early as 1653 that the Incas 'worshipped and offered sacrifices to any natural things that were found to differ somewhat from others of the same kind'. This was true of ancient American Indians everywhere. The Ute Indians (as probably the Anasazi before them) see the reclining figure of a chief in the long ridge of Ute Mountain, Colorado. Apaches see the profile of a sleeping ancestral hero in the shape of a peak in the Chisos Mountain by the Rio Grande in Texas. The ancient Yucatan Mayans worshipped at an extraordinary tree-shaped stalagmite in the ritual cave of Balankanche and at a zoomorphic rock in the Loltun cave. And the Anishinabe (Ojibwa) Indians of Manitoba still make offerings at a rock in Whiteshell Provincial Park that is a remarkable simulacrum of a resting buffalo.[17] There must be a virtually inexhaustible number of examples.

Sometimes, acoustic and visual factors combine, as at Ninaistakis ('the Chief Mountain') in Glacier National Park in the Montana Rockies, hard by the border with Canada. This peak is sacred to the Blackfeet Indians and other Indian peoples of the region. It is home to the Thunderbird spirit, and is the focus of many surrounding vision questing sites (some are near its summit). It is a distinctive landmark, looking from some angles like a chief's ceremonial head-dress and it has simulacra on one of its rock faces resembling a woman with a baby in her arms, to which a Blackfeet legend relates. When the wind blows at the appropriate velocity the mountain 'sings' as air is funnelled through fissures and rocky spires near its summit.[18]

Trees do not figure very prominently in American Indian religious lore, and they are in any case more transient than geological features, but the cosmological image of the World Tree, the cosmic axis, was known to numerous ancient American Indian societies (the tree-shaped stalagmite at Balankanche was worshipped by the ancient Maya as an expression of their World Tree). Trees could be involved in ceremonial activity, though usually in the form of a pole – the Lakota Sun Dance pole is a case in point. A sacred (*waken*) tree – usually a cottonwood – is sought and 'captured', and then given highly formalized ceremonial observance, being addressed as if it were a human being. A 'good woman' is chosen to complete the felling of the tree. It is stripped of branches and foliage, except for the topmost branch fork and leaves which comprise the tree's 'scalp' – if any other branches are left, the tree's ghost may haunt the sun dancers. It is finally carried to the dance ground where it is laid with its top towards the sunset direction and dressed with a variety of symbolic objects, such as feathers, rawhide images, the fat of buffalo loin and many more items. The tree is then erected. 'At the top of the tree they tie a red blanket and then they paint the *waken* tree on the sides of the four winds.'[19] While the tree for the Lakota Sun Dance pole was 'captured' afresh every year, the Omaha had a permanent sacred pole that related to a key tribal myth and was used repeatedly in religious ceremonies.[20] Although it was one of the tribe's most sacred objects, in 1888 the pole was deposited with the Peabody Museum. It was returned to the Omaha a full century later.

Selected water sites were identified as sacred by many American Indian peoples. Springs, lakelets, even stretches of rivers were venerated, and waterfalls, too, were often sanctified, typically as vision quest sites. The Jivaro (Shuar) people of the Amazon, for example, make pilgrimages to sacred waterfalls that are used for vision questing (sometimes with the aid of hallucinogens) as part of a boy's spiritual development.[21] Running Eagle Falls in Glacier National Park, Montana, is sacred to the Blackfeet Indians. The legend associated with the feature states that during a vision quest there a young woman acquired the power to become a female warrior who became noted as a rescuer of other Blackfeet braves in battle.[22] Some water sites were truly major sacred places. Lake Titicaca in Bolivia, for instance, was believed by the peoples of the Andes to be the place where the creator god Viracocha emerged; shrines going back to the time of Tiahuanaco have been found on the sacred Island of the Sun in the lake. Similarly, the Pueblo Indians of Taos, New Mexico, believe that their point of emergence was Blue Lake, an ancient place of worship situated at 4260m (14,000ft) in the mountains above Taos. The lake was described by Mabel Dodge in the early 1920s: 'Bottomless, peacock blue, smooth as glass, it lies like an uncut, shining jewel... This Blue Lake is the most mysterious thing I have seen in nature, having an unknowable, impenetrable life of its own, and a definite emanation arises from it.'[23] In 1906 this sacred turquoise lake, *Ba Whyea*, was wrested from the Indians' control by the United States Government through the agency of the Forest Service. It was only restored to them in 1969 after a long legal struggle. The Blue Lake area can now be visited only by enrolled members of the Taos Pueblo.

Of all sacred sites, the most venerated places of ancient America were mountains and caves. As already described (see Chapter Seven), some American Indians *dreamed* their sacred mountains, which were viewed as being actual spirit entities. The Paiute Indian, Jack Stewart, referred to Birch Mountain, California, as 'my mountain' and considered it as an elder, his spiritual mentor: 'When I was still a young man, I saw Birch Mountain in a dream. It said to me: "You will always be well and strong. Nothing can hurt you and you will live to an old age." After this Birch mountain came and spoke to me whenever I was in trouble and told me that I would be all right.'[24]

Many American Indian societies viewed their relationship with their sacred hills and mountains much as Jack Stewart did on his more personal level, though it was a relationship that spanned generations and centuries rather than a single lifetime. Examples would include San Francisco Peak, which it has already been noted, is sacred to the Pueblo Indians, being a vision quest location, a resource area for sacred plants, and home of the *kachinas*; known to the Navajo as *Dook'o'ooslud*, it is their sacred mountain of the west too.

Devil's Tower in Wyoming is sacred to numerous Indian tribes, and a pilgrimage site for the Sioux who prefer it to be known as Bear's Lodge (*Mato Tipila*). This dramatic, flat-topped volcanic plug, its vertical, deeply grooved sides rising almost 300m (1000ft) above the surrounding landscape, became known to moviegoers world-wide as the site of the encounter between humans and extra-terrestrials in the film *Close Encounters of the Third Kind*. It is a mecca for rock climbers. But Indians go there for religious purposes: 'Those who use the butte to pray become stronger. They gain sacred knowledge from the spirits that helps us preserve our Lakota culture and way of life.'[25] The Indians are unhappy about the thousands of climbers every year who, from a spiritual standpoint, show disrespect in scrambling up the butte's sides, making a noise hammering in their pitons and calling to one another. Another bone of contention is the removal of prayer bundles from Devil's Tower, and Indians resent being photographed by tourists when they are praying or vision questing. 'The absence of solitude and privacy is keenly felt,' Andrew Gulliford reports.[26]

Other sacred eminences in the northern United States include Montana's Sweetgrass Hills. Sacred to many Indian tribes, including the Blackfeet, Gros Ventre, Salish and Chippewa Cree, these distinctive hills rise to 920m (3000ft) above the surrounding prairie, and contain many vision quest sites. They also contain gold, and there has been a struggle to prevent the issuance of prospecting permits. To the Indians, it is the sweetgrass that is valuable, and this is collected and distributed widely for ceremonial purposes. In 1992, 500-year-old ceremonial artefacts made from shells collected from distant shores were found deep in a cave in the hills, and it is thought that sacred observances at Sweetgrass Hills go back to very ancient times, perhaps to the Clovis timeline itself. In northern California, the impressive 4369-m (14,200-ft) Mount Shasta, is likewise venerated by all Indian groups who live around its base, including the Wintu, to whom it is the home of 'the little people'. Traditionally, when a Wintu Indian dies, the body is oriented towards Shasta, so the soul can fly there, and from its sacred peak rise to the Milky Way.

In Mexico, the pyramidal structures of the Olmecs, Mayans and Aztecs all symbolized sacred volcanoes, which were considered to be sacred beings who provided water. In a sense, pyramids were effigies. Templo Mayor, the pyramidal temple of Tenochtitlan, was known to the Aztecs as *atl-tepetl*, 'water mountain', and was modelled on the nearby sacred peak of Mount Tlaloc. Volcanic veneration went back a long way in the region: it is clear the pyramids of Teotihuacan echo the shapes of the two chief mountains in the vicinity (see Plates 8 and 9), and the initial foundations of the largest pyramid in all the Americas, at the ancient urban and pilgrimage centre of Cholula, are 2000 years old. The contours of the Cholula pyramid imitate those of Popocatapetl, the active volcano whose massive bulk only 29km (18 miles) away dominates the skyline. Excavations by archaeologists on the lower flanks of the mountain have revealed the remains of a village that was overcome by an eruption in AD80. In the patios of the houses the archaeologists uncovered small clay and stone shrines depicting the mountain, each accompanied by a crudely carved face. These shrines were linked by a chimney to a charcoal-filled chamber: smoke would have issued out through the shrines, mimicking an eruption.[27] These shrine effigies were obviously intended to keep the sacred volcano's angry aspects at bay, but such attempts at appeasement are clearly failing. Fifteen hundred years later, the Aztecs held an annual ceremony called *Tepeilhuitl* dedicated to Popocatapetl in which an image of the mountain was fashioned from dough. In another ceremonial feast, several mountains were modelled in dough, including Popocatapetl, and each was given a human face. Today, Popocatapetl rumbles ominously again, and local Indians are once more making effigies of the volcano, and leaving offerings in caves high on its slopes.

Mountain veneration was no less important in the Andes. Indeed, it was important enough for human beings to be sacrificed on the peaks in Inca times. In 1995, at nearly 6300m (21,000ft) on the volcanic Mount Ampato in Arequipa, Peru, high-altitude archaeologist Johan Reinhard discovered the deep-frozen body of a young Inca girl, wonderfully preserved. The girl had been aged about 14 years at death and her body was curled into a foetal position. The ice-mummy was nicknamed, variously, 'Juanita' and 'the Ice Maiden'. With enormous difficulties, Reinhard and his assistant, Miguel Zarate, got the 500-year-old body down from the mountaintop and into a deep-freeze cabinet. Later laboratory examination showed that the girl had died from a blow striking her above her right temple. She had been dressed in a striped cloak fastened with a broad belt. Beneath, she was wearing a long tunic drawn together by a woven belt patterned with intricate geometric designs. She had eaten a vegetable meal about seven hours prior to death. Reinhard returned to the mountain peak with a larger and better-equipped expedition. They found pits below the summit containing the frozen bodies of two other children, each aged about ten years. One had a feather head-dress that had fallen over its face. Associated with the mummies were 50 ceramic bowls, wooden beakers and figurines. There had been a ceremonial platform, and the archaeologists found the remains of the camp used by the people who had accompanied the children to the summit and sacrificed them there. In 1999, Reinhard along with archaeologist Constanza Ceruti and their team, found three more sacrificial children on the even higher peak of Llullaillaco, a volcano in north-west Argentina.[28] They first of all discovered two stone shelters near the summit, with an adjacent area edged by a low stone wall. Within this delimited space they detected a small, buried chamber containing the frozen body of a boy dressed in a bright red tunic and curled up so his face was resting on his knees. Next, they found the ice-mummy of a teenage girl with braided hair, sitting in a cross-legged posture. She came to be called the 'Maiden'. Finally, the investigators uncovered the body of a younger girl whose frigid remains had been struck by lightning at some point since her death. Consequently, she was nicknamed 'Lightning Girl'. Over a hundred objects were found buried with the children. The youngsters had remained deep frozen for five centuries, without any thawing and re-freezing; their brains were well preserved, their lungs still contained air, blood remained in their hearts and blood vessels, and it was possible to extract DNA. It seems they had not been struck, strangled or had their throats cut, as was generally the case with Inca human sacrifices, but had been left to die from exposure. The bodies of all three children showed high levels of cocaine, with the Maiden's levels being particularly high. This suggests that they were fed considerable quantities of coca leaves so that they could drift more easily into death.

It was no mean feat on the part of those who conducted the summit ceremonies and sacrifices to have reached such altitudes and returned without modern equipment and clothing, yet over fifty ceremonial platforms and shrines with low stone walls have now been found on Andean summits, testifying to a major tradition of mountaintop ceremonies (not all of them necessarily involving human sacrifice). Reinhard points out that to the Incas the mountains were not merely the homes of gods, they literally *were* the gods. This mountain worship could take on bizarre forms: according to the Spanish chronicles, some Indians who lived close to conical peaks deformed their heads into similar shapes, probably by using binding techniques, while those who lived beneath squat or ridge-like mountains flattened the tops of their heads.

Caves are the topographical complement to mountains, and they were no less venerated in ancient America. It is easy to see why, as these natural cathedrals of rock are replete with symbolism associated with entering the Earth's womb. Their resonant, gloomy spaces lined with fantastically formed rocks, stalactites and stalagmites provide a perfect environment for the performance of ritual activities and solitary observances, cut off from the light and sound of the everyday world. They are the speleological metaphor for the dark and labyrinthine recesses of the unconscious mind. To the Mescalero Apaches, caves were especially powerful places where an individual could communicate directly with the mountain spirits, and ceremonial items were ritually 'retired' within them.[29] The ancient Mayans, though, had even more of a penchant for ritual caves. They considered subterranean grottoes to be unsullied by human activity – caves were *suhuy*, 'virgin'. One of their concerns was the collection of 'virgin water' for ritual and ceremonial use from the deep reaches of cave systems where few people ever went, and especially where no women visited. The water was obtained from subterranean lagoons and, more often, from water dripping down from cavern roofs or off stalactites – pottery vessels and stone troughs were strategically placed to catch the precious fluid. Such a procedure can be found frozen in time in some of the caverns in the Balankanche system, where vessels were left beneath curtains of stalactites (see Plate 30). A particularly spectacular example was discovered in the Actun Kabal system in Belize where a ceramic vessel left for centuries was found brimming with water, and had a stalagmite growing up off the pot rim itself. The Mayan priest or ritualist who had left the vessel there would have had to ascend a precipitous slope exposed to a drop of 30m (100ft), pass through a spacious chamber, climb a 4.5m (15ft) rock wall, and then negotiate a narrow, winding passage.[30]

It is gradually becoming apparent to archaeologists that the Maya sought and used crystals in caves.[31] Considered as precious objects by the Mayans, in the past and now, crystals are known as *sastu'n*, a term derived from a word meaning transparent, bright or clear. This not only related to their normal appearance, but also to the fact that when quartz crystals are struck or rubbed together rapidly they glow with a surprisingly bright light;

it is not difficult to imagine the dramatic effect such 'lightning stones' would have had when used in this way in rituals taking place in the inky darkness of caverns. The power of crystal was believed by the Mayans to be derived from the power of the earth, so crystals found in caves, closely identified with the earth (some modern Mayan groups believe the Earth Lord dwelled in a cave, for instance), would doubtless have been considered to be especially powerful. It is well documented that Mayan shamans used crystals for curing and divining, practices continuing even to this day. Crystals were gazed into for divination purposes, and when passed over a sick person's body by a shaman were thought to be able to 'pull out' the disease. They were also used to help in finding herbs in woods, or in recovering lost objects. Crystals are kept in bowls of water or liquor when not in use. Crystals thought to have been associated with ritual have been found in major ancient Mayan cave systems such as Nan Tunich and Dos Pilas, as well as lesser caves and rock shelters.

In the way that Mayan pyramids were effigies of or metaphors for mountains, so too caves had their equivalents in Mayan architecture.[32] Typically, the temple on top of a pyramid platform was a cave metaphor, and some pyramids, like the Castillo at Chichen Itza, also have internal chambers. Earlier in time than the Maya, there was the great ritual cave at Teotihuacan, over which the Pyramid of the Sun was later built, and caves in the Tehuacan Valley contained burials reaching back 9000 years. Centuries after the Maya, the Aztecs also venerated caves. They considered caves to be entrances to the underworld, a realm of spirits and death, yet they were also linked to fertility, for prayers were offered inside caves for rain to feed the crops. The Aztecs were obsessed with obsidian, the shiny black glass produced by volcanic action. The hallmark of Aztec craftwork, obsidian was used not only for knife blades and other weapons and tools, but also for magical purposes – black obsidian mirrors were used for divination. Tezcatlipoca, the 'lord of the smoking mirror' was a major, all-knowing Aztec deity, a god of the night and the dark underworld realm, and a master of the subterranean world of the caves. Symbolically, obsidian was associated with the god Tepeyollotli, the jaguar 'heart of the mountain', and that heart was only accessible by a cave opening, often visualized as open jaguar jaws. Scholar Nicholas Saunders says: 'Obsidian in some way "represented" the solidified blood-essence of Tezcatlipoca/Tepeyollotli, who, as the jaguar manifestation of Tezcatlipoca, inhabited and symbolized both caves and mountains.'[33]

Various forms of cave worship would have been conducted at countless places and times throughout ancient America. Indeed, caves, mountains, lakes, springs, trees, rocks and examples of all the features of the natural environment were pressed into religious use, expressing that animistic connection with the land so characteristic of the American Indian.

CHAPTER NINE

MYSTIC MARKINGS AND SPIRIT SIGNS

Very few ancient American Indian cultures left any writing, but many nevertheless left their mark – quite literally – on rock surfaces and on the very land itself. Rock art is tantalizing and puzzling, while the ground figures comprise one of the deepest mysteries bequeathed to us by the inhabitants of ancient America. Both types of marking can speak of rich spiritual and visionary experiences, and grant us a glimpse into the inner world of the ancient New World.

The Nature of Rock Art

For a long time the study of ancient rock art has been the Cinderella of archaeology, It is now slowly emerging as an effective way to look inside the minds of prehistoric peoples world-wide. Rock art is, in effect, visual and symbolic 'writing' rather than 'art' in the sense of mere decorated rock surfaces. The trick is in trying to decipher it.

There are two basic forms of rock art, 'petroglyphs' and 'pictographs'. Petroglyphs are images incised directly into the rock surface (Figure 9.1). This is accomplished in a variety of ways, including engraving the rock, pecking lines and shapes into it using smaller rocks to hammer in the indentations, or, probably the most common method, removing the naturally occurring dark

Fig. 9.1. Petroglyphs at Painted Rocks (now Painted Rocks State Park) on the Gila River, Arizona. (After J.R. Browne, 1865)

'desert varnish' by scratching, scraping or abrading, leaving a light-on-dark image. (Desert varnish is the term given to the black-brown sheen that develops on rock surfaces over long periods of time, especially in arid regions – but not exclusively so. It is caused by the oxidization of airborne particles from the environment that settle on the rocks and are then cemented into place by enzymes produced by bacteria living on the rock.)

Pictographs are painted images produced on rock surfaces by applying coloured pigments using brushes made from animal hair, plant fibre, sticks, fingers, or by spraying from the mouth or through a blowing tube. Coloured pigments were, in the main, mineral-based, obtained from oxides in rocks or clays, and from coloured stone such as serpentine and turquoise. These were ground into powder and mixed with a binder such as resin, gum, oils from seeds, egg white, or even blood. In addition, the ancients used charcoal for the black pigment and white pigment was made from kaolin, gypsum or limestone. All these ways of producing engraved and painted rock art were employed in ancient America.

It is very difficult to date rock art categorically. In theory it is possible to radiocarbon date the organic material in pictograph pigments, but petroglyphs have no organic component so they do not allow this approach. Sometimes the age of rock art can be estimated from the growth of lichen on the surface. Or the degree of darkness of an image caused by environmental 'varnishing' can be compared to the pre-existing desert varnish patina on surrounding rock. A variety of experimental technical methods are also being tested in pursuit of the elusive goal of finding a way to achieve absolute dating of rock art. In areas that allow it, comparison of rock art styles, and the survival of any relevant ethnological information can also prove useful.

Stone Ciphers

Ancient American rock art imagery contains: abstract and geometric patterns and shapes; human, animal and plant forms; hybrid human-animal figures; dots; lines; meanders; grids; spirals; circles and concentric rings; star-shapes and other symbols; hand and foot shapes; depictions of ritual objects; images of tools such as spear-throwers; markings representing animal tracks; and scenes from daily and ritual activities. More recent rock art, executed after European contact, depicts images of horses and riders in brimmed hats. Certain themes and imagery can dominate some individual rock panels, while others present whole collections, or are confusions of images superimposed one on another.

The placing of rock art was significant; it was not a matter of idle doodling on any rock surface that came to hand. A cluster of rock art images might signify a vision quest spot, a venerated boulder or cave, or even the foot of a sacred hill or mountain. It can mark places exhibiting simulacra qualities; a case in point is Painted Rock on the Carrizo Plain in central southern California, which displays vulva symbolism. It is an isolated U-shaped sandstone outcrop that 'has been almost universally identified as resembling a massive vagina on the landscape' notes rock art archaeologist, David Whitley.[9] This outcrop contains one of the largest and most elaborate concentrations rock art in the whole region.

Overall, there are tens of thousands, perhaps hundreds of thousands, of rock art images throughout the Americas. In North America, the Canadian Shield has over four hundred pictographic sites, mainly on riverside cliff-faces, dating back perhaps two thousand years. Painted in bright red ochre, they show human and animal figures, and 'medicine' objects such as drums and medicine bags. Some panels are high up on sheer cliff-faces, with no indication of how the artist could suspend himself there to do the painting: clearly, the spots where the imagery was placed were of prime importance, no matter the difficulties involved. There are also petroglyphs in Canada, the best-known example being the Peterborough Petroglyphs site in southern Ontario, which is comprised of a horizontal limestone slab incised with hundreds of images. Petroglyphs dominate most other rock art locations in North America, which are scattered throughout the various states. Some individual rocks in Wisconsin and other northern mid-west states, for instance, have carved images of simple human forms, geometric markings such as rows of grooves and diamond shapes, complex abstract forms, and bird images, especially of the 'thunderbird' type with beaked head turned to one side and wings outstretched displaying long feathers. There are a few pictographs, too, usually simple red abstract markings made with iron oxide pigmentation.[2] Without doubt the greatest concentration is in the south-west of the United States (see Plates 31 and 32), if one includes southern Texas and California within that region. To give some idea, in New Mexico there are over 21,000 petroglyphs at the Three Rivers Petroglyph site near Tularosa and over 15,000 more at the West Mesa Petroglyph Park near Albuquerque. In addition, the Coso Mountains in southern California, close to the state line with Nevada, have been described as having one of the most 'spectacular concentrations of rock art sites in North America – if not the world'.[3] Yet even these examples barely scratch the surface of the numbers of petroglyphs that exist overall in this vast region. Pictographs are also to be found, most notably, in coastal southern California. Multicoloured hallucination-like images painted by Chumash Indians occupy hundreds of sandstone caves and rock shelters, places that were retreats for Chumash shamans. The brushland and canyons now designated the Seminole Canyon State Historical Park in Texas, at the confluence of the Rio Grande and the Pecos Rivers near the Mexico border, contains rock shelters housing – as we shall see – some of the eeriest pictographs in ancient America. The rock art of the south-west embraces many styles, reflecting the work of different cultural groups in various eras. Its chronology is thought to range from 7000 or more years ago up to the historic era.

In Mexico and Central America, pictographs possibly dating back to the Archaic era (7000–1500BC) have been found in caves, including the Santa Marta Cave in Chiapas and the cave of Espiritu Santo in El Salvador. The Olmec produced cave paintings dating from c.900BC. These have been found in three caves – Juxtlahuaca, Oxtotitlan, and Cacahuaziziqui, all in mountains about 160km (100 miles) south of Mexico City. At Juxtlahuaca, the paintings are large scale and situated towards the rear of the deep cave, thousands of metres (yards) from the entrance. 'Their remote setting is unquestionably deliberate and strongly suggests a ritual motivation,' opines art historian Andrea Stone.[4] One panel is executed in brilliant red, yellow and black, and features a were-jaguar towering over a small, bearded seated figure. The jaguar-man is sporting a head-dress and costume items similar to those depicted in Olmec monumental sculpture. Images in other panels include a feathered serpent.

Following the Olmec era, the Mayans painted more extensively than other ancient Mexican cultures on the walls of a great many of their ritual caves. Many of the human figures in these have bold, dark outlines executed in a fluid manner that gives them an almost cartoon-like quality (see Plate 33). Subject matter includes large human heads, perhaps images of gods, and figures seemingly of gods or priests in ritual garb. Some figure groups depict what may be rituals associated with the sacrifice of captives, others show what appear to be transvestites – or, perhaps more accurately, ritualists posing as women, and 'ithyphallic' figures (displaying an erect penis) are not uncommon. In addition to figurative subjects, there are abstract signs and symbols and hand prints. The chronology of the paintings extends throughout the Mayan era, often within the same cave – the Loltun cave in Yucatan being one example where this happens. There are also Mayan petroglyphs, a celebrated example being the larger-than-life-sized relief carving of a warrior, priest, or god on the rock face immediately adjacent to one of the entrances to the Loltun cave. Experts have guesstimated its date at between AD50 and 200. Inside the cave system, as in other caves, the Maya carved glyphs and symbols on stalagmites and odd-shaped rocks that have fallen to the ground from cavern ceilings.

The extent of the rock art of South America is not yet properly known. There are paintings on cave walls at Cerro Sechin, Peru, that are thought to date well before 1000BC, and petroglyphs are abundant in parts of the Amazon Basin. There, rocks are engraved with imagery ranging from concentric circles to winged figures. 'The Indians associate many of them with various concepts in their magical and religious beliefs,' states F. Thrupp.[5] The great anthropologist of the Colombian Amazon, G. Reichel-Dolmatoff, noted that several landmarks in the north-west Amazon were thought by the Indians to be where humans had their points of origin. These places, Reichel-Dolmatoff further noted, tended to be huge rocks or boulders situated at waterfalls and often covered with ancient petroglyphs.

Meanings

Confronting rock art in the field is both a dramatic and challenging experience. It is almost like listening to a cacophony of whispers, incantations and faint murmurings from the spirits of the ancient people who stood before these same rocks and told of their dreams, visions, perceptions and beliefs. How can we extract meaning from the rock markings?

Informed interpretations are the best that can be expected, and various explanations have been put forward. One is that rock art simply depicts actual scenes, the sort of function we traditionally ascribe to much of art today. There can be no doubt that this is true in some cases, for historical-period rock art shows Europeans on horseback, while earlier examples show ritual scenes and even astronomical phenomena observed in the heavens. But relatively little rock art is narrative in this fashion, and even where the simple description of, say, an animal or an object seems to be involved, rock art archaeologists have come to learn that the image may have been intended as a metaphor, as we shall see later. Another, more widely applicable interpretation is that the images depict mythological themes relevant to the people who produced the art; that they were mythological storybooks of a kind, or celebrations of mythological characters. There can be little doubt that something of this nature is true in a good many cases, for certain characters depicted on rock art panels have been identified as gods, culture heroes and other mythological beings. A famous case is that of the hunchback flute-player, who figures in known Pueblo Indian lore and, as Kokopelli, is a known Hopi *kachina*, yet his depiction goes back hundreds if not thousands of years at some rock art sites in the south-west. A relatively small number of rock art sites seem related to astronomy – both as markers for sun-watching positions, and also as basic calendars in which rock imagery and shadows interact (see Chapter Five). Some rock art is emblazoned on landmarks and other prominent landscape features and seems to have acted as a signpost on established trails and at the confluence of rivers. According to research in Utah by rock art specialists, petroglyphs and even pictographs accumulated at such spots because the locations were special in themselves (in the way crossroads in Old Europe were considered magical locations). The rock art also acted as navigational guides.[6] Waymarked trails would have been connected with pilgrimage or mythic migration routes as well as with more mundane purposes. It is known that some rock art markings relating to travellers' clans were made on boulders and rock faces along religious pilgrimage routes, as Hopi ethnology confirms.[7] There is little doubt about the validity of yet another interpretation – that much rock art marked locations that were considered to be imbued with supernatural power, or inhabited by spirits, as has already been indicated. This links to vision quest spots and shamanism, which in turn brings up what is proving to be a powerful new interpretation of much rock art: namely, that it relates to the visionary experiences of entranced shamans.

Visions in Stone

It is now felt by a growing number of rock art specialists that the geometric and abstract symbols that pepper petroglyph and pictograph panels – the dots, spots, spirals, arcs, grids and similar markings – are depictions of the patterns produced by brain processes during certain stages of trance.[8] Called 'entoptic' patterns, these are universal mental images because everyone shares the same 'hard-wiring' of the cerebral cortex. These geometric patterns can appear as glowing, moving images with eyes closed, or seem to be projected onto surrounding surfaces when entranced persons open their eyes. Considerable scientific study has gone into the nature of these trance-induced visual effects. The pioneering work in linking this neuroscientific material with rock art was accomplished by South African archaeologists working with Bushman rock art. From careful analysis of the rock art, along with the study of previously ignored Bushman ethnology, and the experiences of shaman-healers in surviving Bushman groups, the experts found that these entoptic patterns are the hallmarks of trance-based rock art linked to shamanism.[9] Archaeologists and anthropologists working in the Americas discovered that the same rules applied to rock art there. For example, Reichel-Dolmatoff found that Amazonian Indians like the Tukano had developed techniques to prolong the entoptic stage of their ayahuasca drug visions, and used the patterns as the basis for their artwork.[10] (Although the patterns themselves are universal, the meanings ascribed to them differ from culture to culture, and the Tukano used the entoptic patterns for their own symbolic use.) Archaeologist David Whitley, who initially worked with the South African group, has done an enormous amount of work on Californian and Great Basin rock art, the ethnological records relating to the Indian peoples who made it, and has made powerful strides in understanding how it relates to shamanism.

In shaman-inspired rock art of this nature, the animal and human figures, the hallucinatory were-animals, and even some of the scenes that are depicted, relate to the spirit world – the visionary realms of the shamanic ecstatic trance and the out-of-body soul flight to the spirit world. (This could also account for the rock art with mythological themes.) The shimmering spirit figures of the otherworld develop out of the entoptic patterns, and during certain stages of trance can intermix with them. It is significant that much ancient American shamanic experience was aided by the use of hallucinogenic drugs, because such substances are known to strongly enhance entoptic effects and, of course, to produce extremely powerful visionary states. A review of just some examples will be sufficient to indicate the ways these visionary (or hallucinatory) elements have manifested themselves in ancient American rock art.

The Chumash rock shelter paintings in California are unquestionably tied in with shamanic experience, as is known from ethnological data. One way this is shown in Chumash art, as in rock art elsewhere, is by the appearance of distorted human forms and were-animals, both of which are thought to depict the powerful changes in body-image that can occur in trance states, especially drug-induced ones. Modern people taking mind-altering substances have reported feeling as if they were turning into animals, or that their limbs, neck or other parts of their anatomy were seemingly stretching to fantastic lengths. Also, some figures in Chumash pictographs are shown with a dazzle of dots surrounding their contours, and these are likely to represent entoptic effects, judging by the experience of one subject who took a *Datura* preparation. He not only saw vivid visions while under the direct influence of the drug, but the effect lasted for weeks afterwards. 'Everything he looked at appeared to be surrounded by tiny white dots.'[11] Chumash shamans took the highly hallucinogenic jimson weed (*Datura*) during their vision quests, and their rock art reflects this.

Winged figures occur widely in ancient American rock art. This is again a probable reference to body-image transformation common in trance, but specifically linked to the sensation of the out-of-body soul or spirit flight that is the crux of the shamanic experience. 'Many of the figures most abundant in the petroglyphs of the Vaupes [Colombian Amazon] represent, it is believed, supernatural beings with wings,' say Richard Evans Schultes and Robert Raffauf. 'Part of this use of wings may be the result of the experiences of ancient Indians who made the engravings – experiences of flying through the air, a very frequent initial symptom of intoxication with hallucinogens.'[12] The ritual hallucinogen still used in this region is ayahuasca, which, we recall, is recognized as a 'drug for flying'. A related and equally widespread motif is that of human figures shown with claw feet or bird heads, with or without wings. 'Bird symbolism is prevalent in shamanic symbolism throughout the world,' south-western rock art scholar, Polly Schaafsma, has pointed out[13] The hybrid half-man, half-bird form expresses the experience of spirit flight. In some cases, these figures may be depictions of priests or shamans in ritual bird costumes, but that does not change the trance origin of the experience expressed by the imagery.

David Whitley has made an intensive study of the Coso Mountains in southern California, and has been able to securely tie in the petroglyphs there with the practice of shamanism.[14] His detailed study of the ethnology of the area has revealed that the mountain range was a major centre for rain shamans belonging to the Numic-speaking Shoshone, Paiute and Kawaiisu Indians. Shamanic pilgrimage to the Cosos goes back many generations, perhaps covering thousands of years, with the last known rain shaman travelling there as recently as the 1940s. There are a great many rock art sites in the mountains and they mark places where the supernatural force the Indians called *poha* was strongest, and were where the shamans conducted their vision quests. They also record the shamans' visions. A recurring Coso motif is the bighorn or mountain sheep, often shown being shot by a human figure with a bow and arrow. Most previous interpretations of this imagery had centred around the idea that it represented hunting scenes or was 'hunting magic' to secure success for the hunters. But Whitley's in-depth work shows that literal interpretations cannot be relied on when dealing with rock art, for, in actuality, such petroglyph motifs derive from an Indian belief complex related to rainmaking: bighorn sheep were the spirit animals of rain shamans, and there was folklore that associated the death of a bighorn with rainfall. The shaman made rain by 'killing a bighorn', a metaphor for his entering trance in order to gain supernatural power to aid him in controlling the weather. Like the Chumash, these shamans also used preparations made from jimson weed to deepen and extend their trance states. Some of the sheep depictions are shown with human feet, a reference to the magical transformation of the entranced shaman into his power animal. In the Cosos there are petroglyphs showing the outline of human figures containing elaborate geometric patterns – Whitley reads these as being 'portraits' of shamans in trance states, the patterning being entoptic-based.

During his rock art studies of the Cosos and the Great Basin region, Whitley has noted that petroglyphs sometimes seem deliberately associated with cracks and crevices in rock surfaces (a phenomenon noted with rock art in other parts of the world as well). It seems that in the shamanic world-view the spirit world was thought to exist behind rock faces, just as the *manitous* in Canada were thought to dwell inside cliffs. In trance, the shaman's spirit could pass through cracks into the world beyond the rock surface, and spirits could likewise travel in the other direction to enter the human world. (Part of this belief might have been augmented by the phenomenon of echoes, which in the ancient world generally were thought to be the calls of spirits.) One particularly instructive petroglyph noted by Whitley on a cracked rock near Blythe, California, shows a human figure forming out of a wiggly line which itself is emerging from the split in the rock. He interprets this as showing a rattlesnake shaman turning back into human form on his return from the spirit world behind the rock surface. Rock art researcher Dennis Silfer has noticed similar examples. In one case, at Three Rivers, a petroglyph of a pair of upside down legs seems 'to portray a person (shaman or spirit-being?) diving into the earth through an opening between boulders'. At another New Mexico petroglyph site, depictions of arms and open hands 'reach out and wave from cracks in the basalt boulder'.[15]

In the Seminole Canyon area and the immediate surrounding region of the Lower Pecos in Texas, some of the most powerful links between rock art and shamanism have become apparent. There are pictographs in rock art shelters there, and their styles reflect various eras. The oldest is the Pecos River Style. Tests on the organic binder of the iron oxide

Fig. 9.2. Sketch of the 'White Shaman' pictograph, Seminole Canyon, Texas. The depiction of an out-of-body experience during a peyote trance?

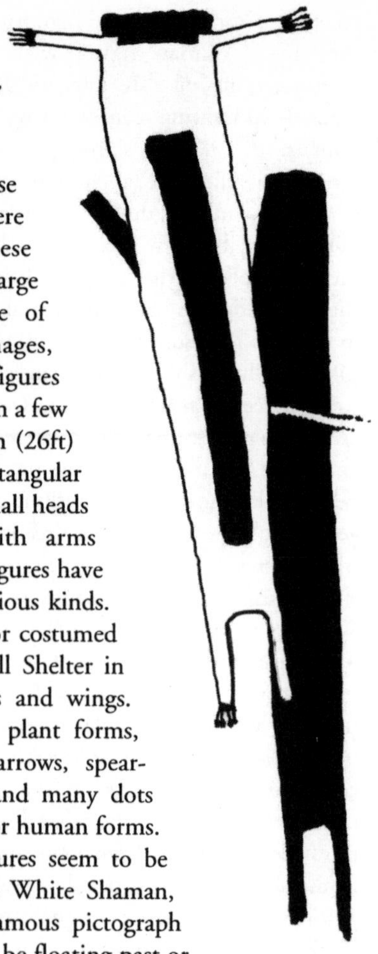

mineral pigments indicate dates for these paintings around 2000BC, and there may well be older examples. These pictographs are mostly in the form of large rock-wall panels containing a range of monochrome and polychrome images, including highly stylized human figures known as 'shamans' that can range from a few inches high up to awesome effigies 8m (26ft) tall. Many of the figures have long rectangular bodies with short straight legs, very small heads when not absent entirely, and with arms reaching outwards. Sometimes these figures have what appear to be head-dresses of various kinds. Some other figures are were-animals or costumed shamans, such as one in the Fate Bell Shelter in Seminole Canyon, which has antlers and wings. There are depictions of animal and plant forms, serpentine lines, geometric forms, arrows, spear-throwers, what appear to be darts, and many dots floating freely or surrounding animal or human forms. Many of the rectangular shaman figures seem to be floating upwards; one, known as the White Shaman, which gives its name to the most famous pictograph panel in Seminole Canyon, appears to be floating past or out of a dark form of similar shape to itself (Figure 9.2). This has been interpreted as 'the entranced spirit... leaving his body'. [16] The region is within the natural growing area of the peyote cactus, and, as noted in Chapter Seven, peyote buttons thousands of years old have been found in rock shelters in the Lower Pecos region. In addition, archaeologist Carolyn Boyd has made a very detailed study of the imagery within the rock paintings, and has found that it has both direct and indirect parallels with the rituals associated with the Huichol pilgrimage to the Wirikuta Plateau in Mexico to obtain the mescaline-containing cactus. [17] The Huichols also produce textile imagery that has distinct echoes of the Pecos River Style murals. There can be no reasonable doubt that these remarkable but disturbingly eerie pictographs depict the effects of peyotism, the visions and experiences of shamans in mescaline-induced trance.

Signs on the Land

It is highly probable that many of the mysterious ground markings found at locations scattered throughout ancient America have a similar affiliation with shamanism. These ancient 'geoglyphs' encompass a range of styles and means of construction, from a strange effigy with kaleidoscope eyes and fractal-like body etched into a Chilean desert, to crazy patterns of stones laid out on bare tablerock in Canada.

There were three main methods of geoglyph construction in America. Some geoglyphs were etched into desert surfaces by cutting through the 'skin' or 'desert pavement'. This skin was formed by a cement of surface pebbles that had been darkened by desert varnish. Removing this skin revealed a brighter underlying surface of silts or sand. These kinds of geoglyphs are sometimes referred to as 'intaglios'. Another key technique was to form the image by laying out small rock cobbles, either placing them on the surface of exposed rock areas or by pressing them into desert surfaces. A geoglyph of this type is usually called a 'petroform'. The third basic method was to create images by means of earthworks, such as ridges, ditches and mounds. Some examples of this sort of feature are labelled 'effigy mounds'. Some geoglyphs were produced by variations on these methods, and there are less common techniques. For example, some features were formed by removing, say, pebbles in a landscape littered with small volcanic stones to leave a cleared area, or a shape was produced by clearing, smoothing, tamping or stomping an area.

The basic types of geoglyphic imagery are varied, and somewhat similar to the content of rock art, but not exactly so. They break down into four main categories: human, animal and other representational forms; geometrical shapes; meandering lines and irregular shapes or enclosures; and dead straight lines laid out with ruthless precision. They can occur separately, or intermixed at the same site.

Geoglyphs occur unevenly throughout the Americas, in isolated examples or in clusters, often in the same general areas as rock art. It is certain that many remain to be discovered, but a great many geoglyph locations have been discovered, scattered in all parts of the Americas. There are too many to itemize here, but any list of the main concentrations would have to include the Whiteshell Provincial Park area of Manitoba; Ohio, Wisconsin and Iowa; the Gila River area of southern Arizona; the Colorado River Valley between Arizona and California, the Mojave Desert region including Death Valley; and various sites in the Andes such as the desert tablelands known as 'pampas' in the Nazca area of Peru, the altiplano of Bolivia, and the Atacama Desert of north-west Chile. All these areas were territories of peoples who practised shamanism in one form or another, and all made sacramental use of mind-altering drugs. In the following pages I present a brief sample of geoglyph sites of various kinds in order to get a little closer to identifying some of their secrets.

Desert Designs

David Whitley's ethnological studies have revealed that the whole territory eastwards from the Coso Mountains across Panamint Valley and the adjacent Death Valley to Charleston Peak outside Las Vegas was known to the Shoshone as *tiwiniyarivipi* – 'where the stories begin and end' or 'mythic land, sacred country'. [18] Many geoglyphs are secreted in remote locations across that magic land, and take various forms. One example is situated in Death Valley on a low volcanic hillock near the salt bed known as The Devil's Golf Course. The small hill rises out of the flat floor of the Valley like an island. [19] It has a cover of small volcanic rocks and pebbles, and cutting across it is a path made by the careful clearance of this rock litter (see Plate 34). Although the path traverses the whole hill, it comes from nowhere and goes to no destination in the surrounding terrain – it belongs just to the hill and is a sacred path. A leading investigative archaeologist of the Death Valley features, Jay von Werlhof, notes that to the Indian mind certain trails or paths had power: 'While geoglyphs and trails did have separate particular roles, generically they fulfilled similar spiritual purposes.'[20] The course of this path passes through or by the remains of various ritual features on the hill, including three stone mounds in a cleared area forming a shrine or sacred enclosure. Where the path enters and exits the cleared area small arrangements of stone are laid out, interpreted as 'spirit breaks' to protect the shrine area from any unwanted supernatural influences passing along the path. Also in the complex are vision quest sites, and scatters of quartz, which was a vitally important magical stone to the Indians here as much as it was to the Mayans, and at numerous geoglyph locations it is possible to find evidence of its use. A different kind of Death Valley geoglyph is to be found atop a mesa-like fan not far from Nevares Spring. The top is devoid of vegetation, and is covered by a dark veneer of pebbles lightly cemented in place by the effects of the harsh conditions. Laid out on this is a long meandering line of small stones, undisturbed for untold centuries (see Plate 35). As well as cleared ritual paths and petroforms like these examples, intaglios are to be found in the valley, such as a long curving line scraped on a mesa top at Mustard Canyon. Alongside it is a small circular arrangement of stones that Werlhof calls a 'ritualistic shaman's hearth'. [21]

There are dozens of geoglyphs of these various kinds in the valley, and many more in the neighbouring Panamint Valley. They often comprise complexes of alignments, meanders, grids and irregular enclosures, and can extend for hundreds of metres (yards). What could have been their purpose? Werlhof thinks that, essentially, they were about weather magic (as were the petroglyphs in the Cosos). People inhabited Death Valley from about nine thousand years ago, when a cool period caused a shallow lake to occupy the valley floor. Eventually warmer, arid conditions developed, and by about two thousand years ago the lake had dried up. Werlhof pictures a scene in which the shamans of Indian groups living in this increasingly arid environment struggled to put a brake on the worsening conditions. 'Attempting to rearrange forces, or to keep them static, was part of the shaman's way,' he points out. He continues: 'Even though the climatic transition must have been gradual, oral traditions... probably kept alive the apparently edenistic epoch that had slipped past and disappeared into history... to bring back the favourable past, must well have engrossed the dream hours of the shamans... The symbols employed in earthen art, as well as the act of placing them conspicuously on the earth, seemingly reflect an enormous effort to induce rejuvenation of a dying ecosystem.'[22]

It may seem strange to us that the laying out of ground markings should be seen as a magical act, but we know from the ethnology of the Yuman Indians in southern Arizona along the Gila River, where there are also concentrations of geoglyphs, that their shamans did make marks on the ground as part of their deployment of supernatural power. In war, for example, the shaman might scratch a line in the ground between the contending parties. 'The line represented a mountain, the long Sierra Estrella,' the ethnologist Leslie Spier wrote. 'While the line that was drawn may have been a mark beyond which the enemy were dared to come, it was thought of as a mountain magically raised to give protection.' [23] The same form of magic was used to thwart opponents in inter-tribal races: one runner would run ahead of another and draw a line across the path so his rival would imagine it to be a deep canyon or a mountain that prevented him continuing. In one recorded instance, a Maricopa shaman drew a line across the course of a race between runners of the Maricopa and Pima tribes. 'The Maricopa racer got by, but when the Pima came up, he stood stock still: he did not know what to do.'[24] The Pima had to be led around the 'mountain' – that is, the line – so he could continue the race. It was at such times, so it is said, that people found out who were shamans.

Whitley's research leads him to another interpretation of the Panamint and Death Valley geoglyphs, though it may in fact complement the above observations. Drawing on available ethnology and new fieldwork, he notes that vision questing was a multi-stage ritual that involved days of fasting, praying, the making of rock art, and 'ritual exertion'. This latter involved running, swimming (where possible) and the creation of stone structures – cairns and ground figures or alignments.[25] It also involved the breaking of quartz crystals to release their magic 'lightning', and for tools for making petroglyphs. In this view, then, the geoglyphs were adjuncts to the vision quest.

South from Death Valley, intaglio figures that seem to have had a different function are to be found in the Colorado River region, which covers immediate areas of south-eastern California and south-western

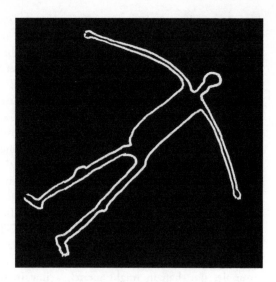

Fig. 9.3. Plan of one of the Blythe geoglyphs of a human figure, possibly representing the creator being, Masthamo.

Arizona. Probably the most famous of the desert figures is the 'Giant' on a terrace above the river near Blythe, California (Figure 9.3). This intaglio is about 52m (170ft) long, and is part of a complex of other geoglyphs, which include two other large human figures, a cat-like creature, a concentric circle and a spiral. Another giant figure can be found on the desert near Winterhaven, south of Blythe, near the Mexico border. On the Arizona side of the river near Parker, there is an intaglio of a rattlesnake with twin rocks representing its eyes. There are many more figurative and abstract images scattered on either side of the Colorado River. It is thought that many of the human and animal figures relate to characters and events in Yuman mythology, and especially to the god and culture hero Mastamho, who is thought to be represented by the Blythe Giant. He, it is said, created the world in general, and the Colorado River specifically. The intaglios are thought to have been made over many centuries; scientific attempts at dating the desert varnish on them suggest the earliest may range from *c.*1000BC to AD900. Some of the intaglios are now thought to have been stations on a Yuman pilgrimage route. This ran from *Avikwal* (Pilot Knob) at the southern end of the river – mythically, the spirit house where the dead dwell – to *Avikwaʼame* or Spirit Mountain further north (Newberry Peak, located in the southernmost tip of Nevada) – built by Mastamho, and from where he created the world. 'At the various ceremonial stops along this route, an officiating shaman would instruct the participants in mythic history and ritually re-enact mythic events,' David Whitley explains.[26] The pilgrimage route re-traced the path of Masthamo in his mythic travels and activities, much as an Australian Aboriginal dream journey route or 'songline' re-traces the travels of a Dreamtime being. Spirit Mountain is a major petroglyph site.

The mountain was noted far and wide as a place of great supernatural power, envisaged as being linked in a network of spectral threads (see below). Possibly over thousands of years, it was visited by shamans who, in trance, re-experienced the mythic events of the creation and met the mythic beings involved.

The practice of making desert markings was widespread throughout ancient America, as a visit to a broad region of the Atacama Desert around Pintados in northern Chile can confirm. In this arid land there are hundreds of intaglios of llamas, lizards, birds, cats, fish, crosses, chequer-boards and other geometric patterns, and some human-like forms. They can be found alone or clustered in groups of up to 65 geoglyphs. Most of them fall along ancient llama caravan routes that ran east–west between the Andes and the Pacific coast, and north–south between desert oases. Some geoglyph groups even depict long lines of llamas and related camelid animals, such as alpacas. Sizes of the geoglyphs range from a few metres (yards) to over 115m (350ft) in height, the tallest being the so-called 'Atacama Giant'. There is some evidence that they may date to *c*.500BC, but so far there appears to be little that is known about them for certain.

Earthen Enigmas

The greatest known concentration of effigy mounds is in the upper mid-west of the United States. The core area is Wisconsin, but it extends into parts of Iowa, Illinois and Minnesota. In Wisconsin alone, it is estimated that there were originally over a hundred main groups of effigy mounds comprising some 15,000 of the features. One collection, the Harper's Ferry Great Mound Group, once comprised almost 900 mounds. Although most effigy mounds are now lost, having been ploughed out or built over, some still survive and can be seen in well preserved areas such as Effigy Mounds National Monument, just across the Mississippi in Iowa (Figure 9.4).

Fig. 9.4. A 19th-century survey showing a range of effigy mound shapes in a Wisconsin cluster. (After R.Taylor, 1840)

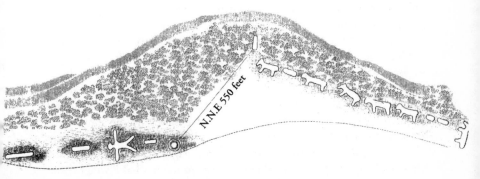

The mounds depict a variety of animals, including birds, bears, wolves, long-tailed creatures called 'panthers' and 'lizards', turtles and deer, together with some hybrid human–bird forms and nine complete human figures. There is an even greater number of mounds with geometric ground plans that have been categorized as linear, oval, conical and biconical. In south-western Wisconsin there are additionally 'chain' or compound mound groups consisting of long strings of conical mounds connected by linear embankments. Effigy mounds are now known to have been built between about AD700 and 1200 by what archaeologists call the Late Woodland culture. These people continued and developed earlier mound-building traditions. Effigy mound experts, Robert Birmingham and Leslie Eisenberg, describe how 'sometime after AD700, the construction of mounds greatly accelerated, and Late Woodland people throughout southern Wisconsin and parts of adjoining states began a spectacular custom that involved

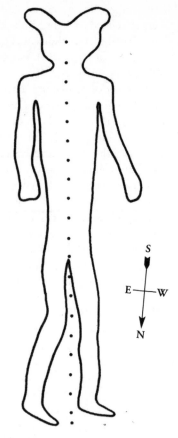

Fig. 9.5. Nineteenth-century plan of Man Mound, Baraboo, Wisconsin. The dots down the length of the figure are 3m (10ft) apart.

sculpting hilltops and other prominent locations into sometimes huge ceremonial complexes that consisted of effigy mounds.'[27]

Each of the mounds seems to have been constructed in a single building effort. It appears that mounds were sometimes built over intaglio versions of the effigy dug a metre (yard) or more into the ground. Evidence suggests that an intaglio was left open for some time, presumably for various ceremonial activities, and was then filled with ash, charcoal and coloured soils in preparation for the actual building of the mound. In general, the mounds tend to be under 2m (6ft) in height, but can extend very much farther. The largest surviving bird-image is in the grounds of the Mendota State Hospital near Madison, Wisconsin, and has a wingspan of just under 212m (700ft). From the ground, it is impossible to appreciate its overall form, with beaked head turned to one side, and its wings outstretched. Aerial photography has revealed the vestigial remains of a bird effigy elsewhere with a 0.4-km (¼-mile) wingspan. A preserved human effigy, Man Mound (Figure 9.5), near Baraboo, Wisconsin, is a little over 61m (200ft) long, while a now-destroyed man mound near Lake Monona, Madison, extended for over 214m (700ft)).

So, what were the mounds all about? First of all, most of the human effigies are shown with horns. These are thought to indicate buffalo-horn head-dresses, commonly associated with shamans in Indian cultures of the region known to ethnology. Also, Red Horn, a culture-hero in local Winnebago (Ho-Chunk) myth, who undergoes a shamanistic death–rebirth cycle, is believed to be depicted in 1000-year-old pictograms in the remote Gottschall Rock Shelter in south-west Wisconsin. It could be that Red Horn is represented in the man mounds, for the creek that runs in front of the cave joins with the Wisconsin River 13km (8 miles) away, where a cluster of man–bird and bird effigy mounds existed. It has already been noted that bird symbolism is redolent of shamanism, and that hybrid man–bird effigies specifically speak of shamanism (Figure 9.6). The meanings of the various effigy mound shapes remain elusive, giving rise to numerous speculations.

Fig. 9.6. Man-bird and bird effigy mounds in Wisconsin. (After surveys by I.A. Lapham and W.H. Canfield, 1850)

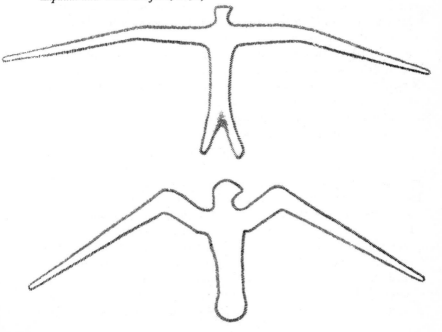

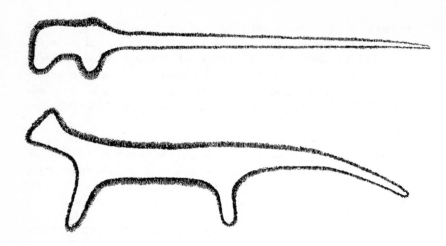

Fig. 9.7. Two examples of long-tailed effigy mounds. (After I.A. Lapham, 1849)

Nevertheless, detailed study of the motifs on Late Woodland pottery, together with a better appreciation of Winnebago myth and the interpretations offered by living elders, is giving current scholars some ideas to work on. It seems that the creatures depicted in the shapes of the effigy mounds fall into categories that express the Upperworld (air) and Lowerworlds (earth and water) of Late Woodland cosmology. Upperworld creatures are birds and humans, and so the shamanic man-bird forms must fall into this category. The bird effigies are often of the thunderbird type, the beneficent deity whose eyes flash lightning and wings cause the thunder. These bird-related effigies are typically found among the hills and bluffs of western Wisconsin. This portion of the state lies beneath the 'Mississippi flyway' – the migration route of waterfowl and other birds.[28] Lowerworld earth effigy creatures include bears, buffalo, wolves, deer and elk. These are mainly found in western and central parts of Wisconsin. Finally, Lowerworld water creatures are represented principally by the long-tailed effigy forms (Figure 9.7). These were for a long time identified as 'panthers' and 'lizards', but the new appreciation of Indian mythology now points to them being water spirits. Long-tailed water-spirit effigy mounds are concentrated in the low-lying eastern part of Wisconsin, which has an abundance of lakes, swamps and marshes. At first, one group of long-tailed mounds, the so-called Lizard Mound Group near West Bend, Wisconsin, seemed to confound this distribution pattern, sitting as it does on a plateau well away from major bodies of water. However, it was then realized that the site is located exactly on the headwaters of a branch of the Milwaukee River, and is surrounded by numerous springs – springs were considered by virtually all ancient American Indians as powerful places, entrances to the spirit world.

It now appears that these cosmological divisions may have also been reflected in Late Woodland society, as some Winnebago Indians even today have a clan structure in which each clan is divided into three groups or societies – thunderbird, bear and water spirit.[29]

The meaning of the geometric mounds remains a mystery. A few speculations have been offered, but all are rather weak or inconclusive as yet. The structuralist might note that these mounds could be the equivalent in earthen form of the entoptic patterns in rock art, although that does not address the question of what meanings the Late Woodland people might have ascribed to them.

What of the function of the effigy mounds? Most of them contained burials, usually deposited in the head or heart region of the effigy. Also found in the mounds are arrangements of stones, showing evidence of fire and burning, that are interpreted as altars. Small clay and rock receptacles of unknown purpose are commonly discovered inside the mounds, and, like burials, usually occupy heart or head areas of an effigy. These receptacles were sometimes placed inside mounds that contained no burials. In some cases, effigy mounds contain nothing at all – no burials, receptacles or altars – so it is clear that the *primary* purpose of the mounds could not have been for burial, although death rituals were often associated with them. The suggestion that these mounds were used for burial functions does not explain why they were in the shapes of mythological beings. Nor, as is the situation with virtually all geoglyphs, why they had to be on such a scale that they could not be appreciated at ground level but only from some distance up in the air. There are three ways to answer this conundrum, in ascending order of likelihood in the opinion of the present author. First, the effigies did not have to be seen but, for symbolic purposes, simply *known* to be in that form. Second, the effigies were meant to be signs to the gods, not human beings. Third, the effigies were part of the spiritual geography of Late Woodland shamanism, and related to concepts concerning the entranced shaman's aerial journey or spirit flight. This latter is an approach to which we shall return. All three ideas have the merit of belonging to the kind of world-view possessed by ancient American Indians, whereas populist modern notions of 'ancient astronauts' do not, and instead represent a kind of cultural imperialism by imposing modern notions on the past and erasing older perceptions in the process. It is just as harmful as physically destroying or damaging ancient monuments.

Whatever their purpose, it is assumed by many scholars now that the mound complexes were used for ceremonial purposes, or at least that the building of a mound was attended by ceremonial activities, of which burial was only a part. 'The similarity of mound forms, mound arrangements, and other customs attending mound construction found among the large effigy mound area argues for a shared sacred knowledge that may have been controlled by a society (perhaps secret) of religious specialists, such as shamans, who directed the mound-building ceremonials,' Birmingham and Eisenberg conclude.[30]

The various Woodland-era cultures were, of course, preceded by the shamanic Hopewell culture, responsible, we recall, for huge geometric earthworks in Ohio and adjacent states whose purpose has never been deciphered. It cannot be doubted that some vestigial Hopewell influence passed up the centuries to the Late Woodlanders.

Although the upper mid-west has the greatest concentration of effigy mounds, they occur elsewhere in the Americas. For instance, there are stone effigy mounds in Putnam County, Georgia, in the south-east of the US, the best-known being the Rock Eagle mound. Made of quartz boulders and cobbles of other stone, the mound is in the shape of a bird – a raptor of some kind – with its head turned towards the east. It has a wingspan of 37m (120ft). It will also be recalled that the great mound at Poverty Point, Louisiana, is thought by many to have originally been in the shape of a bird. And it has already been noted that far to the south, in Mexico, the Olmec centre of San Lorenzo was built on a man-made earthwork in the shape of a bird, possibly a condor, 1.2km (¾ mile) long. The full extent of such features in ancient America is still to be discovered.

Something about Straightness

The most famous of geoglyphs are the so-called 'Nazca lines' in Peru (see Plate 36). They are intaglios situated on a 48-km (30-mile) stretch of desert tableland or pampa between Nazca and Palpa. Ruler straight, they extend for up to 10km (6 miles), are of varying widths. In some places they run in parallel to one another and at others go off at all angles. Tests have shown that it would have been relatively easy to make the lines, but the question remains why do so? The network of lines seem to criss-cross the desert at random, but there is an order of a kind embedded within them: they meet or diverge at dozens of 'ray', 'line' or 'star-like' centres, as they are variously called, and at least one line from each links with another. The line markings are thought to date from the Nazca culture of c.AD600, but there is evidence to indicate that some markings are older, and some younger than that date. There are similar lines relatively nearby on other Andean desert areas.

The Nazca lines share the desert with other kinds of intaglio markings, such as the images of monkeys, spiders, lizards, birds, whales and flowers, as well as geometric forms such as spirals and irregular, abstract shapes. These geoglyphs range from about 15m (50ft) to over 300m (1000ft) in length. They are unicursal in nature, meaning that each one is formed by a single line that can be traced throughout the figure without hindrance – it doesn't stop at a dead end or cross over itself (Figure 9.8). For this reason, there have been suggestions the figures could be dance or processional

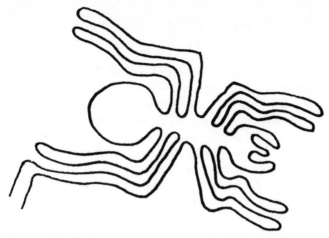

Fig. 9.8. Plan of a Nazca spider geoglyph, showing unicursal nature. The geoglyph is 46m (150ft) in length.

patterns. In addition to these, there are large trapezoid areas that the straight lines connect to in various ways.

The straight lines have puzzled observers for generations. It is relatively easy to advance theories for figurative geoglyphs, but there is something so unforgiving about the simplicity of a straight line. A clearly deliberate, obsessively straight line. Dozens of them. What can their purpose possibly have been? Astronomical notions have been proffered, but they are unconvincing. A map of water sources is another suggestion, which may in part be correct but simply does not explain the profusion of markings. Marking places of burial on the pampa has also been a proposed explanation, but, again, it hardly accounts for the complexity of the markings. Yet another idea is that the lines are ritual paths oriented towards holy mountains, water-giving mountains – the mountain gods, and gods that were mountains, as the Incas still believed many centuries later. There is almost certainly something in this, but it is only a cultural development of a deeper issue. It is not enough on its own. There are other theories too, but however worthy they may be, and however clever the wordplay or conceptual juggling by the theorists, none of them quite accounts for the *straightness*. It is the most obvious feature, yet the one most readily overlooked or side-stepped by almost all the scholars interested in these features.

Another issue concerns whether the Nazca lines are really geoglyphs, or simply pathways. Researchers have found deeply-rutted tracks within the cool, clean exactitude of some of the straight lines. [31] The Nazca 'lines' were *walked*. Some align towards the ruins of Cahuachi off to one side of the pampa, a place that is believed to have been an oracle and pilgrimage centre.[32] Others seem to start nowhere in particular and end at no destination we can recognize as meaningful. But are the lines *simply* pathways? No. At the very least they are sacred paths, not mundane trails, and they are made in the same fashion and occur in the company of undoubted geoglyphs. So, they are both paths and geoglyphs. The conundrum is the same as the one Werlhof addressed in Death Valley: 'While geoglyphs and trails did have separate particular roles, generically they fulfilled similar spiritual purposes.' He notes that the Mojave Indians treat both geoglyphs and sacred trails as having been made by the same spirit creators.[33] To explore this conundrum further, we have to follow the straightness, the deliberate and obsessive straightness, not become corralled within individual cultures, chronologies or types of feature. There is something about straightness, and it can only be seen as a whole phenomenon. As soon as that approach is taken, a bevy of examples present themselves from all over ancient America. (As we briefly note some of these, we will become aware that straight path-lines simply marked on the ground gradually turn into more substantial, engineered structures such as causeways. The form becomes more concrete, as if the geoglyph has grown out of the land, but the ghost of the strange straightness persists.)

Far to the south of the Nazca 'lines', there are straight lines in the Atacama Desert of Chile.[34] Hundreds of kilometres (miles) to the south-east, there are networks of straight pathways on the altiplano of Bolivia. These path-lines are, in the main, formed simply by clearing vegetation and rocks along an exact straight course, punctuated by shrines and other *huacas*. Some of these features are 32km (20 miles) in length, longer than anything at Nazca. Some do indeed go to mountain peaks, and Indians still process along some of them, in Indian file, to the summits to make offerings to the gods, or to the mountain. Farther to the east, beyond the Andes, researchers are finding mainly straight causeways and linear structures in various parts of the Amazon. The straightness cannot be adequately accounted for by utilitarian explanations. The field observations of archaeologist William Denevan are to the point: 'The straightness of most of the causeways is impressive... While the engineering needed to maintain a straight road in flat open terrain is relatively simple, building a long straight road to a destination that cannot be seen is not easy... Most of the stone causeways are on well-drained ground where a wide, well-beaten pathway would suffice. The raised, permanent road, then, takes on other significance.'[35]

Some 2700km (1700 miles) north of Nazca, as the crow flies, in northern Colombia, the Kogi Indians walk ancient stone paths as a religious observance. The Kogi *mamas* or shamans also travel these roads in their dreams, or trances, because the physical roads are deemed to be the traces of spirit paths in the otherworld. With their dreamy shamanic vision, they can see spirit paths continuing straight on beyond where the physical paths

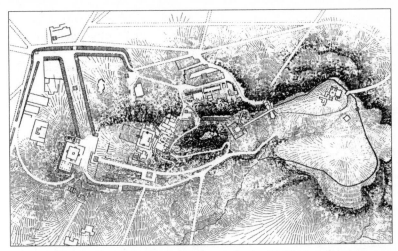

Fig. 9.9. Nineteenth-century plan of La Quemada citadel, Mexico, showing some of the ancient straight causeways (depicted as white lines) of varying widths around the base of the hill. The causeways extend outward into the landscape for long distances. (C. Nebel, 1839)

terminate.[36] Farther north, in Mexico, the obsessive straightness turns up again as Mayan causeways. Known as *sacbeob* or 'white ways' in Mayan, these features in their prime ran straight as arrows through the Yucatan jungle, linking Mayan ceremonial cities – the one between Coba and Yaxuna in northern Yucatan is 100km (62 miles) long, though most of it is now in jumbled, ruinous form. The causeways also ran between features within the cities. Yes, they were roads, but they were also sacred ways, with altars placed along them. 'They facilitated the movement of its population for sacred, secular, and military purposes,' dedicated field researcher William Folan remarks, noting the *multi-function* concept of roads held in the American Indian mind.[37] That the causeways had deeper meaning is indicated by the fact that Mayan lore to this day tells of mythological underground *sacbeob*, and other – invisible – ones called *Kusan Sum* that run through the air. One of these aerial routes is said to run between the ancient Mayan cities of Dzibilchaltan and Izamal.

Farther northwards, in Mexico, there are several straight-road systems, such as the one around the citadel of La Quemada in Zacatecas, northern Mexico (Figure 9.9). This ceremonial complex used by the Chalchihuites people between AD600 and 800 is built on a twin-peaked rocky hill that rises in isolated grandeur above the flat floor of the Malpaso Valley. The remnants of dead-straight stone roads criss-cross the valley floor all around the citadel (see Plate 37). First examined by engineers in the 19th century, these slightly raised paved causeways were found to have occasional altar-like features along them, to link ceremonial areas, or to run to natural features such as caves or distant mountains. Archaeologist Charles Trombold, who has been conducting a special investigation into La Quemada, comments that the causeways cannot be treated as ordinary roads, but had to be associated with ritual activities. These must have been important because the causeways represent a great deal of planning and organizational effort. 'They represent the tip of a cultural iceberg,' he astutely observes.[38]

The tips of similar 'cultural icebergs' also appear in North America, most famously, in the form of the ceremonial roads around the Anasazi ritual centre of Chaco Canyon, in New Mexico. These Chacoan roads converge on or radiate out of the canyon, and are engineered features up to 10m (32ft) wide, a curious fact in that the Anasazis had neither beasts of burden nor wheeled vehicles. NASA infrared aerial photography has further revealed that some sections of roads have up to two parallel sections running alongside, like modern multi-lane highways. The roads connect with structures referred to as Great Houses, whose architecture appears to have been designed to accommodate them. They are thought to have been ceremonial buildings used only occasionally, at times of religious ceremonies. Some Chacoan roads are known to extend for tens of kilometres (miles), and perhaps farther – elements of Anasazi roads have been found in all the Four Corner states of Utah, Arizona and Colorado, as well as New Mexico. It is thought that the road system may have linked the major ceremonial *kivas* in the Anasazi centres scattered across the 640-km (400-mile) wide San Juan Basin. It may well have been that the roads served multiple purposes, including the mundane one of transport, but there can be no doubt that religious activity also featured. Some of the roads are marked by animal sculptures and shrines, and scatters of pottery found along them suggest ceremonial breakage, a common ritual practice in many cultures of antiquity. 'The most common feature of the Chaco roads is their straight-line course, which is maintained in spite of topographic obstacles,' states NASA archaeologist, Thomas Sever, who has made a special study of the features. 'The purpose for the straightness is not entirely clear and has never been satisfactorily answered.'[39] He noted that the Anasazi road makers were not following the most efficient course, judging by modern standards, deliberately taking their roads straight through or over obstructions in the landscape.

There are other examples of straight roads and tracks in North America, such as the Miwok trails in the California sierras said to be 'airline straight' in their directness, and there are doubtless further examples waiting to be discovered by diligent research. There are also more elliptical associations with sacred straightness – the Hopis, for instance, had their ceremonial runners speed to horizon sun shrines in a line as straight as a sunbeam (see Chapter Five).

The hallmark of these roads is their distinctive straightness. It was part of what made them sacred and special. 'If there is one attribute that characterizes New World road systems, it is straightness,' asserts Trombold.[40] It is a characteristic that spanned centuries, cultures and vast distances, and raises questions as to how this diffusion happened, questions that cannot be entertained here. They were roads, but they clearly had ceremonial purposes, and at root possessed religious, mythological or sacred connotations. 'Roads constructed in extraordinary ways may reflect ritual or symbolic concerns,' advised John Hyslop, a great investigator of Inca and other Andean road systems. 'Attempts to interpret all aspects of prehistoric roads in purely materialist terms are bound to fail.'[41] This was hinted at in the 1920s by the Navajo elder, Hosteen Beyal, who told Neil Judd, an archaeologist investigating Chaco Canyon, that the Chacoan roads were not really roads, although they looked like them.[42] If he expanded on this cryptic statement, Judd made no direct record of it, but the archaeologist did thereafter start referring to the roads as 'ceremonial highways', and promised a book on the subject which, alas, never appeared.

It is the straightness that is the key mystery to be solved whether dealing with the Chacoan roads, the Nazca lines, or any of the other examples. There are a few clues. One is that, like geoglyphs, the 'lines' and 'roads' appear in territories that belonged to people who had shamanistic religions. Another is that Amazonian Indians, when shown pictures of the Nazca geoglyphs, apparently associate them with their own visions under hallucinogens such as ayahuasca. In 1977, American anthropologist Marlene Dobkin de Rios came right out and said it: giant effigy mounds, or geoglyphs like the Nazca features, were made to be comprehensible only from the air because entranced shamans were believed to literally fly on their aerial journey to the spirit world.[43] The images of animal familiars and sacred signs were landmarks in a mindscape emblazoned on the physical ground, a spiritual geography laminated onto the land. They were to guide the out-of-body shaman, or to act as signs of power to warn off enemy shamans and sorcerers (for there were always great rivalries and magical battles between shamans of different tribes). Dobkin de Rios suggested that the geometric and linear patterns related to entoptic imagery. In this view, the straight line, apart from being a distinctive expression of supernatural power with its geometric perfection contrasting with the contours of the natural landscape, was symbolic of the experience of leaving the body. Modern accounts of out-of-body and near-death experiences, often include the description of a tunnel. This is, in fact, an entoptic effect. If Dobkin de Rios's theory is correct, then the ancient American Indians chose to represent their out-of-body experiences as a straight line. There is comparative cultural support for this. The Bushman rock art of southern Africa expresses spirit flight in shamanic ecstasy in the form of a line coming out of a figure's head, or running along the ground.[44]

This conceptual linkage between lines and spirit flight is graphically illustrated in a marvellous ethnological account secured around the end of the 19th century from Papago Foot, a shaman of the Gila River area in Arizona. When he was a young man, Papago went on a vision quest to a sacred cave in a butte near Tempe, and smoked a special 'reed' cigarette that put him into a sleep, or trance, during which he had a powerful vision. A spirit appeared to him in human form, saying he would help him become a shaman. 'The spirit tied a cobweb from that butte to Tempe Butte, and thence to Four Peaks, to the San Francisco Mountains... and thence to Avikame at Needles. He travelled on that cobweb and had various cures revealed to him at each butte.'[45] Ethnologist Leslie Spier further confirmed that the Indians 'think of the buttes as connected by strings... The dreamer thinks he is moved along the string through the air...'[46] The 'strings' and 'cobwebs' stretched through the air were surely the spectral version of lines marked on the ground. In the same way, the *Kusan Sum* of the Maya are invisible forms of the physical *sacbeob* or straight causeways, and the invisible spirit paths of the Kogi are related to their physical pathways. We do not know what the spectral version of the Nazca lines were, for that culture is lost to us.

The Gila River region, to which Papago Foot belonged, has a concentration of geoglyphs. One spot close to the river, a low mesa called Sears Point, contains several ground markings. A geoglyph there takes the form of a straight line scoured on the ground. It is so old that what would once have been a yellow line shining out bright against the dark pebbles of the desert pavement has itself become darkened, turning it into a much more subtle feature. At the eastern end of the line is a rock with a notch in it. At the other, western, end of the line there is a vision quest bed, marked by a semi-circle of rocks. To anyone sitting within this vision quest bed, the peak of a mountain sacred to the Yuman and Pima Indians, also inhabitants of the area, is visible in the notch in the rock. When one looks down the line from the other end, the line points towards a notch in a ridge that exactly frames the peak of another known sacred peak. At the summer and winter solstices, the sun can be seen to, respectively, rise and set over these peaks when viewed along the ground line.[47] In the way old Jack Stewart 'dreamed' his power mountain, or Papago Foot travelled in spirit to the sacred mountains by means of a cobweb, so Yuman shamans flew to the sacred peaks in dreams or visions inspired by jimson weed. They cajoled power mountains to side with them in battles with other tribal groups, and at auspicious times they visited the mountains to gain supernatural power. We can be sure that the sun rising or setting over the peaks at the solstices would represent such auspicious moments, and that the straight line on the Sears Point mesa was a 'dream trajectory' along which the shaman travelled in spirit to the mountains.

The explanation for the line-paths is to be found somewhere within this complex mixture of ideas. The courses of shamans' spirit flights were expressed in lore as invisible routes through the air, or as lines marked on the ground. These lines became expressions of supernatural power, and took on 'exoteric' importance – that is, one the ordinary tribal members could understand – as ritual routes. In more rigidly structured ancient American societies, this linear symbol of supernatural power was appropriated by chiefs or kings. The form of the line-paths became more monumental to express kingly or state power that was underpinned by religious authenticity (similar to the way many chiefs and kings in ancient America and elsewhere sought validity by claiming divine ancestry). That religious authority originated in the solitary experience of the shaman going on his ecstatic spirit flight.

* * *

Ancient Americans dreamt these and other strange dreams for untold generations until they were interrupted by the arrival of the Europeans. This 'Old World' America was rudely awoken from its dreamtime, and became the 'New World' of strangers. What had been another, very different way of thinking – of being – in the world, was eclipsed, and with startling rapidity fell into decline. We are left with the ruins of ancient America's inner world just as surely as we are left with the ruins of its lost civilisations. But something of the old understandings can still be salvaged by those with the will and wit to seek them out. Much of this book has been couched in the past tense, but the truth is that there are American Indian groups still extant who can trace their heritage back many centuries, even if only in a fragmentary way. Shamans still have visions, and aspects of old lifeways survive. The spiritual insights of ancient America can be of great value to the modern mind. The meanings behind rock art and the markings on the land can be read, to some degree, and may yet reveal mysteries of human consciousness currently beyond our knowledge. The ruins of the old cities and settlements are still yielding information, some of which may rewrite the history books of the whole world. But the authentic physical and spiritual relics are fragile and fragmented, and it is open to question whether the whispers of the spirits of this ancient land of the west will ever be fully heard before they fall silent forever.

REFERENCES & NOTES

(Dates in brackets after some titles indicate date of first publication. Numbers in parentheses at the ends of some entries denote specific page reference of a quoted passage or, occasionally, a particular item of information.)

PART ONE
Chapter 1
1. Crawford, Michael H., *The Origins of Native Americans*, Cambridge University Press, Cambridge, 1998.
2. Hrdlicka, A. 'Melanesians and Australians and the Peopling of America', Smithsonian Miscellaneous Collections, vol. 94, no. 11, Washington D.C.,1935.
3. Williams, Stephen, *Fantastic Archaeology*, University of Pennsylvania Press, Philadelphia, 1991.
4. *Ibid.* (151)
5. Von Daniken, Erich, *Chariots of the Gods?*, (1968), Putnam, New York, 1969. (119)

Chapter 2
1. Townsend, Richard F., *The Aztecs*, Thames & Hudson, London, 1992.
2. Coe, Michael D., *Mexico*, (1962), Thames & Hudson, London, 1994 edition, 1997. (115)
3. Boas, Franz, *Race, Language and Culture*, (1940), The Free Press, New York, 1966. (437)
4. This folk motif is even more widespread than Boas realized, for it also occurs in Wales – see *Radnorshire in History, Topography, and Romance*, by W. Bowen Hamer, 1914. In the Welsh version, a man, Pengrych, tries to escape three pursuing elves after he abducts a fairy maiden. He first takes a lump of salt from a bag given to him by a mysterious old woman and throws it at the nearest elf, who dissolves like ice and turns into a pool of water. Next, he takes out a ball of sulphur and tosses it back at his next nearest pursuer. That creature, too, dissolves into a pool of water. The third object in the bag was iron, inimical to fairies, but Pengrych loses

it and instead has to despatch his final pursuer with an iron-bladed knife. The third pursuer lets out a dreadful howl and falls to the ground, becoming a system of water spouts. This legend purports to explain the origins of the spa waters at Llandrindod Wells.
5. The Ainu are an interesting case in themselves. They are a non-Mongoloid type people having light skin colour, round eyes, and thick wavy hair, prompting speculation that they could originally have been of Caucasoid origin. They inhabited the Japanese archipelago from at least 5000BC.
6. Boas, 1940/1966, *op. cit.* (444)

Chapter 3
1. Crawford, Michael H., *The Origins of Native Americans*, Cambridge University Press, Cambridge, 1998.
2. *Ibid.*
3. Campbell, Joseph, *Historical Atlas of World Mythology*, Vol.1, Part 2, Harper & Row, New York, 1988.
4. Fagan, Brian M., *The Journey from Eden*, Thames & Hudson, London, 1990.
5. Crawford, Michael H., 1998, *op. cit.*, citing Dillehay and Collins, 1998. (16)
6. Bahn, Paul, 'Dating the First American', in *New Scientist*, no.1778, 20 July, 1991.
7. Professor Stephen Shennan, University College London, as quoted in 'Brazilian Findings Spark Archaeological Debate', by Alex Bellos, in the *Guardian*, 14 February, 2000.
8. Bellos, *ibid.*
9. Crawford, 1998, *op. cit.* (21)
10. Stanford, Dennis, and Bradley, Bruce, 'The Solutrean Solution – Did Some Ancient Americans Come from Europe?', in *Discovering Archaeology*, February, 2000.

11. Santos, F.R., Pandya, A., Tyler-Smith, C., *et al.*, 'The Central Siberian Origin for Native American Y Chromosomes', in *American Journal of Human Genetics*, 64, February, 1999.

12. Wells, R. Spencer, Yuldasheva, N., Ruzibakiev, R., *et al.*, 'The Eurasian Heartland: A continental perspective on Y-chromosome diversity', in *Proceedings of the National Academy of Science*, vol. 98, no. 18, August 28, 2001.

13. Underhill, Peter A., Shen, P., Lin, A.A., *et al.*, 'Y chromosome sequence variation and the history of human populations', in *Nature Genetics*, vol. 26, November, 2000. (361)

14. Crawford, 1998, *op. cit.* (25)

15. Wright, Karen, 'First Americans', in *Discover*, February, 1999.

16. Downey, Roger, *Riddle of the Bones-Kennewick Man*, Copernicus, New York, 2000.

17. It must be noted that no skeletons yet found are older than the suggested Beringia migrations.

18. Brace, Loring C., Nelson, Russell, A., Seguchi, Noriko, *et al.*, 'Old World sources of the first New World human inhabitants: A comparative craniofacial view', in *Proceedings of the National Academy Science*, vol. 98, no. 17, August 14, 2001 (electronic publication July 31, 2001).

19. *Ibid.*

PART TWO
Chapter 4

1. One of the criticisms made by scholars – and by this author in the past – of those who wanted to see parallels between Egyptian and New World pyramids was that such equivalences were fatuous, for New World pyramids were thousands of years younger than the Egyptian ones. While this critique remains true in most cases, it is now clear it cannot be considered as fully valid. Nevertheless, the pyramids of Egypt and America are somewhat different in kind, and we can actually trace their architectural development in Egypt. Rather, if equivalences have to be sought, American pyramids more readily resemble the pyramid tombs of ancient China.

2. BBC TV, 'Olmec heads' in the *Secrets of the Ancients* series, re-transmitted on British television on 3 March, 2002.

3. Coe, Michael D., *Mexico from the Olmecs to the Aztecs*, Thames & Hudson, London, 1994. (74)

4. *Ibid.*

5. Tate, C., and Bendersky, G., 'Olmec Sculptures of the Human Fetus', *Precolumbian Art Research Institute Newsletter On-Line Publications*, no.30, Winter, 1999. (Also in *Perspectives in Biology and Medicine*, Spring, 1999.)

6. Pohl, John M., *Exploring Mesoamerica*, Oxford University Press, New York, 1999.

7. Coe, 1994, *op. cit.*

8. Pohl, 1999, *op. cit.*

9. Coe, 1994, *op. cit.*

10. Stone-Miller, Rebecca, *Art of the Andes*, Thames & Hudson, London, 1995. (28–9)

11. Von Hagen, Adriana, and Morris, Craig, *The Cities of the Andes*, Thames & Hudson, London, 1998.

12. Pohl, 1999, *op. cit.*

13. Miller, Mary, and Taube, Karl, *The Gods and Symbols of Ancient Mexico and the Maya*, Thames & Hudson, London, 1993.

14. Aveni, Anthony F., *Skywatchers of Ancient Mexico*, University of Texas Press, Austin, 1980.

15. *Ibid.*

16. Kolata, Alan L., *Valley of the Spirits*, John Wiley, New York, 1996.

17. Berrin, Kathleen and Pasztory, Esther (eds.), *Teotihuacan – Art from the City of the Gods*, Thames & Hudson/Fine Arts Museum of San Francisco, London, 1993.

18. Krupp, E.C., *Echoes of the Ancient Skies*, Harper & Row, New York, 1983.

19. Devereux, Paul, *Stone Age Soundtracks*, Vega, London, 2001.

20. (i) Freidel, David, Schiele, Linda, and Parker, Joy, *Maya Cosmos*, William Morrow, New York, 1993. (ii) Christian Ratsch, personal communication.

21. Krupp, 1983, *op. cit.*

22. Lekson, Stephen H., *The Chaco Meridian*, Altamira Press, Walnut Creek, 1999.

Chapter 5

1. Sullivan, William, *The Secret of the Incas*, Three Rivers Press, New York, 1996.
2. Aveni, Anthony F., 'Archaeoastronomy in the Southwestern United States', in *Astronomy and Ceremony in the Prehistoric South-west*, Carlson, John B., and Judge, W. James, (eds.), Maxwell Museum of Anthropology, Anthropological Papers no. 2, University of New Mexico, 1983.
3. Bauer, Brian S., and Dearborn, David, P., *Astronomy and Empire in the Ancient Andes*, University of Texas Press, Austin, 1995.
4. Williamson, Ray A., *Living the Sky*, University of Oklahoma Press, Norman, 1984. (110)
5. Frazier, Kendrick, *People of Chaco*, Norton, New York, 1986.
6. J.G. Bourke, 1881, cited by Williamson, Ray A., and Ambruster, Carol, 'Astronomical Alignments at Cajon Mesa Ruins, Hovenweep National Monument: An Update', in *Archaeoastronomy*, vol. X, 1987-1988. (71)
7. Zeilik, Michael, 'Anticipation in Ceremony: The Readiness is All', in *Astronomy and Ceremony in the Prehistoric South-west*, in Carlson and Judge, (eds.), 1983, *op. cit.*
8. Zeilik, Michael, 'Archaeoastronomy at Chaco Canyon: The Historic-Prehistoric Connection', in *New Light On Chaco Canyon*, Noble, David Grant, School of American Research Press, Santa Fe, 1984. (69)
9. Mixon, Benjamin, and White, Raymond E., 'Skywatchers of the Salt River Valley Hohokam', in *The Astronomy Quarterly*, vol.8, 1991.
10. *Ibid.*
11. Miller, Jay, 'North Pacific Ethnoastronomy: Tsimshian and Others', in *Earth and Sky*, Williamson, Ray A., and Farrer, Claire R., (eds.), University of New Mexico Press, Albuquerque, 1992.
12. Williamson, Ray A., 'Light and Shadow, Ritual, and Astronomy in Anasazi Structures', in Carlson and Judge, (eds.), 1983, *op. cit.* (109-110)
13. Carlson, John B., 'Romancing the Stone, or Moonshine on the Sun Dagger', in John B. Carlson and W. James Judge, (eds.), 1983, *op. cit.*
14. This idea arose from an Ajumawi myth that tells how the creator beings, Jamul (Coyote-man) and Kwahn (Silver-Gray Fox-man) decided to settle a quarrel about who should set the laws and who should be the leader by having a race. They trained for the contest by the racing of shadows.
15. Broughton, Jack M., and Buckskin, Floyd, 'Racing Simloki's Shadow: The Ajumawi Interconnections of Power, Shadow, Equinox, and Solstice', in Williamson and Farrer, (eds.), 1992, *op. cit.*
16. Kroeber, A.L., *The Patwin and their Neighbors*, University of California Publications in Archaeology and Ethnology, vol.29, no.4, 1932.
17. Freidel, Schele, Parker, 1993, *op. cit.*
18. *Ibid.*
19. Urton, Gary, *At the Crossroads of the Earth and the Sky*, University of Texas Press, Austin, 1981.
20. Krupp, E.C., *Echoes of the Ancient Skies*, Harper and Row, New York, 1983.
21. Vergara, Miguel Angel, *Chichen Itza – Astronomical Light and Shadow Phenomena of the Great Pyramid*, Centro de Investigacion Maya Haltun Ha Nolo, Ediciones Alducin, Yucatan, Mexico, undated.
22. *Ibid.*
23. The signs of what appear to have been another timber circle were discovered in 1994 close to ridge mound 72, and so situated on or alongside the Cahokia meridian.

Chapter 6

1. Trento, Salvatore Michael, *The Search for Lost America*, Contemporary Books, Chicago, 1978.
2. *Ibid.* (37)
3. *Ibid.*
4. Neudorfer, Giovanna, transcribed interview in *Ancient Vermont*, Warren L. Cook (ed.), Castleton State College/

Academy Books, Rutland, Vermont, 1978. (123-129)
5. Trento, 1978, *op. cit.*
6. Dix, Byron, 'Possible Calendar Sites in Vermont', in Cook, (ed.), 1978.
7. Reynolds, Peter, and Ross, Anne, 'Summary', in *ibid.* (141)
8. Trento, Salvatore M., *Field Guide to Mysterious Places of Eastern North America*, Henry Holt, New York, 1997.
9. Reynolds and Ross, 1978, *op. cit.*
10. Kirk, Lowell, 'The Bat Creek Stone', in *The Tellico Plains Mountain Press*, undated; see website http://www.telliquah.com/Batcreek.htm
11. *Ibid.*
12. *Ibid.*
13. Willard, Lawrence F., 'Westford's Knight in Stone', in *Mysterious New England*, Yankee, Inc., Dublin, N.H., 1971.
14. Trento, 1978, *op. cit.*
15. http://abcnews.go.com/ABC2000/abc2000science/newworld991019.html

PART THREE
Chapter 7
1. Frank Hamilton Cushing used it in the 19th century, and the anthropologist A.L. Kroeber first used it in 1900. By the 1920s it had become standard for academic purposes. The term, though, has to be understood as being very broad, for there is no such thing as a standard type of shaman – the role can have many differences in the various societies in which it occurs even within the Americas, let alone between the New World and the Old World. The common denominator is that trance ecstasy is involved at some stage.
2. Steward, Julian H., *Two Paiute Autobiographies*, University of California Publications in American Archaeology and Ethnology, Vol.33, no.5, 1934. (423-438)
3. Levy, Jerrold E., Neutra, Raymond, and Parker, Dennis, *Hand Trembling, Frenzy Witchcraft, and Moth Madness*, (1987), University of Arizona Press, Tucson, 1995.

4. Neihardt, John G., *Black Elk Speaks*, (1932), Washington Square Press, New York, 1959.
5. Kroeber, A.L., *Elements of Culture in Native California*, University of California Publications in American Archaeology and Ethnology, Vol.13, No.8, University of California Press, Berkeley, 1922. (300-301)
6. Cushing, Frank Hamilton, *Zuni – Selected Writings of Frank Hamilton Cushing*, Jesse Green (ed. and Introduction), (1979), University of Nebraska Press, Lincoln, 1981. (209)
7. *Ibid.*
8. Kroeber, 1922, *op. cit.* (309)
9. Thompson, Eric S., *Maya History and Religion*, (1970), University of Oklahoma Press, Norman, 1990. (359)
10. Hall, Robert L., *An Archaeology of the Soul*, University of Illinois Press, Urbana, 1997. (131)
11. Arval Looking Horse, cited in *ibid.* (130)
12. Hall, 1997, *op. cit.* (124)
13. Schultes, Richard Evans, and Hofmann, Albert, *Plants of the Gods*, (1979), Healing Arts Press, Rochester, Vermont, 1992. (27-30)
14. Prehistoric rock carvings showing mushrooms and what appear to be mushroom spirits have also been found in Siberia.
15. La Barre, Weston, *The Peyote Cult*, (1938), University of Oklahoma Press, Norman, 1989. (257)
16. Furst, Peter, *Hallucinogens and Culture*, Chandler and Sharp, Novato, 1976. (154)
17. (i) For a more comprehensive and referenced account see Devereux, Paul, *The Long Trip*, Penguin Arkana, New York, 1997; (105-140).
(ii) Recommended specialist works would include: Furst, 1976, *op. cit.*; Schultes and Hofmann 1979/1992, *op. cit.*; La Barre, 1938/1989, *op. cit.*; Schultes, Richard Evans, and Raffauf, Robert F., *Vine of the Soul*, Synergetic Press, Oracle, Arizona, 1992. There are numerous others.
18. Spindler, Louise, 'Great Lakes: Menomini', in Walker, Deward E.,

and Carrasco, David, (eds.), *Witchcraft and Sorcery of the American Native Peoples*, University of Idaho Press, Moscow, Idaho, 1989. (51)

19. Merkur, Daniel, 'Arctic: Inuit', in Walker and Carrasco, *ibid.* (13)

20. Basso, Keith H., 'South-west: Apache', in Walker and Carrasco, *ibid.*

21. Saler, Benson, 'Guatemala: Quiche Maya', in Walker and Carrasco, *ibid.*

22. Cushing, 1979/1981, *op. cit.* (157-160)

23. Shimony, Annemarie, 'Eastern Woodlands: Iroquois of Six Nations', in Walker and Carrasco, 1989, *op. cit.*

24. Colson, Audrey J. Butt, 'Guyana: Akawaio', in Walker and Carrasco, *ibid.*

25. Levy, Jerrold E., Neutra, Raymond, and Parker, Dennis, *Hand Trembling, Frenzy Witchcraft, and Moth Madness*, (1987), University of Arizona Press, Tucson, 1995.

26. (i) Persinger, Michael A., and Lafreniere, Gyslaine, *Space-Time Transients and Unusual Events*, Nelson Hall, Chicago, 1977. (ii) Devereux, Paul, *Earth Lights Revelation*, Blandford, London, 1989. (iii) Devereux, Paul, and Brookesmith, Peter, *UFOs and Ufology*, Blandford, London, 1997. (138-159)

27. Devereux, Paul, and Puthoff, Hal, *Marfa Lights*, International Consciousness Research Laboratories Technical Report, no. 789.5, Princeton, 1995.

28. Spindler, 1989, *op. cit.* (48)

29. Ellis, Florence H., 'Southwest: Pueblo', in Walker and Carrasco, 1989, *op. cit.*

30. *Ibid.*

31. This outbreak of sightings was further complicated by a Mexican TV programme that encouraged a rash of questionable video clips from viewers, and also by a solar eclipse. See Devereux and Brookesmith, 1997, *op. cit.*

Chapter 8

1. Tyler, Hamilton A., *Pueblo Gods and Myths*, (1964), University of Oklahoma Press, Norman, 1986. (170)

2. *Ibid.* (172)

3. Zuni leaders cited in Gulliford, Andrew, *Sacred Objects and Sacred Places*, University Press of Colorado, Boulder, 2000. (93-95)

4. Gulliford, 2000, *ibid.* (77)

5. Snead, James E., and Preucel, Robert W., 'The Ideology of Settlement: Ancestral Keres Landscapes in the Northern Rio Grande', in Ashmore, Wendy, and Knapp, Bernard A., (eds.), *Archaeologies of Landscape*, Blackwell, Oxford, 1999.

6. Keresan pueblos include: Cochiti (*Kotyiti*), San Felipe (*Katishya*), Santa Ana (*Tamaya*), Santo Domingo (*Kewa*), and Zia (*Tsia*).

7. Guchte, Maarten van de, 'The Inca Cognition of Landscape: Archaeology, Ethnohistory, and the Aesthetic of Alterity', in Ashmore and Knapp, 1999, *op. cit.* (156-7)

8. Rajnovich, Grace, *Reading Rock Art: Interpreting the Indian Rock Paintings of the Canadian Shield*, Natural Heritage/Natural History Inc., Toronto, 1994.

9. Mohs, Gordon, 'Sto:lo Sacred Ground', in Carmichael, David L., Hubert, Jane, Reeves, Brian, and Schanche, Audhilde, (eds.), *Sacred Sites, Sacred Places*, Routledge, London, 1994.

10. *Ibid.* (193)

11. Carmichael, David L., 'Places of Power: Mescalero Apache sacred sites and sensitive areas', in Carmichael *et al*, 1994, *op. cit.* (89)

12. Reeves, Brian, 'Ninaistakis – the Nitsitapii's sacred mountain: traditional Native religious activities and land use/tourism conflicts', in Carmichael *et al*, 1994.

13. Gulliford, 2000, *op. cit.*

14. Constance DuBois, 1908, cited in Devereux, Paul, *Stone Age Soundtracks – the Acoustic Archaeology of Ancient Sites*, Vega, London, 2001.

15. Devereux, 2001, *ibid.*

16. Guchte, 1999, *op. cit.* (163)

17. For a deeper text-and-picture exploration of the subject of simulacra, see Michell, John, *Simulacra*, Thames and Hudson, London, 1979, and

Devereux, Paul, *The Sacred Place*, Cassell, London, 2000.

18. Reeves, 1994, *op. cit.*

19. Thomas Tyon (1910-11) cited by James R. Walker, (1917) in DeMallie, Raymond J., and Jahner, Elaine A., (eds.), *Lakota Belief and Ritual*, (1980), University of Nebraska Press, Lincoln (Nebraska), 1991. (176-180)

20. Devereux, Paul, *Living Ancient Wisdom*, Rider, London, 2002.

21. Harner, Michael J., *The Jivaro*, University of California Press, Berkeley, 1972.

22. Gulliford, 2000, *op. cit.*

23. Mabel Dodge, cited in Gulliford, *ibid.* (159)

24. Jack Stewart, cited in Steward, Julian H., *Two Paiute Autobiographies*, University of California Publications in American Archaeology and Ethnology, Vol.33, No.5, Berkeley, 1934. (426)

25. Cited in Gulliford, 2000, *op. cit.* (163)

26. *Ibid.* (166)

27. Plunket, Patricia, and Urunuela, Gabriela, 'Appeasing the Volcano Gods', in *Archaeology*, July/August 1998.

28. Douglas, Kate, 'High Society', in *New Scientist*, no. 2320, 8 December, 2001.

29. Carmichael, 1994, *op. cit.*

30. Stone, Andrea J., *Images from the Underworld*, University of Texas Press, Austin, 1995.

31. Brady, James E., and Prufer, Keith M., 'Caves and Crystalmancy: Evidence for the Use of Crystals in Ancient Maya Religion', in *Journal of Anthropological Research*, vol.55, 1999.

32. Brady, James E., and Ashmore, Wendy, 'Mountains, Caves, Water: Ideational Landscapes of the Ancient Maya', in Ashmore and Kanpp, 1999, *op.cit.*

33. Saunders, Nicholas J., 'At the mouth of the obsidian cave: deity and place in Aztec religion', in Carmichael *et al*, 1994, *op. cit.*

Chapter 9

1. Whitley, David S., 'Finding rain in the desert: landscape, gender and far western North American rock art', in Chippindale, Christopher, and Tacon, Paul S.C., (eds.), *The Archaeology of Rock Art*, Cambridge University Press, Cambridge, 1998. (20)

2. Birmingham, Robert A., and Green, William, (eds.), 'Wisconsin Rock Art', *The Wisconsin Archeologist*, vol. 68, no. 4, December, 1987.

3. Whitley, David, S., *A Guide to Rock Art Sites*, Mountain Press, Missoula, 1996. (49)

4. Stone, Andrea J., *Images from the Underworld*, University of Texas Press, Austin, 1995. (47)

5. F. Thrupp, 1981, cited in Schultes, Richard Evan, and Raffauf, Robert F., *Vine of the Soul*, Synergetic Press, Oracle, Arizona, 1992. (233)

6. Hartley, Ralph, and Vawser, Anne M. Wolley, 'Spatial behaviour and learning in the prehistoric environment of the Colorado River drainage (south-eastern Utah), western North America', in Chippindale and Tacon, 1998, *op. cit.*

7. Welsh, Liz and Peter, *Rock-Art of the South-west*, Wilderness Press, Berkeley, 2000.

8. Seigel, Ronald K., and West, L.J., *Hallucinations*, John Wiley, New York, 1975.

9. (i) Lewis-Williams, J.D., and Dowson, T.A., 'The Signs of All Times', in *Current Anthropology* 29, no. 2, April, 1988. (ii) Lewis-Williams, J.D., and Dowson, T.A. *Images of Power*, Southern Book Publishers, Johannesburg, 1989.

10. Reichel-Dolmatoff, 'Drug-Induced Optical Sensations and Their Relationship to Applied Art among Some Colombian Indians', in Greenhalgh, Michael, and McGraw, Vincent, (eds.), *Art in Society*, Duckworth, London, 1978.

11. Cited in Patterson, Alex, *Rock Art Symbols of the Greater South-west*, Johnson Books, Boulder, 1992. (84)

12. Schultes and Raffauf, 1992, *op. cit.* (233)

13. Schaafsma, Polly, 1986, cited in Patterson, 1992, *op. cit.* (49)

14. (i) Whitley, David S., 'By the Hunter, for the Gatherer: Art, Social Relations and Subsistence Change in the Prehistoric Great Basin', in *World Archaeology* 25, no. 3, February, 1994. (ii) Whitley, David S., *A Guide to Rock*

Art Sites, Mountain Press, Missoula, 1996.

15. Silfer, Dennis, *Signs of Life – Rock Art of the Upper Rio Grande*, Ancient City Press, Santa Fe, 1998. (28-9)

16. Stieber, Tamar, 'The Little-Known Treasures of the Lower Pecos', in *American Archaeology*, Spring, 2002. (17)

17. Boyd, Carolyn E., 'Pictographic evidence of peyotism in the Lower Pecos, Texas Archaic', in Chippindale and Tacon, 1998, *op. cit.*

18. Whitley, personal communication.

19. Because these sites are exceedingly delicate, exact locations are not being given in this book because of a very real fear of inadvertent damage by over-enthusiastic visitors, or deliberate damage by the ignorant and careless, as has happened to at least one Death Valley site. The reader's indulgence is requested, because while it is appreciated that he or she is likely to be careful and genuinely interested, there is no control over information once it has been released.

20. Werlhof, Jay von, *Spirits of the Earth*, Imperial Valley College Museum, El Centro, 1987. (13)

21. *Ibid.* (180)

22. *Ibid.* (29)

23. Spier, Leslie, *Yuman Tribes of the Gila River*, (1933), Dover Publications, New York, 1978. (169-170)

24. *Ibid.* (335)

25. Whitley, personal communication.

26. Whitley, 1996, *op. cit.* (124-5)

27. Birmingham, Robert A., and Eisenberg, Leslie E., *Indian Mounds of Wisconsin*, University of Wisconsin Press, Madison, 2000. (109)

28. *Ibid.*

29. *Ibid.*

30. *Ibid.* (134)

31. Clarkson, Persis B., 'The Archaeology of the Nazca Pampa, Peru: Environmental and Cultural Parameters', in Aveni, Anthony, (ed.), *The Lines of Nazca*, The American Philosophical Society, Philadelphia, 1990.

32. Silverman, Helaine, 'The Early Nasca Pilgrimage Center of Cahuachi and the Nazca Lines: Anthropological and Archaeological Perspectives', in *ibid.*

33. Werlhof, 1987, *op. cit.*

34. Morrison, Tony, *Pathways to the Gods – The Mystery of the Andes Lines*, Michael Russell, Wilton, 1978.

35. Denevan, William M., 'Prehistoric roads and causeways of lowland tropical America', in Trombold, Charles D., (ed.), *Ancient Road Networks and Settlement Hierarchies in the New World*, Cambridge University Press, Cambridge, 1991. (235-240)

36. Alan Ereira, personal communication.

37. Folan, William, 'Sacbes of the northern Maya', in Trombold, 1991, *op. cit.* (224)

38. Trombold, Charles D., 'Causeways in the context of strategic planning in the La Quemada region, Zacatecas, Mexico', in Trombold, (ed.), 1991, *op. cit.* (165)

39. Sever, Thomas, unpublished dissertation.

40. Trombold, (ed.), 1991, *op. cit.* (5)

41. Hyslop, John, 'Observations about research on prehistoric roads in South America', in Trombold, (ed.), 1991, *op. cit.* (29-30)

42. Cited in Frazier, Kendrick, *People of Chaco*, W.W. Norton, New York, 1986. (111)

43. Dobkin de Rios, Marlene, 'Plant Hallucinogens, Out-of-Body Experiences and New World Monumental Earthworks', in Du Toit, Brian M., (ed.), *Drugs, Rituals and Altered States of Consciousness*, A.A. Balkema, Rotterdam, 1977.

44. Dowson, Thomas A., *Rock Engravings of Southern Africa*, Witwatersrand University Press, Johannesburg, 1992.

45. Spier, 1933/1978, *op. cit.* (247)

46. *Ibid.*

47. Hoskinson, Tom, 'Saguero Wine, Ground Figures, and Power Mountains: Investigations at Sears Point, Arizona', in Williamson, Ray A., and Farrer, Claire R., (eds.), *Earth and Sky*, University of New Mexico Press, Albuquerque, 1992.

INDEX

Italic page numbers refer to illustrations in the text; the *Plates* are separately numbered.